300 BEST Comfort Food RECIPES

300 BEST Comfort Food RECIPES

Johanna Burkhard

Robert ROSE

300 Best Comfort Food Recipes

For complete cataloguing information, see page 374.

Disclaimer
The recipes in this book have been carefully tested by our kitchen and our tasters. To the best of our knowledge, they are safe and nutritious for ordinary use and users. For those people with food or other allergies, or who have special food requirements or health issues, please read the suggested contents of each recipe carefully and determine whether or not they may create a problem for you. All recipes are used at the risk of the consumer.

We cannot be responsible for any hazards, loss or damage that may occur as a result of any recipe use.

For those with special needs, allergies, requirements or health problems, in the event of any doubt, please contact your medical adviser prior to the use of any recipe.

Design & Production: PageWave Graphics Inc.
Editor: Carol Sherman
Photography: Mark T. Shapiro
Food Stylist: Kate Bush
Props Stylist: Charlene Erricson
Color Scans: Colour Technologies

The publisher and author wish to express their appreciation to the following supplier of dishes, linens and accessories used in the food photography:

The Kitchen and Glass Place
840 Yonge Street, Toronto, Ontario, Canada M4W 2H1
Tel: (416) 927-9925

Cover image: Chicken-Vegetable Cobbler (see recipe, page 150)

We acknowledge the financial support of the Government of Canada through the Book Publishing Industry Development Program (BPIDP) for our publishing activities.

Published by: Robert Rose Inc.
120 Eglinton Ave. E., Suite 1000, Toronto, Ontario, Canada M4P 1E2
Tel: (416) 322-6552 Fax: (416) 322-6936

Printed in Canada
1 2 3 4 5 6 7 8 9 10 FC 09 08 07 06 05 04 03 02

Contents

Acknowledgments

A COOKBOOK IS never a solo effort and I would like to sincerely thank my family, friends and colleagues who lent a generous hand in crafting this book.

Thanks to my former food editor, Julian Armstrong of *The Gazette* newspaper in Montreal, for her guidance and wisdom over the years, and to Linda Kay, for her devoted friendship and inspiration in my writing career.

I would also like to thank the creative team of publisher Bob Dees, for his ingenuity and marketing skills; editor Carol Sherman, an absolute delight to work with, and for her meticulous attention to detail; Andrew Smith, Joseph Gisini and Kevin Cockburn of PageWave Graphics for the superb book design and layout; food stylist Kate Bush, props stylist Charlene Erricson and food photographer Mark Shapiro for the wonderful photography.

Warmest thanks to my family for sharing my passion with food; to Hans for his continued support and encouragement over the years.

This book is dedicated to my children, Nicole and Patrick, who are now adults and have set up their own homes and kitchens — a heartfelt thanks for the many happy, loving memories and meals we shared around the table with many more to come.

Introduction

I REMEMBER COMING home from school to the fragrant aroma of a pot roast in the oven or a smoky ham and pea soup simmering away on the back burner. Everyone has a cupboardful of food memories that evoke a sense of family and home. We call them our comfort foods.

For some, it might mean a special occasion spent with family, such as Thanksgiving with roast turkey and sage bread dressing, or celebrating a birthday with chocolate fudge cake and ice cream. For others, it may recall childhood memories of having a cold and how much better we felt with mom's Jell-O or soothing chicken soup. Yet for others, it can be as simple as a winning dish, perhaps a favorite potato salad, at a summer picnic. For me, comfort food means all the things that evoke a sense of nurturing with a good measure of love and care stirred into the pot. And, of course, how great they all taste.

Whatever the memory or reason, comfort foods all have one special thing in common — they make us feel good. My goal in writing *300 Best Comfort Food Recipes* is to help recreate the "feel good" times and draw people back to the kitchen to soul-satisfying recipes that everyone enjoys — pot roast, macaroni and cheese, date squares. These are traditional dishes that are so much a part of our food heritage and culture, yet these recipes are rarely found grouped in one book.

This book not only includes classic dishes that have never lost their appeal, such as *Old-Fashioned Beef Stew, Thyme-Roasted Chicken with Garlic Gravy* and *Cinnamon Apple Crumble Pie*, but I also include new comfort foods that families are enjoying today. These recipes have become a staple in contemporary kitchens and include such dishes as *Wild Mushroom Risotto, Bistro Lentils with Smoked Sausage* and *Lemon Tiramisu*, which all have the comfort food prerequisites of being reliable and tasting great.

Comfort foods are trusting foods. How many times have you labored over a stove to make a wonderful meal only to have groans of disappointment from your family over what you've cooked? With comfort foods — everyone is rewarded including the cook. As a parent, I know that my kids' idea of comfort food includes many of the old favorites, but also embraces the fast-food tastes they're so accustomed to. I've also included recipes for the younger set with many of their special comfort foods — *Taco Pitas*, *Turkey Fajitas* and *Flatbread Pizzas*. These recipes are simple to make and will entice kids to get in the kitchen and help with the preparation.

We shouldn't dismiss the importance of time spent around the table with our children. The time we spend around the table is one of the most important tools we have to communicate with our families. I believe the return of comfort foods may be attributed in part to the boomer generation and a re-establishing of these social food events that are so important in keeping families connected, especially when children are involved.

Cooking today is as much about the demands on our time as about what we're serving for dinner. We're all trying to balance jobs with a busy family life and very often dinner plays second fiddle to juggling work schedules, homework and a host of activities that demand our time. Yet suppers need to be appetizing and nutritious. With our hectic schedules and the frantic pace our kids maintain, it's almost impossible to make a meal from scratch every night. Who has the time anymore? A simple suggestion is to set aside time with your family — perhaps two or three nights a week and plan a dinner of your family's favorite comfort dishes. It doesn't have to be fancy — even just a good bowl of a homemade soup is all it takes to become a special event. The *300 Best Comfort Food Recipes* offers a collection of recipes geared to cooks who want recipes that are simple and reliable, yet reassuringly familiar. Many of these dishes are personal favorites that have become standards in my house. In about the same time that it takes to order a pizza and have it delivered, you can have a delicious dinner on the table. As for the hectic pace — it can sometimes take over our lives. Once in a while we need to slow the pace and take the time to make a leisurely meal — to tuck a pot of molasses baked beans in the oven and just sit back and enjoy the soothing aroma for its restorative effect.

Don't feel guilty if you're not making a meal from scratch every night. I don't. There's just not enough time in our busy lives. Between our hectic schedules and the frantic pace our kids maintain, we don't need the added pressure of having to perform in the kitchen on a nightly basis. That's why many of the recipes in this book provide for next-day encores that can be reheated in the microwave oven or prepared ahead, so that when you do have a spare hour, you can assemble a meal and stash it away in the freezer.

Spending time in the kitchen has other benefits, too. Cooking with our children provides nurturing time we share together. It also reinforces the importance of teaching our children how sound eating habits can make a lifelong difference to their health. Most of the recipes in the book follow today's guidelines for healthy eating, calling for fresh ingredients and moderate use of fat. Several of the recipes are vegetarian, inspired by my daughter's decision when a teenager to no longer eat meat. You'll find recipes here for *Black Bean and Corn Soup*, *Spicy Noodles with Vegetables and Peanut Sauce* and *Vegetable Minestrone with Sun-Dried Tomato Pesto* — sure to become favorite comfort foods for any vegetarian or, for that matter, the entire family.

Nowadays, so many people don't even know cooking basics. The attraction of convenience products and the proliferation of quick restaurant outlets mean we are spending less time in the kitchen. Even making a basic meat loaf is an event. Baking banana bread is a lost art. *300 Best Comfort Food Recipes* is intended to put you at ease in the kitchen. This is the only cookbook you are ever going to need in your kitchen because it covers all of the basics and includes the most-popular, sought-after comfort food recipes. Directions are easy to follow and recipes call for ingredients that are readily available in supermarkets. I even provide practical information, such as recipe shortcuts and other serving suggestions, to help get dinner on the table. As well, this introduction includes Basic Equipment needed for a well-stocked kitchen, Easy Steps for Preparing a Recipe, How to Save Time Shopping, Time-Saving Strategies in the Kitchen and Ways to Streamline your Kitchen.

There's no greater pleasure than the hours spent around the table sharing a meal with family and friends. Whether it's something as simple as a bowl of *Hearty Beef and Barley Soup* accompanied by a warm slice of *Honey Oatmeal Bread* or as elaborate as a holiday meal featuring *Baked Ham with Citrus-Mustard Glaze*, I hope this book inspires you to get back in the kitchen and create some special memories around your table — and perhaps establish some new food traditions of your own.

BASIC EQUIPMENT

We all have a few dud kitchen tools stashed away in our cupboards bought in the hopes of turning us into cooking pros. Before you get tempted to buy yet another kitchen relic, make sure that you have the basics in your kitchen to help with cooking jobs. Though expensive, it pays to buy the very best quality cookware you can afford for a lifetime of great cooking and baking.

SKILLETS, POTS AND PANS

A large 12-inch (25 cm) heavy nonstick skillet is vital for all the stovetop cooking we do today. Also practical is a less expensive, medium 8-inch (20 cm) nonstick skillet for eggs, pancakes and small-batch cooking.

In addition to a range of saucepans from 1 quart (1 L) for boiling eggs to a 3 quart (3 L) large saucepan for potatoes, a Dutch oven is a must-have for cooking stews, chilies and braising meats. (A Dutch oven is a large wide pot with handles and a tight-fitting cover that usually comes in a 5-quart (5 L) size.) Choose one that is heavy-bottomed, stainless steel or enameled cast iron. You will also want to have an 8-quart (8 L) stockpot for cooking pasta, big-batch soups and stocks. A shallow large roasting pan for roasting turkeys, baked hams and chicken is also ideal. (I prefer a dark roasting pan that attracts heat and produces rich brown gravies versus a shiny aluminum pan.)

CUTTING AND CHOPPING EQUIPMENT

A quality chef's knife with a sharpening steel is a cook's best friend. The perfect knife should fit like a glove in your hand, so test the grip and weight before buying. Paring knives for cutting and peeling, a serrated bread knife and sturdy kitchen shears round out the basic cutting and chopping essentials.

For cutting boards, you'll need one large wooden board for chopping vegetables and another plastic one for raw meats and poultry. A large wooden pastry board is optional, but great to own if you enjoy baking.

BAKING EQUIPMENT

An 8-inch (2 L) square baking pan and a 13-by 9-inch (3.5 L) baking pan are required for baking great bars and squares. (Please note this important distinction: a baking pan refers to a metal pan while a baking dish refers to glass. Use the correct piece of equipment specified in recipes for best baking results.)

It would be next to impossible to bake a layer cake without two 9-inch (23 cm) round cake pans; for heavier cakes, such as coffeecakes and cheesecakes, you'll need a 9-inch (23 cm) springform pan, while a tart requires a 10-inch (25 cm) metal pan with removable bottom. For loaves and yeast breads, you'll need two 9-by 5-inch (2 L) loaf pans, along with a muffin pan or two.

When it comes to cookie and baking sheets, lightweight ones warp in a hot oven so choose heavy ones instead. Rimmed baking sheets also can be used to roast vegetables and meats. You'll also need several wire racks for cooling cakes, cookies and breads.

GLASSWARE AND CASSEROLE DISHES

Every kitchen should have an assortment of ovenproof glassware for baking, roasting, microwaving and as storage containers for the refrigerator and freezer.

The basics include two 9-inch (23 cm) glass pie plates, an 8-inch (2 L) square glass baking dish and a 13-by 9-inch (3 L) glass baking dish for lasagna, baking and roasting. For casseroles, one to two 8-cup (2 L) casserole dishes and a 12-cup (3 L) casserole dish should round out the selection.

BOWLS

You'll also need an assortment of stainless steel and glass mixing bowls in various sizes. You can never have too many of these stashed away in your cupboard especially for marathon baking and batch-cooking sprees.

UTENSILS

Here is a checklist of other kitchen essentials:

- 1 heavy rolling pin
- Spoons: wooden, slotted and a set of measuring spoons
- Soup ladle
- Spatulas: rubber and metal
- Wire whisk
- Tong
- Pastry brush
- Microplane grater
- Box grater
- Fine metal sieve
- Colander
- Measures: set of metal measures for dry ingredients and glass measures for liquids from 1 cup (250 mL) to 8 cups (2 L)
- Bulb baster
- Juice squeezer
- Vegetable peeler
- Can opener
- Corkscrew/bottle opener
- Oven mitts/potholders
- Black pepper mill

ELECTRICAL EQUIPMENT

The top two kitchen appliances in the kitchen are a food processor and microwave oven. Also essential is an electric hand mixer for whipping cream and egg whites.

A blender is optional, though practical for smooth puréed soups and drinks. If you are a serious baker, a stand mixer is a definite asset in your kitchen.

EASY STEPS FOR PREPARING A RECIPE

1. Read the entire recipe carefully before you start.
2. Assemble all the ingredients on the counter.
3. Set out necessary cooking equipment such as saucepans, skillets and wooden spoons. Preheat the oven and prepare cooking utensils — for example, grease a casserole dish or line a baking sheet with foil. This eliminates hunting through a drawer in the middle of a recipe to find a piece of equipment or waiting for the oven to preheat once the dish is ready to go.
4. Chop onions, garlic and vegetables before you start cooking and place on a plate, tray or sheet of waxed paper within easy reach. Measure herbs, spices and seasonings; place in small custard cups or on plates.
5. Clean up as you go. Not only does this save time, you'll find it's far more efficient to work in an uncluttered kitchen.

HOW TO SAVE TIME SHOPPING

1. Before you go — get organized. How many times have you wandered the aisles of a supermarket randomly picking up familiar foods? This is a recipe for costly impulse buys. Getting organized before you go shopping will make your life easier in the kitchen and save you money.
2. Make a list. Decide what meals you are going to make. Scan your pantry and refrigerator and jot down missing staples. Add to that any other items called for in recipes. Organize your shopping list according to the supermarket layout, grouping food items, such as fresh meats, dairy, produce and canned goods together, so you won't have to backtrack.
3. Go shopping at the right time. You're likely to purchase more groceries than you intended if you shop when you're hungry. Try also not to shop when you're tired or not in the mood — shopping is a weekly necessity so make it as pleasant and enjoyable as possible.
4. Take advantage of time-saving products. Items such as pasta-ready tomato sauces, precut vegetables and shredded cheeses cost more but are worth the price when it comes to saving time in the kitchen.
5. Try warehouse and bulk shopping. Buying in bulk can save you money — and time. However, the cost savings can evaporate

if the products aren't used at peak freshness. Plan carefully when purchasing in bulk so you don't overbuy.

6. Make shopping a family event. Get your family involved in the kitchen — and in the shopping routine. Cooking is an important life skill that goes hand in hand with food selection and buying. Children, in particular, need to know how to make wise food choices.

TIME-SAVING STRATEGIES IN THE KITCHEN

1. Wash lettuce as soon as you get home from the supermarket. Fill a sink with cold water, swish the leaves around and scoop them out into a salad spinner to dry. Wrap lettuce in a clean, dry kitchen towel and place in a plastic bag or store right in the salad spinner in the refrigerator.
2. Peel a week's worth of onions. Store in a plastic bag in the refrigerator. Not only will you save time prepping onions for recipes, the cold temperature will help minimize tears when you chop them.
3. You can also keep handy bags of chopped onions and sweet or hot peppers in the freezer to add to soups, casseroles and stews. Freeze for up to three months.
4. Separate a head of garlic into cloves and remove skins. Place in covered container in refrigerator; use within a week.
5. Peel ginger and store in a glass jar filled with sherry in the refrigerator. Use the ginger-flavored sherry in recipes.
6. To get a head start on another meal, cook extras such as rice, pasta and potatoes. Pack in covered containers; label and date. Store in the refrigerator for up to three days.
7. Double a recipe, where indicated, and freeze for another meal. Use masking tape and a permanent marker to label and date all freezer foods. Take stock of the foods often so items will be used at peak quality.
8. Batch-cook on weekends so you can rely on the refrigerator or freezer for make-ahead meals.
9. Don't let forgotten leftovers in the refrigerator become costly throw-aways. Place in a covered container, label and date. Store on a designated shelf in the refrigerator so everyone in the family will know where to find them.
10. Take advantage of your microwave to shortcut recipes such as steaming vegetables for stir-fries, melting butter and chocolate and making quick sauces.

WAYS TO STREAMLINE YOUR KITCHEN

1. Knick-knacks or non-essential appliances clutter a kitchen counter. Keep only essential cooking equipment, such as a food processor and coffee maker, handy on your counter. Keep less-used items in the cupboard within easy reach.
2. Get a jug or crock for wooden spoons, tongs and spatulas and keep on the counter next to the stove.
3. Organize your kitchen drawers to keep similar utensils and kitchen tools together — for example, paring knives with vegetable peelers.
4. The same goes for cooking equipment, such as saucepans, mixing bowls and baking equipment, stored in cupboards. Have equipment used on a regular basis in easy reach; store all others in the back of cupboard.
5. Place your cutting board next to the sink; this will allow you to wash produce easily. Place a bowl nearby to dispose of vegetable waste for outdoor composting or for the garbage bin.
6. Organize your pantry so you can find items easily — and quickly see what's missing when making a grocery list. Group canned and packaged goods, such as pastas, on the same shelf. Arrange bottled vinegars and oils together along with condiments such as ketchup and sauces such as soy.
7. Make sure everyone in the family is familiar with the kitchen set-up so that when it's their turn to clean up or put groceries away, everything will be put in the right place.

Appetizers

MAKES 40 APPETIZERS

Want a great start to a meal? Begin here. I always have containers of this delicious mushroom spread in my freezer ready to defrost in the microwave when friends or family drop by. The same applies for the bread, which I slice, pack into plastic bags and freeze.

TIPS

Mushroom-walnut filling can be frozen for up to one month.

To wash or not wash mushrooms? You can wipe them with a damp cloth, if you wish. However, I feel it's important to wash all produce that comes into my kitchen. I quickly rinse mushrooms under cold water and immediately wrap in a clean, dry kitchen towel or paper towels to absorb excess moisture.

Toasted Baguette Slices Cut 1 thin baguette into ⅓-inch (8 mm) thick slices. Arrange on baking sheet; brush lightly with 2 tbsp (25 mL) olive oil or melted butter. Bake in 375°F (190°C) oven for 5 minutes or until edges are lightly toasted. Spread toasts with mushroom mixture just before baking to prevent them from turning soggy.

Creamy Mushroom Walnut Toasts

Preheat oven to 375°F (190°C)
Baking sheet

1 lb	mushrooms (an assortment of white, oyster and portobello), coarsely chopped	500 g
2 tbsp	butter	25 mL
⅓ cup	finely chopped green onions	75 mL
2	cloves garlic, minced	2
½ tsp	dried thyme leaves	2 mL
4 oz	cream cheese or goat cheese, cut into pieces	125 g
⅓ cup	freshly grated Parmesan cheese (plus extra for topping)	75 mL
⅓ cup	finely chopped walnuts	75 mL
2 tbsp	finely chopped fresh parsley	25 mL
	Salt and freshly ground black pepper	
40	toasted baguette slices (see Tip, left)	40

1. In a food processor, finely chop mushrooms in batches using on-off turns.
2. In a large skillet, heat butter over medium-high heat. Add mushrooms, green onions, garlic and thyme; cook for 5 to 7 minutes or until mushrooms are softened. Cook 1 to 2 minutes more, if necessary, until all moisture has evaporated. (Mixture should be dry and almost crumbly.) Remove from heat.
3. Add cream cheese, stirring until smooth. Add Parmesan cheese, walnuts and parsley. Season with salt and pepper to taste. Transfer to a bowl; cover and let cool.
4. Spread toasted baguette slices with a generous teaspoonful (5 to 7 mL) of mushroom mixture. Arrange on baking sheet. Sprinkle tops with additional Parmesan cheese. Bake in preheated oven for 8 to 10 minutes or until edges are toasted.

MAKES 36 APPETIZERS

Get a head start on your party preparations with these tasty appetizers designed to be stored in the freezer. When the festivities are about to begin, just pop them into a hot oven.

TIPS

To freeze, spread bread slices with cheese mixture; arrange in a single layer on baking sheets and freeze. Transfer to a rigid container, separating layers with waxed paper; freeze for up to one month. No need to defrost before baking.

Wear rubber gloves when handling jalapeño peppers to avoid skin irritation.

Cheddar Jalapeño Toasts

Preheat oven to 375°F (190°C)
Baking sheets

8 oz	aged Cheddar cheese, shredded	250 g
4 oz	cream cheese, cubed	125 g
2 tbsp	finely diced red bell pepper	25 mL
2 tbsp	minced jalapeño peppers or 1 tbsp (15 mL) minced pickled jalapeño peppers	25 mL
2 tbsp	finely chopped fresh parsley	25 mL
36	baguette slices, cut 1/3-inch (8 mm) thick	36

1. In a food processor, purée Cheddar and cream cheese until very smooth. Transfer to a bowl; stir in red pepper, jalapeño peppers and parsley.

2. Spread bread slices with a generous teaspoonful (5 mL) of cheese mixture; arrange on baking sheets.

3. Bake in oven for 10 to 12 minutes (up to 15 minutes, if frozen) until tops are puffed and edges toasted. Serve warm.

MAKES 24 APPETIZERS

Everyone likes to have a breezy appetizer in their repertoire. This is one of mine. It takes no time to prepare and tastes great.

TIP

Make this spread up to three days ahead, cover and refrigerate. Assemble appetizers just before serving or toasts will soften.

Easy Artichoke Cheese Melts

Preheat oven to 375°F (190°C)
Baking sheet

1	jar (6 oz/170 mL) marinated artichokes, well drained and finely chopped	1
1/2 cup	shredded Monterey Jack, Gouda or Cheddar cheese	125 mL
1/4 cup	freshly grated Parmesan cheese	50 mL
1/4 cup	light mayonnaise	50 mL
24	baguette slices, cut 1/3-inch (8 mm) thick, lightly toasted (see Tips, page 16)	24
1/4 cup	finely diced red bell pepper	50 mL
8	Kalamata olives, cut into thin slivers	8

1. In a bowl, combine artichokes, Monterey Jack, Parmesan and mayonnaise. Spread over toasts; top with red pepper and olive slivers.
2. Arrange on a baking sheet; bake for 10 to 12 minutes or until tops are bubbly and edges are golden. Serve warm.

Creamy Spinach Dip

MAKES 3 CUPS (750 ML)

Here's a dip that's so much tastier than the ones made with salty soup mixes. Serve with vegetable dippers such as carrot, pepper, cucumber, celery, broccoli, fennel and cauliflower. I use any leftovers as a dressing for pasta or potato salads, or as a spread for sandwiches.

1	package (10 oz/300 g) fresh or frozen spinach	1
1 cup	crumbed feta cheese (about 4 oz/125 g)	250 mL
1/3 cup	chopped green onions	75 mL
1/4 cup	chopped fresh dill	50 mL
1	clove garlic, minced	1
1 tsp	grated lemon zest (see Tips, left)	5 mL
1 1/2 cups	sour cream (regular or light)	375 mL
1/2 cup	light mayonnaise	125 mL

1. Remove tough stem ends from fresh spinach; wash in cold water. Place spinach with moisture clinging to leaves in a large saucepan. Cook over high heat, stirring, until just wilted. (If using frozen spinach, see Tips, page 22.) Place spinach in a colander to drain. Squeeze out moisture by hand; wrap in a clean, dry towel and squeeze out excess moisture.
2. In a food processor, combine spinach, feta, green onions, dill, garlic and lemon zest. Process until very finely chopped.
3. Add sour cream and mayonnaise; process, using on-off turns, just until combined. Transfer to a serving bowl, cover and refrigerate until ready to serve. Serve in a bread bowl (see Tips, left), if desired, and accompany with vegetable dippers.

TIPS

To grate lemon zest, use a zester to remove the zest in thin shreds and finely chop with a knife. When lemons are bargain-priced, stock up for the future. Grate the zest and squeeze the juice; place in separate containers and freeze.

To make a bread bowl for serving: Using a serrated knife, slice 2 inches (5 cm) off top of small (1 lb/500 g) unsliced round whole wheat or sourdough bread. Hollow out loaf, reserving contents, leaving a shell about 1 inch (2.5 cm) thick. Spoon dip into bread bowl. Cut reserved bread into strips or cubes and serve along with vegetable dippers.

MAKES 3 CUPS (750 ML)

This dip will draw raves from a gang of starving teens or a crowd around the TV set when the ball game is in progress. In our house, we usually can't agree if we want the dip hot or mild. The solution? I use mild salsa as the base and once the dip is made, divide it into two bowls. I leave one mild and add plenty of hot sauce or minced pickled jalapeños to spice up the other. Give the dip a quick reheat in the microwave if it cools — assuming it lasts that long, of course!

TIP

Pita Crisps

A lower-fat alternative to tortilla chips are pita crisps. To make them: Separate three 7-inch (18 cm) pitas into rounds and cut each into eight wedges. Place in single layer on baking sheets; bake at 350°F (180°C) for 8 to 10 minutes or until crisp and lightly toasted. Let cool. Store in covered container. The pita crisps can be made one day ahead.

Warm Salsa Dip

1	can (19 oz/540 mL) white kidney beans, drained and rinsed	1
1 cup	mild or hot salsa	250 mL
2	cloves garlic, minced	2
1 tsp	ground cumin	5 mL
1 tsp	dried oregano leaves	5 mL
4 oz	cream cheese, cubed and softened	125 g
1 cup	shredded mozzarella cheese or Monterey Jack or white Cheddar cheese	250 mL
	Tortilla chips or pita crisps (see Tip, left)	

1. In a bowl, mash beans with a fork until quite smooth.

2. In a medium saucepan, combine beans, salsa, garlic, cumin and oregano. Place over medium heat, stirring often, until piping hot.

3. Stir in cream cheese; stir until dip is smooth. Add mozzarella; stir until melted. Serve warm with tortilla or pita crisps.

Microwave Method

1. Combine all the ingredients in microwave-safe bowl. Microwave at Medium-High, stirring twice, for 5 to 7 minutes, or until heated through and cheese is melted. Serve warm with tortilla or pita crisps.

5-Minute Crab Dip

MAKES 1½ CUPS (375 ML)

With a can of crab meat in the pantry and cream cheese in the fridge, you're all set to make a quick dip in 5 minutes flat. You can make it in the microwave or just as easily on the stovetop over medium heat.

8 oz	cream cheese	250 g
1	can (6 oz/170 mL) crab meat, drained, liquid reserved	1
¼ cup	finely chopped green onions	50 mL
2 tsp	fresh lemon juice	10 mL
½ tsp	Worcestershire sauce	2 mL
¼ tsp	paprika	1 mL
	Hot pepper sauce	

1. Place cream cheese in a medium-size microwave-safe bowl; microwave at Medium for 2 minutes or until softened. Stir until smooth.
2. Stir in crab, green onions, 2 tbsp (25 mL) reserved crab liquid, lemon juice, Worcestershire sauce, paprika and hot pepper sauce to taste. Microwave at Medium-High for 2 minutes or until piping hot. Serve warm.

TIP

Serve with Melba toast rounds or crisp vegetable dippers.

VARIATION

5-Minute Clam Dip

Substitute 1 can (5 oz/142 g) drained clams for the crab. Stir in 1 minced garlic clove, if desired.

MAKES 3 CUPS (750 ML)

When you've got the gang coming over, serve this warm dip and watch it disappear. I like to accompany it with white or blue corn tortilla chips.

TIPS

If you want a hot version, use 2 fresh or pickled jalapeño peppers. Or for a mild version, use 1 can (4 oz/113 g) green chilies, drained and chopped.

To defrost spinach, remove packaging and place in a 4-cup (1 L) casserole dish. Cover and microwave at High, stirring once, for 6 to 8 minutes or until defrosted and hot. Place in a sieve and press out excess moisture.

Warm Spinach and Cheese Dip

1	package (10 oz/300 g) fresh or frozen chopped spinach	1
8 oz	cream cheese, softened	250 g
1 cup	mild or medium salsa	250 mL
2	green onions, finely chopped	2
1	clove garlic, minced	1
1/2 tsp	dried oregano leaves	2 mL
1/2 tsp	ground cumin	2 mL
1/2 cup	shredded Monterey Jack or Cheddar cheese	125 mL
1/2 cup	milk (approx.)	125 mL
	Salt	
	Hot pepper sauce	

1. Remove tough stem ends from fresh spinach; wash in cold water. Place spinach with moisture clinging to leaves in a large saucepan. Cook over high heat, stirring, until just wilted. (If using frozen spinach, see Tips, left.) Place spinach in a colander to drain. Squeeze out moisture by hand; wrap in a clean, dry towel and squeeze out excess moisture.
2. In a medium saucepan, combine spinach, cream cheese, salsa, green onions, garlic, oregano and cumin. Cook over medium heat, stirring, for 2 to 3 minutes or until smooth and piping hot.
3. Stir in cheese and milk; cook for 2 minutes or until cheese melts. Add more milk to thin dip, if desired. Season with salt and hot pepper sauce to taste. Spoon into serving dish.

Microwave Method

1. In an 8-cup (2 L) casserole dish, combine spinach, cream cheese, salsa, onions, garlic, oregano and cumin; cover and microwave at Medium for 4 minutes, stirring once. Add cheese and milk; cover and microwave at Medium-High, stirring once, for 2 to 3 minutes, or until cheese is melted. Season with salt and hot pepper sauce to taste.

MAKES 2 CUPS (500 ML)

This creamy dip relies on lower-fat dairy products and zesty herbs, so it clocks in with a lot less fat and calories than you might imagine. Make it at least a day ahead to let flavors develop. Serve with fresh veggies.

TIPS

Other fresh herbs, including basil, can be added according to what you have in the fridge or growing in your garden. If you're fond of fresh dill, increase the amount to 2 tbsp (25 mL).

This dip also makes a great dressing for pasta and potato salads. Store in a covered container in the fridge for up to one week.

Do-Ahead Herb Dip

1 cup	creamed cottage cheese	250 mL
1/2 cup	plain yogurt or sour cream	125 mL
1/2 cup	light mayonnaise	125 mL
1/3 cup	finely chopped fresh parsley	75 mL
2 tbsp	finely chopped fresh chives or minced green onions	25 mL
1 tbsp	chopped fresh dill	15 mL
1 1/2 tsp	Dijon mustard	7 mL
1 tsp	red wine vinegar or lemon juice	5 mL
	Hot pepper sauce	

1. In a food processor, purée cottage cheese, yogurt and mayonnaise until very smooth and creamy.
2. Transfer to a bowl; stir in parsley, chives, dill, mustard, vinegar and hot pepper sauce to taste. Cover and refrigerate.

SERVES 8

Variations of the popular bean dip always make the party circuit. Here's my updated version. It has an oregano-bean base, a creamy jalapeño cheese layer and a vibrant fresh topping of tomatoes, olives and cilantro.

TIP

Fresh cilantro, also called coriander and Chinese parsley, lasts only a few days in the fridge before it deteriorates and turns tasteless. Wash cilantro well, spin dry and wrap in paper towels; store in plastic bag in the fridge. Leave the roots on — they keep the leaves fresh.

Always Popular Layered Bean Dip

8-inch (20 cm) shallow round serving dish or pie plate

1	can (19 oz/540 mL) red kidney beans or black beans, drained and rinsed	1
1	clove garlic, minced	1
1 tsp	dried oregano leaves	5 mL
1/2 tsp	ground cumin	2 mL
1 tbsp	water	15 mL
1 cup	shredded Monterey Jack or Cheddar cheese	250 mL
3/4 cup	sour cream	175 mL
1 tbsp	minced pickled jalapeño peppers	15 mL
2	tomatoes, seeded and finely diced	2
1	Haas avocado, peeled and diced (optional)	1
2	green onions, finely chopped	2
1/3 cup	sliced black olives	75 mL
1/3 cup	chopped fresh cilantro or parsley	75 mL

1. In a food processor, combine beans, garlic, oregano, cumin and water; process until smooth. Spread in serving dish.
2. In a bowl, combine cheese, sour cream and jalapeño peppers. Spread over bean layer. (Can be assembled earlier in day; cover and refrigerate.)
3. Just before serving, sprinkle with tomatoes, avocado (if using), green onions, olives and cilantro. Serve with tortilla chips or pita crisps (see Tip, page 20).

MAKES 2 CUPS (500 ML)

I like to serve this tasty easy-to-make spread with warm squares of focaccia or pita crisps.

TIP

Dip can be made up to three days ahead.

VARIATION

Instead of fresh basil, increase chopped parsley to 2 tbsp (25 mL) and add $\frac{1}{2}$ tsp (2 mL) dried basil leaves to the onions when cooking.

Italian White Bean Spread

2 tbsp	olive oil	25 mL
1	small onion, finely chopped	1
2	large cloves garlic, finely chopped	2
1 tbsp	red wine vinegar	15 mL
1	can (19 oz/540 mL) white kidney beans, drained and rinsed	1
2 tbsp	finely chopped oil-packed sun-dried tomatoes	25 mL
1 tbsp	chopped fresh parsley	15 mL
1 tbsp	chopped fresh basil leaves	15 mL
	Freshly ground black pepper	

1. In a small saucepan, combine oil, onion and garlic; cook over medium-low heat, stirring occasionally, for 5 minutes or until softened (do not brown). Add vinegar and remove from heat. In a food processor, purée kidney beans and onion mixture until smooth.
2. Transfer to a bowl. Stir in sun-dried tomatoes, parsley and basil; season with pepper to taste. Cover and refrigerate.

MAKES GENEROUS 2 CUPS (500 ML) WITH 24 PITA BITES

You can buy hummus, the classic spread from the Middle East, in most supermarkets, but I find it so easy to make in my home kitchen. Serve it as a dip with pita wedges or use as a sandwich spread.

TIP

Thin hummus, if desired, by stirring in additional water.

Hummus

1	can (19 oz/540 mL) chickpeas, rinsed and drained	1
1/3 cup	tahini	75 mL
2 to 3	cloves garlic, chopped	2 to 3
1/4 cup	olive oil	50 mL
1/4 cup	fresh lemon juice	50 mL
2 tbsp	water	25 mL
2 tbsp	finely chopped fresh parsley	25 mL
	Salt and freshly ground black pepper	

1. In a food processor or blender, purée chickpeas, tahini, garlic, olive oil, lemon juice and water until smooth.

2. Transfer to a bowl; stir in parsley and season with salt and pepper to taste.

Hummus Pita Bites

2	7-inch (18 cm) thin soft pitas, split	2
1 cup	hummus	250 mL
1/2	small seedless cucumber	1/2
1/2	small red bell pepper, cut into thin strips	1/2

1. Spread the rough sides of each pita generously with hummus, leaving a small border.

2. Cut cucumber into 5-inch (12 cm) long strips, each 1/4-inch (0.5 cm) thick. Place a few cucumber and red pepper strips along edge of pita halves and roll into a tight bundle. Wrap each in plastic wrap and refrigerate up until serving time.

3. To serve, trim ends and slice into 1-inch (2.5 cm) pieces. Place cut side up on a serving plate.

MAKES 2½ CUPS (625 ML)

Here's a modern spin to an old standby, chicken liver spread. Even if you're not a big fan of liver, you'll be instantly won over when you try this lightly sweetened pâté with currants and Port. Serve with warm toasted baguette slices.

TIPS

Make the pâté up to three days ahead. Cover surface with plastic wrap and refrigerate. Or pack into containers and freeze for up to one month.

The taste of freshly grated nutmeg is so much better than the pre-ground variety. Whole nutmeg can be found in the spice section of your supermarket or bulk food store. Look for inexpensive nutmeg graters in kitchenware shops.

Party Pâté

3 tbsp	dried currants	45 mL
3 tbsp	ruby Port	45 mL
1 lb	chicken livers	500 g
½ cup	water	125 mL
2 tbsp	butter	25 mL
1	medium onion, finely chopped	1
1 cup	peeled, chopped apples	250 mL
¾ tsp	salt	4 mL
½ tsp	dried sage leaves	2 mL
½ tsp	freshly ground black pepper	2 mL
¼ tsp	freshly grated nutmeg (see Tips, left)	1 mL
⅓ cup	butter, cut into small cubes	75 mL
	Toasted baguette slices (see Tips, page 16)	

1. In a small glass dish, combine currants and Port; microwave at High for 1 minute until plump. Set aside.
2. Trim chicken livers and cut into quarters. Place in a large nonstick skillet with water; bring to a boil over medium heat, stirring often, for 5 minutes or until no longer pink. Drain in sieve; transfer liver to food processor.
3. Rinse and dry skillet; add 2 tbsp (25 mL) butter and melt over medium heat. Add onion, apples, salt, sage, pepper and nutmeg; cook, stirring often, for 5 minutes or until softened.
4. Add onion-apple mixture to liver in bowl of food processor; purée until very smooth. Let cool slightly. Add butter cubes to liver mixture and purée until creamy. Add reserved currants and Port; pulse, using on-off turns, until just combined.
5. Spoon into a serving bowl. Cover surface with plastic wrap and refrigerate until firm, about 4 hours or overnight. Serve with baguette slices.

MAKES 24 APPETIZERS

Here's another last-minute idea for tasty bites to serve when friends drop over. These small nibblers are a throwback to the cocktail/lounge scene of the 1960s, when appetizers often meant cold cuts wrapped around a pickle. I like them because they can be assembled in a few minutes and are a colorful addition to a tray of warm appetizers.

TIP

This recipe can be varied according to what you have on hand. Thin slices of salami or ham folded in half, cocktail onions and marinated artichoke pieces make for other easy combinations.

Antipasto Nibblers

24	stuffed green olives or Kalamata olives	24
8 oz	Fontina cheese, cut into 3/4-inch (2 cm) cubes	250 g
1	small red bell pepper, cut into 1-inch (2.5 cm) squares	1
1	small green bell pepper, cut into 1-inch (2.5 cm) squares	1
1 tbsp	olive oil	15 mL
1 tbsp	balsamic vinegar	15 mL
	Freshly ground black pepper	
2 tbsp	chopped fresh basil leaves or parsley	25 mL

1. Thread 1 olive, 1 cheese cube, then 1 pepper square on cocktail toothpicks. Arrange in attractive shallow serving dish. Cover and refrigerate until serving time.
2. In a small bowl, whisk together oil and balsamic vinegar; pour over kabobs. Season generously with pepper; sprinkle with basil and serve.

MAKES ABOUT 48 ROUNDS

Here's an updated version of the classic cheese ball, an appetizer that dominated the party scene in the 1950s and 1960s. This recipe may seem to call for a lot of peppercorns, but it's not all that peppery. It just has a lively zip.

TIPS

To crack peppercorns, place in a heavy plastic bag and, on a wooden board, crush using a rolling pin or heavy skillet.

Cheese logs can be frozen for up to one month. Defrost in the refrigerator for several hours before slicing.

VARIATION

Cheddar Walnut Rounds

Substitute 1/3 cup (75 mL) finely chopped walnuts or pecans for cracked peppercorns.

Cheddar Pepper Rounds

8 oz	aged Cheddar cheese, shredded	250 g
4 oz	cream cheese	125 g
2 tbsp	brandy or sherry	25 mL
1/4 cup	finely chopped fresh parsley	50 mL
1 tbsp	cracked black peppercorns (see Tip, left)	15 mL

1. In a food processor, combine Cheddar cheese, cream cheese and brandy. Process until mixture is very smooth. Transfer to a bowl; refrigerate for 3 hours or until firm.
2. Divide mixture into two pieces; wrap each in plastic wrap. Roll on a flat surface and shape into a smooth log measuring about 6 inches by 1 1/2 inches (15 by 4 cm).
3. Place parsley and cracked peppercorns on a plate. Unwrap cheese logs and roll in parsley-peppercorn mixture until evenly coated. Wrap again in plastic wrap and refrigerate until firm.
4. To serve, cut each log into 1/4-inch (0.5 cm) slices and place on small toasted bread rounds, Melba toasts or crackers.

MAKES ABOUT 64

I make double batches of these wonderfully cheese-laden sticks, especially at holiday time. They are perfect as appetizers and great to serve along with soup. To obtain the richest flavor, buy a wedge of authentic Parmigiano Reggiano and have it finely grated for you at the cheese shop.

TIP

Baked straws can be stored in covered container for up to five days. Or freeze unbaked straws for up to two months in a covered container lined with waxed paper. No need to defrost before baking.

Nippy Parmesan Cheese Straws

Preheat oven to 375°F (190°C)
Baking sheet(s), lined with parchment paper

1 cup	freshly grated Parmesan cheese	250 mL
1/2 tsp	paprika	2 mL
1/4 tsp	cayenne pepper	1 mL
1	package (14 oz/400 g) puff pastry (2 sheets)	1

1. In a bowl, combine Parmesan, paprika and cayenne pepper.
2. Sprinkle work surface with 2 tbsp (25 mL) of the Parmesan mixture to cover an area approximately the same size as one pastry sheet. Top with pastry sheet; sprinkle with another 2 tbsp (25 mL) of the Parmesan mixture.
3. Roll out pastry to make a 10-inch (25 cm) square. Sprinkle half the pastry with 2 tbsp (25 mL) of the Parmesan mixture; fold dough over in half. Sprinkle with 2 tbsp (25 mL) more Parmesan mixture. Roll out to make a thin 12-by 10-inch (30 by 25 cm) rectangle. Cut dough in half to make two 12-by 5-inch (30 by 12.5 cm) rectangles.
4. With a sharp knife and using a ruler as a guide, cut pastry into strips measuring 5 by 3/4 inches (13 by 2 cm); twist each strip three or four times to make a spiral. Arrange on prepared baking sheets, pressing the ends onto the sheets to hold them in place.
5. Repeat steps 2 through 4 with second pastry sheet and remaining Parmesan mixture.
6. Freeze for 15 minutes or until pastry is firm. Bake in preheated oven for 14 to 16 minutes or until puffed and golden. Transfer to a rack to cool.

SERVES 4

This makes a very simple but delicious appetizer. If you are expecting a large crowd, buy a larger wheel of Brie and top with generous layer of chutney and chopped walnuts. Bake a few minutes longer or until sides are soft to the touch.

TIPS

Make extra batches of the chutney and pack the hot mixture into sterilized 1-cup (250 mL) preserving jars and fit with two-piece lids. Process in boiling water bath for 10 minutes to ensure a vacuum seal.

A jar of this chutney tied with a colorful swatch of fabric and a pretty ribbon makes a wonderful hostess gift.

It also makes a fabulous condiment to serve with Roast Turkey (see recipe, page 110) or try it with Tourtière (see recipe, page 170).

Baked Brie with Cranberry-Pear Chutney

Preheat oven to 350°F (180°C)
Baking sheet, lined with foil

1	round of Brie cheese (7 oz/200 g)	1
1/4 cup	Cranberry-Pear Chutney (see recipe below)	50 mL
2 tbsp	finely chopped walnuts	25 mL
	Baguette slices	

1. Arrange Brie on prepared baking sheet. Spread top with chutney; sprinkle with walnuts.
2. Bake in preheated oven for 5 to 7 minutes or until sides of Brie are soft to the touch. Using a metal spatula, transfer to a serving plate; surround with bread slices. Serve warm.

Cranberry-Pear Chutney

Makes about 3 cups (750 mL)

3 cups	fresh or frozen cranberries	750 mL
1 1/2 cups	peeled, finely diced pears, such as Anjou	375 mL
1	small onion, finely chopped	1
1 cup	packed brown sugar	250 mL
1/2 cup	orange juice	125 mL
1/2 cup	cider vinegar	125 mL
1/2 cup	golden raisins	125 mL
1 tbsp	grated orange zest	15 mL
1 tsp	ground ginger	5 mL

1. In a large saucepan, combine cranberries, pears, onion, brown sugar, orange juice, vinegar, raisins, orange zest and ginger. Bring to a boil over medium heat.
2. Simmer, uncovered, stirring occasionally, for 15 to 20 minutes or until mixture has thickened and fruit is tender.

MAKES 1¼ CUPS (300 ML)

You can whip up this reliable recipe in only a few minutes using ingredients you keep on hand in the pantry and in the fridge. It's equally good with crackers or vegetable dippers. You'll turn to it, as I have, time and time again.

TIPS

Microwave cold cream cheese at Medium for 1 minute to soften.

Spread can be prepared up to two days ahead, covered and refrigerated.

Rosy Shrimp Spread

4 oz	cream cheese, softened	125 g
¼ cup	sour cream or plain yogurt	50 mL
2 tbsp	prepared chili sauce	25 mL
1 tsp	prepared horseradish	5 mL
	Hot pepper sauce to taste	
1	can (4 oz/113 g) small shrimp, drained and rinsed	1
1 tbsp	minced green onion tops or chopped fresh chives	15 mL

1. In a bowl, beat cream cheese until smooth. Stir in sour cream, chili sauce, horseradish and hot pepper sauce.

2. Fold in shrimp and green onions. Transfer to serving dish; cover and refrigerate until serving time.

Smoked Salmon Mousse (page 33) ➢

MAKES 3 CUPS (750 ML)

This is one of my most-requested recipes. It delivers a wonderful smoked salmon flavor, but uses relatively little of that costly ingredient. My secret? I work magic with canned salmon, which keeps the cost reasonable so I can serve this appetizer more often.

TIPS

I prefer to use canned sockeye salmon (instead of the pink variety) for its superior color and flavor.

The mousse can be prepared up to four days ahead for easy entertaining.

To get more juice out of a lemon, roll on counter top or microwave at High for 20 seconds before squeezing.

Smoked Salmon Mousse

1/3 cup	dry white wine or water	75 mL
1	package (1/4 oz/7 g) unflavored gelatin	1
1	can (7 1/2 oz/213 g) sockeye salmon, drained, skin removed	1
1 cup	sour cream	250 mL
1/2 tsp	grated lemon zest	2 mL
1 tbsp	fresh lemon juice	15 mL
1/4 tsp	salt	1 mL
	Hot pepper sauce to taste	
4 oz	smoked salmon, finely chopped	125 g
2 tbsp	minced green onions	25 mL
2 tbsp	finely chopped fresh dill	25 mL
1/2 cup	whipping (35%) cream, whipped	125 mL
	Dill sprigs and lemon zest for garnish	

1. Place wine in a small bowl; sprinkle gelatin over. Let stand 5 minutes to soften. Microwave at Medium for 1 minute or until dissolved.
2. In a food processor, combine canned salmon, sour cream, lemon zest and juice, salt and hot pepper sauce; process until smooth. Add gelatin mixture; process until combined.
3. Transfer mixture to a bowl. Stir in smoked salmon, green onions and dill; fold in whipped cream.
4. Spoon mixture into a serving dish. Cover loosely with plastic wrap (it should not touch surface of the mousse); refrigerate for 4 hours or overnight. Garnish top with dill sprigs and lemon zest; serve with Melba toast or pumpernickel rounds.

◄ Cheese-Smothered Onion Soup (page 46)

MAKES 24 APPETIZERS

Everyone loves smoked salmon and these popular appetizers are always the first to go at a party.

TIPS

These appetizers can be made earlier in the day or even the day ahead — just cover and refrigerate. Garnish shortly before serving.

Use this cream cheese and mustard spread instead of mayonnaise when you're making finger sandwiches with sliced smoked ham or turkey.

Irresistible Smoked Salmon Bites

4 oz	cream cheese	125 g
1 tbsp	finely chopped fresh dill	15 mL
2 tsp	honey mustard	10 mL
2 tsp	grainy mustard	10 mL
2 tsp	fresh lemon juice	10 mL
6	slices dark rye or pumpernickel bread, crusts trimmed	6
6 oz	sliced smoked salmon	175 g
	Capers and dill sprigs for garnish	

1. Place cream cheese in a bowl; microwave at Medium for 1 minute to soften. Stir well. Blend in dill, honey mustard, grainy mustard and lemon juice.

2. Generously spread mustard mixture over bread slices; layer with smoked salmon. Cut each slice into four triangles or squares, or six rectangles. Garnish with capers and dill. Cover with plastic wrap and refrigerate.

SERVES 8 AS AN APPETIZER OR 4 AS A MAIN COURSE

These spicy wings are always a party hit. They're deliciously messy, so be sure to have plenty of napkins on hand.

TIP

You can also partially cook the wings in the oven for the first 20 minutes and complete the cooking on the barbecue over medium heat.

Honey-Garlic Chicken Wings

Preheat oven to 400°F (200°C)
Baking sheet, lined with foil then brushed with oil

3 lbs	chicken wings, separated and tips removed	1.5 kg
1/3 cup	soy sauce	75 mL
1/4 cup	liquid honey	50 mL
2 tbsp	hoisin sauce	25 mL
2 tbsp	rice vinegar	25 mL
2	large cloves garlic, minced	2
2 tsp	hot pepper sauce or more to taste	10 mL

1. Place chicken wings in a large heavy plastic bag and set in a large bowl. In a small bowl, combine soy sauce, honey, hoisin sauce, vinegar, garlic and hot pepper sauce. Pour over wings, close tightly and seal. Let marinate in fridge for several hours or overnight.
2. On prepared baking sheet, arrange wings in a single layer; bake in preheated oven for 20 minutes. Pour off pan juices and turn wings over.
3. Meanwhile, place marinade in a small saucepan. Bring to a boil over medium heat; cook 3 to 5 minutes or until slightly thickened. Baste wings liberally with marinade.
4. Bake 15 to 20 minutes more or until wings are tender and nicely glazed.

MAKES ABOUT 72 MEATBALLS

Who doesn't love meatballs as an appetizer? As fast as I fill the serving bowls with them, they disappear.

TIP

Cooked meatballs can be made up to one day ahead and kept covered in the refrigerator, or frozen for up to two months. To freeze, place meatballs in a single layer on trays; when frozen, transfer to covered containers. To defrost quickly, place meatballs in a casserole dish and microwave at High for 4 to 5 minutes until just warmed through, stirring once.

Appetizer Meatballs

Preheat oven to 400°F (200°C)
Baking sheet, greased

1 tbsp	vegetable oil	15 mL
1	medium onion, finely chopped	1
2	cloves garlic, minced	2
3/4 tsp	salt	4 mL
1/2 tsp	dried thyme leaves	2 mL
1/2 tsp	freshly ground black pepper	2 mL
1/2 cup	beef stock	125 mL
2 tsp	Worcestershire sauce	10 mL
2 lbs	lean ground beef	1 kg
1 cup	soft fresh bread crumbs	250 mL
2 tbsp	finely chopped fresh parsley	25 mL
1	large egg, lightly beaten	1

1. In a medium nonstick skillet, heat oil over medium heat. Add onion, garlic, salt, thyme and pepper; cook, stirring often, for 5 minutes or until softened. Stir in beef stock and Worcestershire sauce; let cool slightly.
2. In a bowl, combine onion mixture, ground beef, bread crumbs, parsley and egg; mix thoroughly.
3. Form beef mixture into 1-inch (2.5 cm) balls; arrange on prepared baking sheet. Bake in preheated oven for 18 to 20 minutes or until nicely browned. Transfer to a paper towel-lined plate to drain.

MAKES 36 APPETIZERS

This versatile dipping sauce is also good with chicken or pork kebabs, or with chicken wings. For a spicy version, add hot pepper sauce to taste.

Party Meatballs with Sweet-and-Sour Sauce

1/2 cup	orange juice	125 mL
1/4 cup	soy sauce	50 mL
1/4 cup	ketchup	50 mL
1/4 cup	packed brown sugar	50 mL
2 tbsp	balsamic vinegar	25 mL
1	clove garlic, minced	1
1 1/2 tsp	cornstarch	7 mL
36	Appetizer Meatballs (half the recipe, see page 36)	36

1. In a medium saucepan, stir together orange juice, soy sauce, ketchup, brown sugar, vinegar, garlic and cornstarch until smooth. Bring to a boil over medium heat, stirring constantly, until sauce is thick and smooth.

2. Stir in cooked meatballs; cover and simmer for 5 minutes or until heated through.

MAKES 2½ CUPS (625 ML)

Supermarket shelves are lined with great-tasting salsas. Take your favorite salsa, throw in a few roasted vegetables and voila! — you've got yourself a snazzy spread. This versatile sauce makes a wonderful condiment for sandwiches with cold cuts or cheese, or as a pizza topping.

TIPS

Prepare ratatouille salsa ahead. It keeps well in a covered container in the refrigerator for three days or one month in the freezer.

Dice the vegetables into uniform ¼-inch (0.5 cm) pieces.

Medium salsa gives a nice burst of heat to the sauce. If using mild salsa, add hot pepper sauce to taste.

Ratatouille Salsa

Preheat oven to 425°F (220°C)
Baking sheet, greased

1½ cups	diced eggplant	375 mL
1½ cups	diced zucchini	375 mL
1	red bell pepper, diced	1
1 tsp	dried basil leaves	5 mL
1 tbsp	olive oil	15 mL
1½ cups	medium salsa	375 mL
¼ cup	chopped fresh parsley	50 mL
1	clove garlic, minced	1
	Tortilla chips	

1. Spread eggplant, zucchini and red pepper on prepared baking sheet. Sprinkle with basil; drizzle with oil. Roast in oven, stirring occasionally, for about 20 minutes or until vegetables are tender and lightly colored.

2. Transfer to a bowl; stir in salsa, parsley and garlic. Cover and refrigerate. Serve with tortilla chips.

MAKES 24 APPETIZERS

Here's a more appealing version of nachos and cheese — and it's lower in fat.

Ratatouille Nachos

Preheat broiler
Baking sheet

24	round nacho tortilla chips	24
1 cup	Ratatouille Salsa (see recipe, page 38)	250 mL
1 cup	shredded mild Asiago or Provolone cheese	250 mL

1. Arrange nachos in a single layer on baking sheet. Top each with about 2 tsp (10 mL) salsa; sprinkle with cheese. Place under preheated broiler for 2 minutes or until cheese melts. Watch carefully; serve warm.

MAKES 48 TRIANGLES

Phyllo pastry makes great crisp wrappers for a variety of savory fillings. The pastry is used extensively in Mediterranean cooking and fits in perfectly with the modern notion of comfort foods because it delivers taste, style and convenience, too. I make batches of these Greek-inspired appetizers ahead and then freeze them. The only thing left to do is pop them in the oven and serve.

TIPS

To freeze, place unbaked triangles on baking sheets; freeze until firm. Place in waxed paper-lined containers; freeze for up to two months. No need to defrost before baking.

The artichoke filling also freezes well. Pack into containers and freeze for one month.

Artichoke Phyllo Triangles

Preheat oven to 375°F (190°C)
Baking sheet, lightly greased

1 tbsp	olive oil	15 mL
1	can (14 oz/398 mL) artichoke hearts or bottoms, drained well, finely chopped	1
4	green onions, finely chopped	4
2	cloves garlic, minced	2
1 tsp	dried oregano leaves	5 mL
1/4 cup	finely chopped oil-packed sun-dried tomatoes	50 mL
1/4 cup	finely chopped Kalamata olives	50 mL
1 cup	shredded Gruyère cheese	250 mL
1/4 cup	freshly grated Parmesan cheese, (plus extra for topping)	50 mL
	Freshly ground black pepper	
6	sheets phyllo pastry	6
1/3 cup	olive oil or melted butter (approx.)	75 mL

1. In a large nonstick skillet, heat oil over medium-high heat. Add artichokes, green onions, garlic and oregano; cook, stirring, for 3 minutes or until softened. Stir in sun-dried tomatoes and olives. Remove from heat; transfer to bowl and let cool slightly.

2. Stir in Gruyère and Parmesan cheeses; season with pepper. (Recipe can be prepared up to this point, then kept covered and refrigerated, up to three days.)

3. Place one phyllo sheet on work surface. (To prevent remaining sheets from drying out, keep them covered with waxed paper, then a damp kitchen towel.) Brush pastry lightly with oil or melted butter. Cut crosswise into eight strips, each 2 inches (5 cm) wide.

4. Place 1 tsp (5 mL) filling at bottom-left corner of each strip; fold right corner over filling to meet the left side to form a triangle. Continue wrapping pastry around filling, maintaining a triangular shape.
5. Place on prepared baking sheet. Brush top lightly with olive oil. Continue making triangles with remaining phyllo and filling in the same way. Bake in preheated oven for 14 to 16 minutes or until golden.

VARIATION

Spread artichoke filling on lightly toasted baguette slices (see Tips, page 16). Sprinkle with additional Parmesan cheese. Bake in preheated oven for 8 minutes or until heated through.

SERVES 8

Spinach and feta pie, a classic Greek comfort food, can be served warm or at room temperature as an appetizer or part of a buffet.

Spanakopita

Preheat oven to 375°F (190°C)
13-by 9-inch (3.5 L) baking pan, greased

2	bags (10 oz/300 g) fresh spinach	2
6 tbsp	olive oil (approx.)	90 mL
1 cup	sliced green onions	250 mL
2	eggs	2
1½ cups	finely crumbled feta cheese (about 6 oz/175 g)	375 mL
¼ cup	chopped fresh dill	50 mL
	Freshly ground black pepper	
11	sheets phyllo pastry	11

1. Rinse spinach in cold water; remove tough ends. Place in Dutch oven or large saucepan with just enough water clinging to leaves; cook, over medium-high heat, stirring, until just wilted. Drain well and squeeze dry; finely chop.
2. In a large nonstick skillet, heat 1 tbsp (15 mL) oil over medium-high heat; cook spinach and green onions, stirring, for 4 minutes or until spinach is just tender. Let cool.
3. In a bowl, beat eggs; add spinach mixture, feta, dill and season with pepper.
4. Cover phyllo sheets with plastic wrap; place a damp towel on top to prevent drying out. Place one sheet of phyllo on work surface and brush lightly with oil. Fit into baking pan with ends hanging over sides. Layer five more phyllo sheets in pan, brushing each with oil before adding the next. Evenly spread with spinach filling and fold ends over filling. Layer remaining five phyllo sheets on top, brushing each lightly with oil before adding the next. Carefully fold pastry edges under bottom pastry.
5. Using a sharp knife cut the top phyllo layers into squares or diamond pattern. Brush top with oil. Bake in oven for 35 to 40 minutes or until golden. Let cool for 10 minutes before cutting into serving-size pieces.

Soups

SERVES 8

Often called "Jewish penicillin," chicken soup is the perfect antidote to an oncoming cold. But there's more to its restorative powers. Rich and delicious, it can banish the winter blues and make you feel just plain good any day of the year.

TIP

You don't have to slave over the stove to make this soul-satisfying soup. Adding the chicken and the vegetables to the pot at the same time streamlines the process and does away with the chore of making stock first. The results are every bit as pleasing.

Chicken Noodle Soup

3 lbs	whole chicken or chicken pieces, such as legs and breasts	1.5 kg
10 cups	water (approx.)	2.5 L
1	large onion, finely chopped	1
3	carrots, peeled and chopped	3
2	stalks celery including leaves, chopped	2
2 tbsp	chopped fresh parsley	25 mL
½ tsp	dried thyme leaves	2 mL
2 tsp	salt	10 mL
¼ tsp	freshly ground black pepper	1 mL
1	bay leaf	1
2 cups	medium or broad egg noodles	500 mL
1 cup	finely diced zucchini or small cauliflower florets	250 mL
2 tbsp	chopped fresh dill or parsley	25 mL

1. Rinse chicken; remove as much skin and excess fat as possible. Place in a large stockpot; add water to cover. Bring to a boil over high heat; using a slotted spoon, skim off foam as it rises to the surface.
2. Add onion, carrots, celery, parsley, thyme, salt, pepper and bay leaf. Reduce heat to medium-low; cover and simmer for about 1¼ hours or until chicken is tender.
3. Remove chicken with slotted spoon and place in a large bowl; let cool slightly. Pull chicken meat off the bones, discarding skin and bones. Cut meat into bite-size pieces. Reserve 2 cups (500 mL) for soup. (Use remainder for casseroles and sandwiches.)
4. Skim fat from surface of soup; bring to a boil. Add cubed chicken, noodles, zucchini and dill; cook for 10 minutes or until noodles and vegetables are tender. Remove bay leaf. Adjust seasoning with salt and pepper to taste.

MAKES ABOUT 8 CUPS (2 L)

Chicken stock is one of the most indispensable flavoring agents in the kitchen. Commercial stock cubes and powders are loaded with salt and just don't deliver the flavor of homemade stock. But who has time to make stock from scratch these days? If you can spare 5 minutes, I'll tell you how I make my mine.

Quick Chicken Stock

3 lbs	chicken bones (such as neck, backbones and wing tips)	1.5 kg
10 cups	cold water	2.5 L
1	large onion, chopped	1
2	carrots, chopped	2
1	large stalk celery, including leaves, chopped	1
1/2 tsp	dried thyme leaves	2 mL
1	bay leaf	1
1 tsp	salt	5 mL
1 tsp	freshly ground black pepper	5 mL

1. Place chicken bones in a large stockpot. Cover with cold water. Add the remaining ingredients.

2. Simmer, covered, for 2 hours; strain. Refrigerate for three days or freeze for up to three months in containers.

SERVES 6

A good melting cheese with a nice nutty flavor, such as Gruyère or raclette, works very well in this savory soup that will warm you up on cold blustery days. The assertive flavor of onions mellows and sweetens when cooked until golden. This classic makes an easy transition from an everyday dish to an entertainment standout.

TIPS

Buy French bread 3 to 4 inches (8 to 10 cm) in diameter. Or, if using a thin baguette, use two slices of bread in each bowl.

The onion soup base can be made ahead and refrigerated for up to five days or frozen for up to three months.

Hate shedding tears when chopping onions? To minimize the weeping problem, use a razor-sharp knife to prevent loss of juices and cover the cut onions with a paper towel as you chop them to prevent the vapors from rising to your eyes.

Cheese-Smothered Onion Soup

3 tbsp	butter	45 mL
8 cups	thinly sliced Spanish onions (about 2 to 3)	2 L
1/4 tsp	dried thyme leaves	1 mL
1/4 tsp	freshly ground black pepper	1 mL
2 tbsp	all-purpose flour	25 mL
6 cups	beef stock	1.5 L
1 tbsp	olive oil	15 mL
1	large clove garlic, minced	1
6	slices French bread, about 3/4-inch (2 cm) thick	6
2 cups	shredded Gruyère cheese	500 mL

1. In a Dutch oven or large heavy saucepan, melt butter over medium heat. Add onions, thyme and pepper; cook, stirring often, for 15 minutes or until onions are tender and a rich golden color. Blend in flour; stir in stock. Bring to a boil, stirring until thickened. Reduce heat to medium-low, cover and simmer for 15 minutes.
2. Meanwhile, position oven rack 6 inches (15 cm) from broiler; preheat broiler.
3. In a small bowl, combine olive oil and garlic; lightly brush oil mixture over both sides of bread. Arrange on baking sheet; place under broiler and toast on both sides.
4. Place toasts in deep ovenproof soup bowls; sprinkle with half the cheese. Arrange bowls in large shallow baking pan. Ladle hot soup in bowls. Sprinkle with remaining cheese. Place under broiler for 3 minutes or until cheese melts and is lightly browned. Serve immediately.

SERVES 8

My family came from the Netherlands to Southern Ontario in the 1950s and we were raised on this warming Dutch soup. When I lived in Quebec for several years, I discovered pea soup was also a key staple in that province's food heritage and I felt right at home.

TIP

For a wonderful rich flavor, I like to add a meaty ham bone to the soup as it simmers. As most hams sold today in supermarkets are boneless, however, the addition of both chopped smoked ham and chicken stock make a good substitute. Do add a ham bone, though, if you have one, and use water instead of stock. Smoked pork hock is another alternative if a ham bone is not available. Remove ham bone at end of cooking; scrape off any meat and add to soup.

Old-Fashioned Pea Soup with Smoked Ham

2 tbsp	butter	25 mL
1	medium leek, white and light green part only, chopped (see Tips, page 59)	1
1	large onion, chopped	1
2	large cloves garlic, finely chopped	2
3	carrots, peeled and chopped	3
1	large stalk celery including leaves, chopped	1
1 1/2 tsp	dried marjoram leaves	7 mL
1	bay leaf	1
1/4 tsp	freshly ground black pepper	1 mL
8 cups	chicken stock (approx.)	2 L
2 cups	chopped smoked ham	500 mL
1 1/2 cups	dried yellow or green split peas, rinsed and picked over	375 mL
	Salt	
1/4 cup	chopped fresh parsley	50 mL

1. In a Dutch oven or stockpot, melt butter over medium heat. Add leek, onion, garlic, carrots, celery, marjoram, bay leaf and pepper; cook, stirring often, for 8 minutes or until softened.
2. Stir in stock, ham and split peas. Bring to a boil; reduce heat, cover and simmer, stirring occasionally, for about 1 1/2 hours or until split peas are tender.
3. Remove bay leaf. Adjust seasoning with salt and pepper to taste. Stir in parsley. Soup thickens as it cools; thin with additional stock or water to desired consistency.

SERVES 8

Here's a homey satisfying soup that's perfect to serve as the main event on cold, blustery days.

TIPS

This recipe makes a large batch of soup; freeze extra for another meal.

If you have any leftover baked ham, dice into small cubes and add along with the split peas. Another option is to add diced smoked sausage, such as kielbasa, for the last 15 minutes of cooking.

Curried Split Pea Soup

1 tbsp	vegetable oil	15 mL
2	medium onions, chopped	2
4	cloves garlic, finely chopped	4
1 tbsp	mild curry paste or powder	15 mL
1 tsp	ground cumin	5 mL
1 tsp	paprika	5 mL
1/4 tsp	cayenne pepper	1 mL
3	large carrots, peeled and chopped	3
2	large stalks celery including leaves, chopped	2
2 cups	yellow or green split peas, rinsed and sorted	500 mL
1/4 cup	tomato paste	50 mL
10 cups	vegetable or chicken stock	2.5 L
1/3 cup	chopped fresh cilantro or parsley	75 mL
	Salt and freshly ground black pepper	
	Plain yogurt (optional)	

1. In a large Dutch oven or stockpot, heat oil over medium heat. Add onions, garlic, curry paste, cumin, paprika and cayenne pepper; cook, stirring, for 3 minutes or until softened.
2. Add carrots, celery, split peas, tomato paste and stock. Bring to a boil; reduce heat, cover and simmer for about 1 to 1 1/2 hours or until peas are tender.
3. Stir in cilantro; season with salt and pepper to taste. Ladle into bowls; top with a dollop of yogurt, if desired. Soup thickens as it cools, so you may want to thin with additional stock before serving.

SERVES 6

My pantry can be sparse, but I can always count on having these few ingredients on hand to make this last-minute soup to serve with crusty whole-grain bread and cheese.

TIPS

Instead of canned tomatoes, use 4 large ripe tomatoes, peeled and chopped.

To make a creamy tomato-rice soup, add $\frac{1}{2}$ cup (125 mL) whipping (35%) cream along with the parsley.

If you have fresh basil on hand, substitute 2 tbsp (25 mL) of the chopped fresh herb for the dried basil in recipe and add along with parsley.

Basil Tomato-Rice Soup

1 tbsp	olive oil	15 mL
1	large onion, chopped	1
2	stalks celery, chopped	2
2	cloves garlic, finely chopped	2
1 tsp	dried basil leaves	5 mL
1	can (28 oz/796 mL) plum tomatoes, including juice	1
6 cups	chicken or vegetable stock	1.5 L
$\frac{1}{2}$ cup	long-grain white rice	125 mL
1 tsp	granulated sugar (approx.)	5 mL
	Salt and freshly ground black pepper	
2 tbsp	chopped fresh parsley	25 mL

1. In a Dutch oven or stockpot, heat oil over medium heat. Add onion, celery, garlic and basil; cook, stirring, for 5 minutes or until softened.

2. In a food processor, purée tomatoes with juice. Add to pot with stock and rice; season with sugar, salt and pepper to taste. Bring to a boil; reduce heat, cover and simmer for 30 to 35 minutes or until rice is tender. Stir in parsley.

SERVES 6

I always look forward to late summer — when baskets of lush ripe tomatoes are the showpiece in outdoor markets — so I can make this silky smooth soup. In winter, vine-ripened greenhouse tomatoes make a good stand-in, particularly if you use a little tomato paste for extra depth. Just add 1 to 2 tbsp (15 to 25 mL) when puréeing soup.

TIP

If tomatoes aren't fully ripened when you buy them, place in a paper bag on your counter for a day a two. The ethylene gas given off by the tomatoes speeds up the ripening process. Never store tomatoes in the fridge — the cold temperature numbs their sweet flavor. A sunny windowsill may seem like a good place to ripen tomatoes, but a hot sun often bakes rather than ripens them.

Creamy Tomato Soup

Preheat oven to 400°F (200°C)
Large roasting pan

1 tbsp	olive oil	15 mL
6	ripe tomatoes cored and quartered, (about 2 lbs/1 kg)	6
1	medium leek, white and light green part only, chopped (see Tips, page 59)	1
1	small onion, coarsely chopped	1
2	medium carrots, peeled and coarsely chopped	2
1	stalk celery including leaves, chopped	1
2	large cloves garlic, sliced	2
½ tsp	salt	2 mL
¼ tsp	freshly ground black pepper	1 mL
Pinch	freshly grated nutmeg	Pinch
3 cups	chicken or vegetable stock (approx.)	750 mL
1 cup	table (18%) cream	250 mL
2 tbsp	chopped fresh herbs such as parsley, basil or chives	25 mL

1. Drizzle oil over bottom of a large shallow roasting pan. Add tomatoes, leek, onion, carrots, celery and garlic; season with salt, pepper and nutmeg.
2. Roast, uncovered, in preheated oven, stirring often, for 1¼ hours or until vegetables are very tender, but not brown.
3. Add 2 cups (500 mL) stock to pan; purée mixture in batches, preferably in a blender or a food processor, until very smooth. Strain soup through a sieve into large saucepan.
4. Add cream and enough of the remaining stock to thin soup to desired consistency. Adjust seasoning with salt and pepper to taste. Heat until piping hot; do not let the soup boil or it may curdle. Ladle into warm bowls; sprinkle with fresh herbs.

SERVES 4

Thick and creamy, laden with chunks of potatoes and featuring the smoky flavor of bacon, this restaurant favorite is easy to recreate in your home kitchen.

VARIATION

Fish Chowder

Omit canned clams. Increase fish stock to 2 cups (500 mL). Add 12 oz (375 g) cubed fish, such as cod, haddock or bluefish, at end of cooking along with bacon bits. Simmer for 5 minutes or until fish flakes. Add more stock, if necessary, to thin soup to desired consistency.

Clam Chowder

4	slices bacon, chopped	4
1	can (5 oz/142 g) clams, drained, juice reserved	1
1	small onion, finely chopped	1
1	stalk celery, finely diced	1
1	clove garlic, minced	1
1	bay leaf	1
1 1/2 cups	potatoes, peeled, cut into 1/2-inch (1 cm) cubes	375 mL
1 cup	fish or chicken stock	250 mL
2 cups	milk	500 mL
3 tbsp	all-purpose flour	45 mL
2 tbsp	finely chopped fresh parsley	25 mL
	Salt and freshly ground black pepper	

1. In a large saucepan, cook bacon over medium heat, stirring, for 4 minutes or until crisp. Remove; blot with paper towels and set aside.
2. Add drained clams, onion, celery, garlic and bay leaf; cook, stirring often, for 3 minutes or until vegetables are softened.
3. Stir in reserved clam juice, potatoes and stock; bring to a boil. Reduce heat to medium-low, cover and simmer for 15 minutes or until vegetables are tender.
4. In a bowl, blend a small amount of the milk into the flour to make a smooth paste. Stir in remaining milk until smooth and lump-free. Add to saucepan; bring to a boil over medium-high heat, stirring often, until mixture thickens.
5. Stir in bacon bits and parsley; season with salt, if needed, and pepper to taste. Remove bay leaf before serving.

SERVES 6 AS A MAIN COURSE OR 8 TO 10 AS A STARTER

Here's an inviting soup that's fragrant with garlic and brimming with fresh seafood in a rich wine and tomato broth. It delivers pleasure from the first to the last spoonful. When I invite friends over for a relaxed dinner, I like to accompany this soup with crusty bread, followed by a simple salad and a fresh fruit dessert.

TIP

For a less expensive version of this recipe, replace shrimp and scallops with an equal quantity of mild fish. If using frozen fish in block form, remove packaging, place on plate and microwave at Medium for 5 minutes or until partly thawed. Cut into cubes; let stand for 15 minutes until completely thawed.

Mediterranean Seafood Soup

2 tbsp	olive oil	25 mL
1	Spanish onion, chopped (about 1 lb/500 g)	1
3	cloves garlic, finely chopped	3
1	red bell pepper, diced	1
1	green bell pepper, diced	1
1	large stalk celery including leaves, chopped	1
1	bay leaf	1
1 tsp	salt	5 mL
1 tsp	paprika	5 mL
1/4 tsp	hot pepper flakes	1 mL
1/4 tsp	saffron threads, crushed	1 mL
1	can (19 oz/540 mL) tomatoes, including juice, chopped	1
4 cups	fish or chicken stock (approx.)	1 L
1 cup	dry white wine or vermouth or stock	250 mL
1 lb	halibut or other mild white fish, cubed	500 g
8 oz	raw medium shrimp, peeled and deveined, tails left on	250 g
8 oz	scallops, halved if large	250 g
1/3 cup	finely chopped fresh parsley	75 mL

1. In a Dutch oven or large saucepan, heat oil over medium-high heat. Add onion, garlic, peppers, celery, bay leaf, salt, paprika, hot pepper flakes and saffron; cook, stirring often, for 5 minutes or until vegetables are softened.

2. Add tomatoes with juice, stock and wine. Bring to a boil; reduce heat to medium-low and simmer, covered, for 30 minutes. (Recipe can be prepared to this point up to a day ahead, or frozen for up to three months; when reheating, bring back to a full boil.)
3. Stir in halibut, shrimp, scallops and parsley; cover and simmer for 3 to 5 minutes or until fish is opaque. Serve immediately in warm soup bowls.

VARIATION

For a change, try adding steamed mussels. Place 1 lb (500 g) mussels in a saucepan with ¼ cup (50 mL) white wine or water. Place over high heat; cover and steam for 3 to 5 minutes or until shells open. Strain liquid and use as part of the fish stock called for in recipe. Discard any mussels that do not open. Add mussels to soup just before serving (leave in the shells, if desired).

SERVES 4 AS A MAIN COURSE OR 6 AS A STARTER

The trademark ingredients of Creole cooking — onions, green pepper and celery — have been combined in a tomato and cream base to create this luscious fish soup.

TIP

Any kind of fish, such as cod, sole, haddock or bluefish, can be used. If using frozen fish fillets, remove packaging and arrange fish on plate; microwave at High for 3 to 4 minutes or until partially defrosted. Cut fish into small cubes; let stand 15 minutes to complete defrosting.

Creole Fish Soup

1 tbsp	olive oil	15 mL
4	green onions, chopped	4
1	large clove garlic, minced	1
2	stalks celery including leaves, chopped	2
1	green bell pepper, diced	1
1 tsp	paprika	5 mL
½ tsp	dried thyme leaves	2 mL
Pinch	cayenne pepper	Pinch
2 cups	diced peeled potatoes	500 mL
1	can (19 oz/540 mL) stewed tomatoes, including juice, chopped	1
2 cups	fish or vegetable stock (approx.)	500 mL
1 lb	fresh or frozen fish fillets	500 g
½ cup	whipping (35%) cream (optional)	125 mL
	Salt and freshly ground black pepper	

1. In a large saucepan, heat oil over medium heat. Add green onions, garlic, celery, green pepper, paprika, thyme and cayenne pepper; cook, stirring, for 3 minutes or until softened. Add potatoes, stewed tomatoes with juice and stock; bring to a boil. Reduce heat, cover and simmer for 15 minutes or until vegetables are tender.
2. Add fish; simmer for 2 minutes or until fish flakes when tested with a fork. Stir in cream, if using. (Add more stock if soup is too thick.) Season with salt and pepper to taste.

SERVES 4 AS A MAIN COURSE OR 6 AS A STARTER

Cultivated mussels are the perfect fast food. They come debearded (meaning the thread that holds them to stationary objects has already been removed) and require only a quick rinse under cold water before cooking. Just throw them in a pot, steam for 4 to 5 minutes and they're ready to eat.

TIP

To store mussels, place in a bowl and cover with damp paper towels. Never keep in a closed plastic bag or the mussels will suffocate. Also never put in a sink full of water or they will drown. For maximum freshness, use within two days of purchase.

VARIATION

Turkey Chowder

Follow recipe as directed. Omit wine; use 2 cups (500 mL) turkey stock instead of mussel broth. Replace mussels with 1½ cups (375 mL) diced cooked turkey or chicken.

Hearty Mussel Chowder

2 lbs	cultivated mussels	1 kg
1 cup	white wine or water	250 mL
4	slices bacon, chopped	4
1	large leek, white and light green part only, chopped (see Tips, page 59)	1
2	stalks celery, chopped	2
1½ cups	diced peeled potatoes	375 mL
½ tsp	salt	2 mL
¼ tsp	freshly ground black pepper	1 mL
½ cup	diced red bell pepper	125 mL
2 tbsp	all-purpose flour	25 mL
1½ cups	milk or light (5%) cream	375 mL
2 tbsp	finely chopped fresh parsley	25 mL

1. Place mussels and wine in a large saucepan. Cover and place over high heat; bring to a boil. Steam for 4 minutes or just until shells open. Drain, reserving cooking liquid. Add enough water or stock to make 2 cups (500 mL) liquid. Remove mussel meat from shells and place in a bowl; discard any that do not open.
2. In a large saucepan over medium heat, cook bacon, stirring often, for 4 minutes or until crisp. Remove with slotted spoon; drain on paper towels. Drain all but 2 tsp (10 mL) fat from pan. Add leek and celery; cook, stirring, for 3 minutes or until softened. Add potatoes, reserved mussel broth, salt and pepper. Bring to a boil; reduce heat, cover and simmer for 15 minutes or until potatoes are tender. Stir in red pepper.
3. In a bowl, blend flour with ¼ cup (50 mL) milk to make a smooth paste; add remaining milk. Stir into saucepan; bring to a boil and cook, stirring, until thickened. Add reserved mussels, bacon bits and parsley; cook 2 minutes or until piping hot.

SERVES 10 TO 12

This nourishing soup is chockfull of vegetables and excels at chasing away the winter chills. It's soothing both to the body and the soul.

VARIATION
Chicken or Turkey Minestrone
Add 2 cups (500 mL) diced cooked chicken or turkey along with chickpeas. Extras of this soup freeze well for up to three months.

Chunky Minestrone

2 tbsp	olive oil	25 mL
2	medium onions, chopped	2
4	cloves garlic, finely chopped	4
3	medium carrots, peeled and diced	3
2	stalks celery including leaves, chopped	2
1½ tsp	dried basil leaves	7 mL
1 tsp	dried oregano or marjoram leaves	5 mL
½ tsp	freshly ground black pepper	2 mL
10 cups	chicken or vegetable stock	2.5 L
1	can (19 oz/540 mL) tomatoes, including juice, chopped	1
2 cups	small cauliflower florets	500 mL
1½ cups	green beans, cut into 1-inch (2.5 cm) lengths	375 mL
¾ cup	small-shaped pasta such as tubetti or shells	175 mL
1	can (19 oz/540 mL) chickpeas or small white beans, drained and rinsed	1
⅓ cup	chopped fresh parsley	75 mL
	Freshly grated Parmesan cheese	

1. In a Dutch oven or large stockpot, heat oil over medium heat. Add onions, garlic, carrots, celery, basil, oregano and pepper; cook, stirring, for 5 minutes or until softened.
2. Stir in stock, tomatoes with juice, cauliflower and beans. Bring to a boil; reduce heat to medium-low and simmer, covered, for 20 minutes or until vegetables are tender.
3. Stir in pasta; cover and simmer for 10 minutes, stirring occasionally, until pasta is just tender.
4. Add chickpeas and parsley; cook 5 minutes more or until heated through. Ladle soup into heated bowls and sprinkle with Parmesan.

SERVES 8

I always make a double batch of this soup each fall when vegetables are at their prime. I pack it into containers and put in the freezer for easy mid-week meals on chilly days. Any combination of vegetables can be used in this hearty vegetable soup, depending on what's in your fridge. Sun-Dried Tomato Pesto is optional, but it adds a wonderful jolt of flavor and dresses up the soup. You can also use whatever pesto you have on hand.

TIP

Serve with additional Parmesan cheese at the table. Refrigerate soup for up to five days or freeze in airtight containers for up to three months.

Vegetable Minestrone with Sun-Dried Tomato Pesto

1 tbsp	olive oil	15 mL
2	large onions, chopped	2
3	cloves garlic, finely chopped	3
2	carrots, peeled and chopped	2
2	stalks celery, chopped	2
10 cups	vegetable or chicken stock (approx.)	2.5 L
2 cups	shredded cabbage	500 mL
2 cups	small cauliflower florets	500 mL
1/3 cup	short fine noodles or other small-shaped pasta such as shells	75 mL
1 cup	frozen peas	250 mL
1	can (19 oz/540 mL) Romano or navy beans, drained and rinsed	1
3/4 cup	Sun-Dried Tomato Pesto (see recipe, page 224)	175 mL
	Freshly grated Parmesan cheese (optional)	

1. In a large stockpot or 32-cup (8 L) Dutch oven, heat oil over medium heat. Add onions, garlic, carrots and celery; cook, stirring occasionally, for 10 minutes or until softened.
2. Add stock and cabbage; bring to a boil over high heat. Reduce heat, cover and simmer for 20 minutes or just until vegetables are tender. Stir in cauliflower and pasta; simmer, covered, for 8 minutes or just until pasta is tender. Stir in peas and beans; cook for 2 minutes.
3. Ladle into bowls; swirl a generous tablespoon (15 mL) Sun-Dried Tomato Pesto into each. Sprinkle with Parmesan cheese, if desired. Soup thickens slightly as it cools; add more stock, if necessary.

SERVES 6

Use shiitake mushrooms along with less inexpensive brown mushrooms to create this intensely flavored soup that makes a great starter for a special dinner.

Creamy Mushroom Soup

2 tbsp	butter	25 mL
1	large onion, finely chopped	1
2	cloves garlic, minced	2
8 oz	assorted mushrooms, such as shiitake and cremini, sliced	250 g
1½ tsp	chopped fresh thyme or ½ tsp (2 mL) dried thyme leaves	7 mL
2 tbsp	all-purpose flour	25 mL
4 cups	chicken stock	1 L
½ tsp	salt	2 mL
¼ tsp	freshly ground black pepper	1 mL
1 cup	table (18%) cream	250 mL
¼ cup	medium-dry sherry (optional)	50 mL
2 tbsp	chopped fresh chives or parsley	25 mL

1. In a Dutch oven or large saucepan, heat butter over medium-high heat. Cook onion and garlic, stirring, for 2 minutes until softened. Stir in mushrooms and thyme; cook, stirring often, for 5 minutes or until mushrooms are tender.
2. Sprinkle with flour; stir in stock, salt and pepper. Bring to a boil over high heat. Reduce heat to medium-low, cover and simmer for 25 minutes. Let cool slightly.
3. In a food processor or blender, purée soup in batches. Return to saucepan. Place over medium heat; stir in cream and sherry, if using. Adjust seasoning with salt and pepper to taste. Heat until piping hot. Ladle into heated bowls and sprinkle with chives.

SERVES 6 TO 8

With all the glamorous foods out there now, cabbage is often neglected. That's a shame. Cabbage is an excellent partner to soothing potatoes and smoky sausage in this robust soup — which shows just how rich an addition this underrated vegetable can be. Taste it and you'll see.

TIPS

To clean leeks, trim dark green tops. Cut down center almost to root end and chop. Rinse in a sink full of cold water to remove sand; scoop up leeks and place in colander to drain or use a salad spinner.

Store soup in covered container in refrigerator for up to five days.

Leek, Potato and Cabbage Soup

2 tbsp	olive oil	25 mL
2	medium leeks, white and light green part only, chopped (see Tips, left)	2
2	cloves garlic, finely chopped	2
1/4 tsp	freshly ground black pepper	1 mL
1/4 tsp	caraway seeds (optional)	1 mL
3	potatoes, such as Yukon Gold, peeled and cut into 1/2-inch (1 cm) cubes	3
4 cups	finely shredded green cabbage	1 L
6 cups	beef stock	1.5 L
8 oz	kielbasa, or other cooked smoked sausage, cut into 1/2-inch (1 cm) cubes	250 g
1/4 cup	chopped fresh parsley	50 mL

1. In a large saucepan, heat oil over medium heat. Add leeks, garlic, pepper and caraway seeds, if using; cook, stirring, for 4 minutes or until softened.
2. Stir in potatoes, cabbage and stock. Bring to a boil; reduce heat to medium-low and simmer, covered, for 20 minutes or until vegetables are tender.
3. Add sausage and parsley; cook 5 minutes more or until sausage is heated through.

SERVES 6

Watercress adds a vibrant color and nip to the classic combo of creamed potato and leek soup.

TIP

You can make this soup a day ahead and reheat until piping hot. It's also delicious served cold.

Perfect Potato and Leek Soup

1 tbsp	butter	15 mL
2	medium leeks, white and light green part only, chopped (see Tips, page 59)	2
2 cups	diced peeled potatoes	500 mL
1 tsp	dried tarragon or fines herbes	5 mL
2 tbsp	all-purpose flour	25 mL
4 cups	chicken stock	1 L
1	bunch watercress, tough stems removed, chopped	1
1 cup	half-and-half (10%) cream or milk	250 mL
	Salt and freshly ground black pepper	
	Watercress sprigs	

1. In a large saucepan, melt butter over medium heat. Add leeks, potatoes and tarragon; cook, stirring, for 5 minutes or until leeks are softened but not browned. Blend in flour; stir in chicken stock. Bring to a boil; reduce heat, cover and simmer, stirring occasionally, for 20 minutes or until potatoes are very tender.
2. Add watercress; simmer 1 minute until watercress is limp and bright green in color. In a food processor or blender, purée soup in batches until smooth. Return to saucepan. Stir in cream; season with salt and pepper to taste. Heat until piping hot; do not let boil. Ladle into bowls; garnish with watercress sprigs.

SERVES 6

Here's a seductive soup with a Caribbean accent to serve for a special dinner. The surprising combination of earthy root vegetables, married with spices like ginger and curry, gives the soup a delicious Island flare. My friends always go home with the recipe.

TIP

The carrots, sweet potato and rutabaga, cut into ½-inch (1 cm) cubes, should total 4 cups (1 L).

VARIATION

Curried Butternut Squash and Apple Soup

Substitute 5 cups (1.25 L) peeled and cubed butternut squash for the carrots, sweet potato and rutabaga.

Curried Cream of Root Vegetable Soup

2 tbsp	butter	25 mL
1½ cups	diced, peeled apples	375 mL
1	medium onion, chopped	1
2	cloves garlic, minced	2
1 tbsp	minced fresh gingerroot	15 mL
1½ tsp	mild curry paste or powder	7 mL
½ tsp	ground cumin	2 mL
½ tsp	ground coriander	2 mL
¼ tsp	dried thyme leaves	1 mL
Pinch	cayenne pepper	Pinch
2	carrots, peeled and cubed	2
1	sweet potato, peeled and cubed	1
1 cup	cubed rutabaga	250 mL
4 cups	chicken or vegetable stock	1 L
1 cup	table (18%) cream	250 mL
¼ cup	chopped fresh cilantro or parsley	50 mL
	Sour cream or yogurt (optional)	

1. In a large saucepan, heat butter over medium heat. Add apples, onion, garlic, ginger, curry paste, cumin, coriander, thyme and cayenne pepper; cook, stirring, for 5 minutes or until softened.
2. Add carrots, sweet potato, rutabaga and stock. Bring to a boil; reduce heat to medium-low and simmer, covered, for 30 minutes or until vegetables are very tender. Let cool slightly.
3. In a food processor or blender, purée soup in batches until smooth. Return to saucepan; stir in cream and heat through. Do not allow soup to boil or it may curdle. Ladle into bowls; sprinkle with cilantro and add dollop of sour cream or yogurt, if using.

SERVES 6

If you have a vegetarian in your family, this is a recipe you can count on. It's no-fuss to prepare, easy to reheat and makes a complete meal.

TIP

Depending on what I have in the fridge, I make variations on this versatile, tasty soup by using other vegetables, such as carrots and cauliflower.

Cheddar Broccoli Chowder

2 tbsp	butter	25 mL
1	small onion, finely chopped	1
1/4 cup	all-purpose flour	50 mL
3 cups	vegetable or chicken stock	750 mL
2 cups	potatoes, peeled and cut into 1/2-inch (1 cm) cubes	500 mL
1	bay leaf	1
3 cups	finely chopped broccoli florets and peeled stalks	750 mL
1 1/2 cups	milk	375 mL
1 1/2 cups	shredded Cheddar cheese	375 mL
	Freshly ground black pepper	

1. In a large saucepan, melt butter over medium heat. Cook onion, stirring, for 2 minutes or until softened. Blend in flour; stir in stock. Bring to a boil, stirring, until thickened.
2. Add potatoes and bay leaf; reduce heat, cover and simmer, stirring occasionally, for 10 minutes.
3. Add broccoli; simmer, stirring occasionally, for 10 minutes more or until vegetables are tender.
4. Stir in milk and cheese; heat just until cheese melts and soup is piping hot. Do not let the soup boil or it may curdle. Remove bay leaf; adjust seasoning with pepper to taste.

SERVES 6

Looking for a great opener for a meal? Here it is. The sweetness of carrots and orange are balanced by the tang of yogurt in this low-calorie soup.

TIP

Normally yogurt will curdle if you add it to a soup or sauce, but blending it with cornstarch as a binder overcomes this problem.

Creamy Carrot Orange Soup

1 tbsp	vegetable oil	15 mL
1	medium onion, chopped	1
1	large clove garlic, finely chopped	1
2 tsp	mild curry paste or powder	10 mL
4 cups	sliced carrots	1 L
4 cups	chicken stock	1 L
1 cup	orange juice	250 mL
1 cup	plain yogurt	250 mL
1 tbsp	cornstarch	15 mL
	Salt and freshly ground black pepper	
2 tbsp	chopped fresh parsley or chives	25 mL
	Grated orange zest	

1. In a large saucepan, heat oil over medium heat. Add onion, garlic and curry paste; cook, stirring, for 2 minutes or until softened. Add carrots, chicken stock and orange juice. Bring to a boil; cover and simmer for 45 minutes or until carrots are very tender. Let cool 10 minutes.
2. In a food processor or blender, purée in batches; return to saucepan. In a bowl, blend yogurt with cornstarch; stir into soup. Cook over medium heat, stirring, for 5 minutes or until heated through. Season with salt and pepper to taste. Ladle into bowls; sprinkle with parsley and orange zest.

SERVES 4 AS A MAIN COURSE OR 6 AS A STARTER

Sweet, young corn, combined with tender leeks and bell pepper, make a delicately flavored fall soup. Kernels cut from cooked cobs of corn are ideal for this recipe. You'll need about three cobs.

TIP

To cut kernels from the cob easily, stand the ears on end and use a sharp knife.

Corn and Red Pepper Chowder

1 tbsp	butter	15 mL
2	medium leeks, white and light green part only, finely chopped (see Tips, page 59)	2
½ tsp	dried thyme leaves	2 mL
2½ cups	chicken or vegetable stock	625 mL
1½ cups	cooked or frozen corn kernels	375 mL
1	large red bell pepper, diced	1
3 tbsp	all-purpose flour	45 mL
2 cups	milk	500 mL
	Salt and freshly ground black pepper	
2 tbsp	chopped fresh parsley or chives	25 mL

1. In a large saucepan, melt butter over medium heat. Add leeks and thyme; cook, stirring often, for 4 minutes or until softened. Do not brown. Stir in stock and frozen corn, if using. Bring to a boil; reduce heat, cover and simmer for 10 minutes. Add cooked corn, if using, and red pepper; cover and simmer for 5 minutes or until vegetables are tender.

2. In a bowl, blend flour with ⅓ cup (75 mL) milk to make a smooth paste; stir in remaining milk. Stir into saucepan; bring to a boil, stirring, until thickened. Season with salt and pepper to taste. Ladle into soup bowls; sprinkle with parsley or chives.

Creamy Tomato Soup (page 50) ➢

SERVES 6

Of all dried legumes, lentils are my favorite. They're fast and easy to cook — and healthy too! With this soup, I bring the stock to a boil, throw in some vegetables, sit back, relax and savor the aroma. In 40 minutes, I am ladling out bowlfuls of wholesome soup.

TIP

To save time, I chop the mushrooms, onions, carrots and celery in batches in the food processor. If you have any leftover baked ham, chop it and add to the soup along with the stock.

Super Suppertime Lentil Soup

8 cups	chicken or vegetable stock	2 L
1 cup	green lentils, rinsed and sorted	250 mL
8 oz	mushrooms, chopped	250 g
2	carrots, peeled and chopped	2
2	stalks celery including leaves, chopped	2
1	large onion, chopped	1
2	cloves garlic, finely chopped	2
1 tsp	dried thyme or marjoram leaves	5 mL
1/4 cup	chopped fresh dill or parsley	50 mL
	Salt and freshly ground black pepper	

1. In a large Dutch oven or stockpot, combine stock, lentils, mushrooms, carrots, celery, onion, garlic and thyme.
2. Bring to a boil; reduce heat, cover and simmer 35 to 40 minutes or until lentils are tender. Stir in dill or parsley. Adjust seasoning with salt and pepper to taste.

SERVES 6

A generous bowlful of this nourishing soup makes an ideal lunch or light supper. Just add some pita bread or whole-grain crackers.

TIPS

Cold soups taste best when refrigerated overnight, giving the flavors a chance to blend. Always check the seasoning of a cold soup, however. Often you will need to add extra salt, pepper or hot pepper sauce.

To ripen tomatoes, see Tip, page 50.

Spicy Black Bean Gazpacho

1	red bell pepper, coarsely chopped	1
3	green onions, coarsely chopped	3
3	ripe tomatoes, coarsely chopped	3
1	large clove garlic, minced	1
1	can (19 oz/540 mL) black beans, drained and rinsed	1
1	can (19 oz/540 mL) tomato juice	1
2 tbsp	balsamic vinegar	25 mL
1 tbsp	red wine vinegar	15 mL
	Salt and freshly ground black pepper	
1/2 tsp	hot pepper sauce or more to taste	2 mL
1/3 cup	chopped fresh cilantro or parsley	75 mL
	Sour cream or plain yogurt	

1. In a food processor, finely chop red pepper and green onions, using on-off turns; transfer to a large bowl. Add tomatoes to food processor; finely chop, using on-off turns. Add to pepper-onion mixture along with black beans and tomato juice. Add balsamic and red wine vinegars; season with salt, pepper and hot pepper sauce to taste. Cover and refrigerate for 4 hours, preferably overnight.
2. Add about 1/3 cup (75 mL) cold water to thin soup, if desired. Adjust seasoning with vinegars, salt, pepper and hot pepper sauce to taste. Ladle into chilled bowls; sprinkle with cilantro and top with a spoonful of sour cream.

SERVES 6

My idea of a no-fuss dinner is this easy soup served with warm bread. It's especially reassuring to know that when I come home late from work, I can reach in my cupboard and pull out some convenient canned products — and dinner is on the table in no time!

TIPS

Supermarkets are full of beans these days. With this recipe, why not try chickpeas, Romano or white kidney beans?

Soups that call for canned products, such as tomatoes and beans, contain hefty quantities of salt (as do commercial stock bases) so be cautious about adding extra. Instead, rely on your pepper mill for a seasoning boost.

Black Bean and Corn Soup

1 tbsp	olive oil	15 mL
1	medium onion, chopped	1
2	cloves garlic, minced	2
1	green bell pepper, diced	1
1	large stalk celery, diced	1
1 tsp	dried oregano leaves	5 mL
1 tsp	ground cumin	5 mL
1/2 tsp	dried thyme leaves	2 mL
Pinch	cayenne pepper	Pinch
4 cups	chicken or vegetable stock	1 L
1	can (19 oz/540 mL) tomatoes, including juice, chopped	1
1	can (19 oz/540 mL) black beans, drained and rinsed	1
1 cup	corn kernels (fresh, frozen or canned)	250 mL
1 cup	diced smoked sausage, such as kielbasa, or smoked ham (optional)	250 mL
1/4 cup	chopped fresh cilantro or parsley	50 mL

1. In a large saucepan, heat oil over medium-high heat. Add onion, garlic, pepper, celery, oregano, cumin, thyme and cayenne pepper; cook, stirring, for 5 minutes or until softened.
2. Add stock and tomatoes with juice; bring to a boil. Reduce heat to medium-low and simmer, covered, for 20 minutes.
3. Stir in beans, corn and sausage, if using. Cook 5 minutes more or until vegetables are tender. Stir in cilantro; ladle into warm bowls.

SERVES 12

I can't think of a better combination than thick slices of warm bread from the oven and steaming bowls of soup when you come in from the cold. This tried-and-true soup has a hearty beefy-mushroom taste and lots of old-fashioned appeal.

TIP

If I'm going to the trouble of making homemade soup, I like to make a big pot so there are plenty of leftovers for my freezer. Ladle soup into containers and freeze for up to three months.

Hearty Beef and Barley Soup

1 tbsp	vegetable oil	15 mL
1 1⁄2 lbs	meaty beef shanks, trimmed of fat (about 2 or 3)	750 g
1 lb	mushrooms, chopped	500 g
2	large onions, chopped	2
4	cloves garlic, finely chopped	4
2	bay leaves	2
2 tsp	salt	10 mL
1 tsp	dried thyme leaves	5 mL
1⁄4 tsp	freshly ground black pepper	1 mL
12 cups	water	3 L
3⁄4 cup	pearl or pot barley, rinsed	175 mL
4	carrots, peeled and chopped	4
2	large stalks celery including leaves, chopped	2

1. In a Dutch oven or stockpot, heat oil over medium-high heat. Add beef and cook until nicely browned on both sides. Transfer to a plate.
2. Reduce heat to medium. Add mushrooms, onions, garlic, bay leaves, salt, thyme and pepper; cook, stirring often, for 5 minutes or until softened. Return beef to pan. Pour in water and bring to a boil. Reduce heat to medium-low and simmer, covered, stirring occasionally, for 1 hour.
3. Add barley, carrots and celery. Cover and simmer, stirring occasionally, for 1 hour more or until beef is tender.
4. Remove beef with slotted spoon. Discard bones; finely chop the meat and return to soup. Discard bay leaves; adjust seasoning with salt and pepper to taste.

SERVES 6

Here's a main course soup to serve with whole-grain bread and a wedge of cheddar. Vary the soup according to the kinds of vegetables you have in the fridge. I often add small cauliflower and broccoli florets or a handful of chopped fresh spinach.

VARIATION

Instead of sweet potatoes, add 1 cup (250 mL) each diced peeled potatoes and diced carrots. Add along with the rutabaga.

Harvest Vegetable Barley Soup

2 tbsp	butter	25 mL
1	large onion, chopped	1
3	cloves garlic, finely chopped	3
1 1/2 cups	diced peeled rutabaga	375 mL
1/2 tsp	dried thyme or marjoram leaves	2 mL
8 cups	chicken or vegetable stock (approx.)	2 L
1/2 cup	pearl barley, rinsed	125 mL
1 1/2 cups	diced peeled sweet potatoes	375 mL
1 1/2 cups	diced zucchini	375 mL
	Salt and freshly ground black pepper	

1. In a large Dutch oven or stockpot, melt butter over medium heat. Add onion, garlic, rutabaga and thyme; cook, stirring often, for 5 minutes or until vegetables are lightly colored.

2. Stir in stock and barley; bring to a boil. Reduce heat, cover and simmer for 20 minutes. Add sweet potatoes and zucchini; simmer, covered, for 15 minutes or until barley is tender. Season with salt and pepper to taste.

SERVES 4

Serve cupfuls of this colorful soup as an elegant starter to a fall menu. I turn to it when fresh-picked squash are plentiful in the market. I often make extra purée and freeze it in containers. It takes no time at all to make the soup if you have the purée on hand in the freezer. The finished soup also freezes well.

TIP

To make squash purée, cut one small butternut or large acorn squash (about 2 lbs/1 kg) into quarters; remove seeds. Place in large casserole dish with ½ cup (125 mL) water. Cover and microwave at High for 15 to 20 minutes or until squash is tender when pierced with a fork. (Cooking time varies with size and type of squash.) Let stand 15 minutes or until cool enough to handle. Scoop out pulp; place in food processor and purée. Makes about 2 cups (500 mL).

Gingery Squash Soup

1 tbsp	butter	15 mL
1	large onion, chopped	1
2	cloves garlic, finely chopped	2
4 tsp	minced fresh gingerroot	20 mL
2 tbsp	all-purpose flour	25 mL
3 cups	chicken stock	750 mL
2 cups	cooked squash purée (such as butternut or acorn)	500 mL
½ cup	table (18%) cream or whipping (35%) cream	125 mL
1 tsp	grated orange zest	5 mL
	Salt, freshly ground black pepper and nutmeg	
2 tbsp	chopped fresh chives or parsley	25 mL

1. In a large saucepan, melt butter over medium-low heat. Add onion, garlic and ginger; cook, stirring often, for 5 minutes or until onion is softened. Blend in flour; stir in stock and squash. Bring to a boil and cook, stirring, until thickened. Reduce heat, cover and simmer for 10 minutes.

2. In a food processor or blender, purée in batches until smooth. Return to saucepan. Add cream and orange zest; season with salt, pepper and nutmeg to taste. Heat until piping hot. Ladle into bowls; sprinkle with chives.

Sandwiches and Light Suppers

Egg Salad on a Kaiser

MAKES 2 SANDWICHES

This versatile egg salad is great on a Kaiser or tucked into pita pockets with shredded lettuce or sprouts and tomato wedges.

TIP

To hard-cook eggs, place in saucepan; add cold water to cover eggs by 1-inch (2.5 cm). Place over medium-high heat; bring to a boil. Boil for 2 minutes; cover and remove from heat. Let stand for 10 minutes. Drain and chill eggs in cold water.

VARIATION

Egg Salad Tortilla Spirals

Spread egg salad on 2 large (9-inch/23 cm) flour tortillas, leaving a 1-inch (2.5 cm) border. Layer with lettuce. Fold bottom over filling, then sides; roll up tightly. Wrap in plastic wrap and refrigerate for up to one day. To make easy-pick-up sandwiches for kids' lunches, cut into 1-inch (2.5 cm) pieces.

2 tbsp	cream cheese, softened	25 mL
2 tbsp	plain yogurt	25 mL
1 tsp	Dijon mustard	5 mL
1/4 tsp	salt	1 mL
1/4 tsp	freshly ground black pepper	1 mL
3	hard-cooked eggs, finely chopped (see Tip, left)	3
1	small green onion, finely chopped	1
2	whole wheat Kaiser rolls, split	2
	Leaf or Romaine lettuce	
6	thin slices tomato	6

1. In a bowl, combine cream cheese, yogurt, mustard, salt and pepper. Stir in eggs and green onion. (Make ahead, cover and refrigerate for up to two days.)

2. Spread egg salad over top halves of rolls. Arrange lettuce and tomato slices on bottom halves; sandwich together.

MAKES 4 SANDWICHES

I like to add inexpensive eggs to helps stretch more costly canned salmon or solid white tuna when making sandwiches.

TIP

To prevent cucumber from turning soggy, assemble sandwiches the same day they are served.

Dilled Salmon and Egg Salad on Pumpernickel

3	hard-cooked eggs, finely chopped (see Tip, page 72)	3
1	can (7½ oz/213 g) sockeye salmon, drained and flaked	1
¼ cup	light mayonnaise	50 mL
1	large green onion, finely chopped	1
2 tbsp	chopped fresh dill or parsley	25 mL
1 tsp	grated lemon zest	5 mL
¼ tsp	salt	1 mL
¼ tsp	freshly ground black pepper	1 mL
8	slices pumpernickel bread	8
½	seedless cucumber, thinly sliced	½

1. In a bowl, combine eggs, salmon, mayonnaise, green onion, dill, lemon zest, salt and pepper. (Made ahead, cover and refrigerate for up to two days.)
2. Divide salad among pumpernickel slices, spreading evenly. Layer with cucumber slices. Serve open-faced or sandwich together. Cut in half.

MAKES 2 SANDWICHES

Chicken salad sandwich has never been the same in my house since I added some pizzazz to the old standby with crunchy radishes, apples and a hint of curry.

TIP

Simmer 2 boneless chicken breasts (½ lb/ 250 g) in lightly salted water or chicken stock for 10 minutes; remove from heat. Let cool in stock for 15 minutes.

Curried Chicken Salad Sandwiches

8 tbsp	light mayonnaise	125 mL
2 tbsp	bottled mango chutney	25 mL
1 tsp	mild curry paste or powder	5 mL
1 ½ cups	finely diced cooked chicken	375 mL
½ cup	finely diced unpeeled apple	125 mL
⅓ cup	finely diced radishes	75 mL
2 tbsp	finely chopped green onions	25 mL
	Salt	
4	slices thick-cut whole-grain bread	4
	Red leaf or Boston lettuce	

1. In a bowl, blend 6 tablespoons (90 mL) mayonnaise with chutney and curry paste. Stir in chicken, apple, radishes and green onions; season with salt to taste.
2. Spread bread slices with remaining mayonnaise. Spread two bread slices generously with chicken mixture; top with lettuce and remaining bread. Cut in half.

MAKES 2 SANDWICHES

When I'm too busy to cook dinner, I often rely on this simple satisfying sandwich instead of ordering take-out.

Tuna Cheddar Melt

Preheat broiler
Baking sheet

1	can (6.5 oz/170 g) tuna, drained and flaked	1
¼ cup	light mayonnaise	50 mL
¼ cup	finely chopped celery	50 mL
1	green onion, finely chopped	1
1 tsp	fresh lemon juice	5 mL
4	slices whole-grain bread	4
8	thin tomato slices	8
	Salt and freshly ground black pepper	
4	slices Cheddar cheese	4

1. In a bowl, combine tuna, mayonnaise, celery, green onion and lemon juice.
2. Spread bread slices with tuna mixture. Layer with tomato slices; season with salt and pepper. Top with cheddar cheese slices.
3. Arrange on baking sheet; place under broiler for about 3 minutes or until cheese is melted. Serve immediately.

MAKES 2 SANDWICHES

There's nothing better for lunch than a golden grilled sandwich oozing with melted cheese. This version includes ham — however you can omit it and the mustard if you wish.

Grilled Ham and Cheese Sandwiches

2 tbsp	light mayonnaise	25 mL
2 tsp	Dijon mustard	10 mL
4	thick slices home-style white or whole-grain bread	4
4	thin slices smoked ham	4
2 oz	aged Cheddar cheese, sliced	60 g
4 tsp	soft butter	20 mL

1. In a small bowl, combine mayonnaise and mustard; spread over bread slices. Cover each with a slice of ham. Top two of the slices with cheddar cheese and top with remaining bread slices so that cheese is sandwiched between the ham. Spread top bread slices each with 1 tsp (5 mL) butter.
2. In a large nonstick skillet over medium heat, place sandwiches buttered-side down in pan and spread top of bread slices with remaining butter. Grill, for 2 to 3 minutes per side, or until nicely golden and cheese is melted. Cut into halves and serve immediately.

MAKES 2 SANDWICHES

The classic grilled cheese sandwich takes on a Mediterranean spin with basil pesto and Italian cheese.

Grilled Italian Sandwiches

4	thick slices crusty Italian bread	4
3 tbsp	store-bought or homemade Basil Pesto (see recipe, page 224)	45 mL
4	slices Provolone, Fontina or mozzarella cheese	4
6	thin tomato slices	6
	Salt and freshly ground black pepper	
2 tbsp	olive oil	25 mL

1. Lightly spread bread slices with pesto. Layer two bread slices with one slice of cheese. Layer with tomato slices; season with salt and pepper to taste. Top with remaining cheese and bread slices. Brush top bread slices lightly with olive oil.

2. Place oiled-side down in a large nonstick skillet over medium heat; brush sandwich tops with remaining olive oil. Grill, for 2 to 3 minutes per side, or until nicely toasted and cheese is melted. Cut into quarters and serve.

SERVES 2

Bruschetta is an Italian open-faced sandwich. It can be served unadorned with garlic and olive oil or with a myriad of popular toppings such as juicy ripe tomatoes, fresh basil and Parmesan. When summer tomatoes and fresh basil beckon, make bruschettas for a simple light lunch or as an appetizer for a barbecue.

TIP

To serve as an appetizer, use 8 thick slices French bread instead of Italian bread.

Classic Bruschetta with Tomato and Parmesan

Preheat broiler

2	large ripe tomatoes, seeded and diced	2
2 tbsp	coarsely chopped fresh basil	25 mL
1	clove garlic, minced	1
2 tbsp	olive oil	25 mL
1 tsp	balsamic vinegar	5 mL
	Salt and freshly ground black pepper	
4	thick slices crusty Italian bread	4
	Shaved Parmesan cheese	

1. In a small bowl, combine tomatoes, basil, 1 tbsp (15 mL) oil and balsamic vinegar; season with salt and pepper to taste. Gently toss and let stand for up to 1 hour.

2. Toast bread in a grill pan over medium heat or under broiler, for about 2 minutes per side, or until golden brown. Brush bread tops lightly with remaining oil. Arrange on a serving plate.

3. Spoon tomato mixture over warm toast and top with shavings of Parmesan cheese. Serve immediately.

MAKES 4 SANDWICHES

These huge sandwiches are stuffed to overflowing with lots of great things. Grill extra flank or round steak or use store-bought sliced roast beef in this family favorite.

Hot Roast Beef Heroes

Preheat broiler
Baking sheet

4	large crusty rolls	4
1/4 cup	cream cheese, softened	50 mL
2 tbsp	plain yogurt or sour cream	25 mL
2 tbsp	Dijon mustard	25 mL
2	tomatoes, thinly sliced	2
1 tbsp	olive oil	15 mL
1/2	large green bell pepper, cut into thin strips	1/2
1	small onion, thinly sliced	1
1	large clove garlic, minced	1
1 cup	sliced mushrooms	250 mL
1/2 tsp	dried oregano leaves	2 mL
1 cup	thin strips cooked flank or round steak	250 mL
	Salt and freshly ground black pepper	

1. Split rolls along one side and open like a book. (Do not cut all the way through.) Place on baking sheet and broil cut side until toasted.
2. In a bowl, combine cream cheese, yogurt and mustard; spread over cut sides of rolls. Line bottom halves with tomato slices.
3. In a large nonstick skillet, heat oil over high heat; cook green pepper, onion, garlic, mushrooms and oregano, stirring occasionally, for 5 minutes. Add beef; cook, stirring, 1 minute more or until hot. Season with salt and pepper to taste. Spoon into rolls and serve immediately.

SERVES 4

Why order out when it's so easy to prepare these pizza-style sandwiches at home? Make them with leftover grilled steak or store-bought deli roast beef for a fast dinner.

TIP

Prepare sandwich filling ahead, cover and refrigerate. Layer rolls with cheese; spoon in beef filling. Wrap in paper towels and microwave at Medium-High for 2½ to 3 minutes for two rolls, or 1½ minutes for one roll, or until heated through.

Beefy Pizza Subs

Preheat broiler
Baking sheet

1 tbsp	olive oil	15 mL
2 cups	sliced mushrooms	500 mL
1	green bell pepper, cut into thin strips	1
1	medium onion, cut into thin wedges	1
1	large clove garlic, minced	1
1 tsp	dried basil or oregano leaves	5 mL
¼ tsp	hot pepper flakes	1 mL
1½ cups	thinly sliced cooked flank steak or 6 oz (175 g) deli roast beef, cut into strips	375 mL
¾ cup	pizza sauce or tomato pasta sauce	175 mL
	Salt and freshly ground black pepper	
4	crusty rolls	4
6 oz	thinly sliced mild provolone or mozzarella cheese	175 g

1. In a large nonstick skillet, heat oil over medium-high heat. Add mushrooms, green pepper, onion, garlic, basil and hot pepper flakes; cook, stirring, for 5 minutes or until softened. Stir in beef and pizza sauce; cook until heated through. Remove from heat; season with salt and pepper to taste.
2. Cut rolls along one side and open like a book; layer with cheese slices. Place on baking sheet under preheated broiler for 1 minute or until cheese melts. Watch carefully. Spoon beef mixture into rolls and serve immediately.

SERVES 4

"Let's order pizza!" The next time you hear this request from your kids, assemble the ingredients here and get them cooking. Why order out when making pizza at home using store-bought bread bases and sauces is such a breeze? It's more economical, too.

TIPS

This recipe is the perfect solution to deal with the odd bits of vegetables, cheese and deli left in my fridge by week's end. Vary the toppings according to what you have on hand including sliced pepperoni, chopped ham or broccoli.

Four 7-inch (18 cm) pitas or six split English muffins can also be used. If necessary, arrange on two baking sheets; rotate halfway during baking so breads bake evenly. Reduce baking time to 10 minutes.

Flatbread Pizzas

Preheat oven to 400°F (200°C)
Baking sheet

1 tbsp	vegetable or olive oil	15 mL
1	small onion, thinly sliced	1
1	clove garlic, minced	1
1 cup	sliced mushrooms	250 mL
1	small green or red bell pepper, cut into thin strips	1
½ tsp	dried basil leaves	2 mL
½ tsp	dried oregano leaves	2 mL
1	12-inch (30 cm) prebaked pizza base or 9-by 12-inch (23 by 30 cm) focaccia	1
½ cup	pizza sauce (approx.)	125 mL
2 cups	shredded cheese, such as mozzarella, Fontina or provolone	500 mL

1. In a large nonstick skillet, heat oil over medium-high heat. Add onion, garlic, mushrooms, pepper, basil and oregano; cook, stirring, for 4 minutes or until softened.
2. Arrange pizza shell on baking sheet; spread with pizza sauce. Top with vegetables and shredded cheese.
3. Bake in preheated oven for 20 to 25 minutes or until cheese is melted.

MAKES 6 WRAPS

Wraps have become the latest healthy fast food craze. Anything goes when making these California-inspired tortilla-wrapped sandwiches including rice or grains, or grilled meats and vegetables with tangy spreads and salsas. Here is a kid-friendly wrap that's fun to eat and makes a great supper.

TIPS

If you have cooked white or brown rice handy in the fridge, you'll need 2 cups (500 mL) for this recipe.

Omit sausages for a vegetarian version.

These wraps are great to assemble ahead and reheat in the microwave. Wrap sandwiches individually in paper towels. Microwave three at a time at Medium for 4 minutes, or microwave one wrap at Medium for 1½ minutes or until heated through.

All-New Sausage Rice Wraps

Preheat oven to 350°F (180°C)
Baking sheets

1½ cups	chicken or vegetable stock	375 mL
⅔ cup	long-grain white rice	150 mL
12 oz	mild or hot Italian sausages, casings removed (3 sausages)	375 g
2 tsp	olive oil	10 mL
1	small onion, chopped	1
2	cloves garlic, minced	2
1	large green bell pepper, chopped	1
1 cup	chopped mushrooms	250 mL
1½ tsp	dried oregano or basil leaves	7 mL
1 cup	tomato pasta sauce	250 mL
6	large 9-inch (23 cm) flour tortillas	6
1½ cups	shredded part-skim mozzarella or Fontina cheese	375 mL

1. In a saucepan, bring stock to a boil; stir in rice. Reduce heat to low, cover and simmer for 20 minutes or until tender. Uncover; fluff with a fork.
2. In a large nonstick skillet, cook sausage over medium-high heat, breaking up with a wooden spoon, for 5 minutes or until no longer pink. Drain in sieve to remove excess fat; set aside.
3. Add oil to skillet; reduce heat to medium. Add onion, garlic, green pepper, mushrooms and oregano; cook, stirring, for 4 minutes or until softened. Add hot cooked rice, sausage and tomato pasta sauce; cook for 2 minutes or until heated through.

4. Place tortillas on baking sheets; sprinkle with cheese. Bake for 4 minutes or until cheese is melted. Spread about ¾ cup (175 mL) filling in a 2-by 5-inch (5 by 12 cm) rectangle along bottom half of each tortilla. Fold 1 inch (2.5 cm) of the right and left sides over filling. Starting from bottom, roll up tortillas around filling. Serve warm.

MAKES 4 WRAPS

I've taken the classic BLT and fashioned it into a wrap, adding fresh basil to the mayonnaise for a thoroughly modern twist.

VARIATION

Club Wrap

Cut 2 grilled or cooked chicken breasts into thin strips. Spread tortillas with basil mayonnaise; layer with tomato, lettuce, chicken and bacon. Roll tortillas as directed.

It's a BLT Wrap!

8	slices bacon, cut into quarters	8
1/3 cup	light mayonnaise	75 mL
2 tbsp	chopped fresh basil or 1/2 tsp (2 mL) dried	25 mL
4	large 9-inch (23 cm) flour tortillas	4
2	large tomatoes	2
4 cups	shredded romaine lettuce	1 L

1. Place bacon on a microwave-safe rack or on a large plate lined with a double layer of paper towels; loosely cover with another layer of paper towels. Microwave at High for 5 minutes or until cooked and almost crisp. Let cool.
2. In a bowl, combine mayonnaise and basil. Spread over tortillas leaving a 1-inch (2.5 cm) border around edge. Cut tomatoes in half crosswise and gently squeeze out seeds; slice thinly. Layer tortillas with tomato slices, lettuce and bacon. Fold 1-inch (2.5 cm) of the right and left sides of tortilla over filling. Starting from the bottom, roll up tortillas around filling. Serve immediately or cover in plastic wrap and store in the refrigerator for up to one day.

MAKES 6 FAJITAS

I love this recipe because it's a quick and easy main dish, yet it calls for only a few ingredients. It's ideal to serve for an impromptu dinner. I set out bowls of the cheese, sour cream and salsa, and let everyone help themselves.

TIPS

Turkey can also be barbecued. Marinate as directed and brush with 1 tbsp (15 mL) oil; grill over medium heat for 3 minutes per side or until no longer pink.

To warm tortillas, wrap in foil in 350°F (180°C) oven for 15 to 20 minutes. Or grill tortillas over medium heat for 30 to 60 seconds per side.

VARIATION

Chicken Fajitas

Instead of turkey, use 4 boneless, skinless chicken breasts; using a sharp knife, cut each chicken breast horizontally along one long side to make two thin pieces.

Turkey Fajitas

1 lb	boneless turkey breast, cut into 1/4-inch (0.5 cm) slices	500 g
1 tbsp	fresh lime juice	15 mL
1	clove garlic, minced	1
1/2 tsp	dried oregano leaves	2 mL
1/2 tsp	ground cumin	2 mL
1/2 tsp	ground coriander	2 mL
1/2 tsp	salt	2 mL
Pinch	cayenne pepper	Pinch
2 tbsp	olive oil	25 mL
1	medium red onion, thinly sliced	1
1	small red bell pepper, cut into thin 2-inch (5 cm) strips	1
1	small green bell pepper, cut into thin 2-inch (5 cm) strips	1
6	large 9-inch (23 cm) flour tortillas, warmed	6
	Salsa, sour cream, shredded lettuce and shredded cheddar cheese for garnishes	

1. In a bowl, toss turkey with lime juice, garlic, oregano, cumin, coriander, salt and cayenne pepper. Marinate for 15 minutes at room temperature, or longer in the refrigerator.
2. In a large nonstick skillet, heat 1 tbsp (15 mL) oil over high heat; cook turkey for 2 to 3 minutes per side, or until lightly browned and no longer pink in center. Transfer to plate; keep warm.
3. Add remaining oil to skillet; cook onion and peppers, stirring, for 3 minutes or until tender-crisp. Remove from heat. Cut turkey into thin diagonal strips; toss with onion-pepper mixture. Spoon turkey mixture down center of each tortilla; add a small spoonful of salsa and sour cream, if desired, and sprinkle with shredded lettuce and cheese. Roll up.

MAKES 4 QUESADILLAS

Here's my modern rendition of grilled cheese: thin flour tortillas replace sliced bread, mozzarella substitutes for processed cheese and chunky salsa stands in for the ketchup. And the beans? They're optional, but make a wholesome addition.

TIPS

I often serve these warm cheesy wedges with soup for an easy dinner. They're also great as a snack that both kids and grownups applaud.

Use mild salsa to appease those with timid taste buds, but add a dash of hot pepper sauce to the filling for those who like a burst of heat.

Cheese and Salsa Quesadillas

1/2 cup	salsa, plus additional for serving	125 mL
4	large 9-inch (23 cm) flour tortillas	4
1 cup	canned black or pinto beans, drained and rinsed	250 mL
1 cup	shredded mozzarella, Monterey Jack or Cheddar cheese	250 mL

1. Spread 2 tbsp (25 mL) salsa on half of each tortilla. Sprinkle with 1/4 cup (50 mL) each of the beans and the cheese. Fold tortillas over and press down lightly.
2. In a large nonstick skillet over medium heat, cook tortillas, two at a time, pressing down lightly with the back of a metal spatula, for about 2 minutes per side, until lightly toasted and cheese is melted. Or, place directly on barbecue grill over medium heat until lightly toasted on both sides.
3. Cut into wedges and serve warm with additional salsa, if desired.

MAKES 6 QUESADILLAS

Quesadillas sound complicated, but they are really just grilled sandwiches made with flour tortillas. The sky's the limit when it comes to fillings. This version, using roasted vegetables and goat cheese, is easy and delicious.

TIPS

Don't be intimidated by the fennel. It's simple to handle; just trim the top and cut in half lengthwise. Remove and discard the tough core.

Wraps can be assembled ahead. Cover in plastic wrap and refrigerate. Just pop them on the grill or in a nonstick skillet until toasted and cheese melts. Keep an eye on them — they cook quickly.

Breezy Californian Quesadillas

Preheat oven to 400°F (200°C)
Baking sheet, greased

1	small red onion, diced	1
1	large red bell pepper, diced	1
½	fennel bulb, cored and diced	½
1 tbsp	olive oil, plus extra for grilling	15 mL
½ tsp	salt	2 mL
½ tsp	freshly ground black pepper	2 mL
¼ cup	chopped Kalamata olives	50 mL
1 tbsp	balsamic vinegar	15 mL
2 tbsp	chopped fresh basil	25 mL
6	small 7-inch (18 cm) flour tortillas	6
6 oz	creamy goat cheese or cream cheese, softened	175 g

1. Spread onion, red pepper and fennel on baking sheet. Drizzle with oil; season with salt and pepper. Roast in preheated oven for 20 minutes, stirring occasionally, until vegetables are tender-crisp. Transfer to a bowl. Stir in olives and vinegar. Cover and refrigerate. (Can be made up to three days ahead.) Stir in basil.

2. Spread each tortilla with 2 tbsp (25 mL) of the goat cheese. Sprinkle each half with ¼ cup (50 mL) of the vegetable mixture; fold over filling, pressing down lightly. (Can be assembled ahead, wrapped in plastic wrap and refrigerated for up to 4 hours.)

3. Brush quesadillas lightly with oil. Place on greased grill over medium heat or cook in batches in a large nonstick skillet over medium heat for 2 minutes on each side or until toasted. Cut each into six wedges. Serve warm.

MAKES 6 ENCHILADAS

Instead of turning chicken leftovers into a week's worth of cold sandwiches, whip up this fast-fix dinner with loads of family appeal.

TIP

You can assemble this dish a day ahead of baking; just top with salsa and cheese prior to popping in the oven.

VARIATION

Cooked turkey or 1½ cups (375 mL) small cooked shrimp can be used instead of chicken.

Amazing Chicken Enchiladas

Preheat oven to 350°F (180°C)
13-by 9-inch (3 L) baking dish, greased

4 oz	cream cheese	125 g
½ cup	plain yogurt or sour cream	125 mL
2 cups	cooked chicken, cut into thin strips	500 mL
3	green onions, finely chopped	3
2	tomatoes, seeded and diced	2
¼ cup	chopped fresh cilantro or parsley	50 mL
6	large 9-inch (23 cm) flour tortillas	6
1½ cups	mild or medium salsa	375 mL
1 cup	shredded Cheddar or Monterey Jack cheese	250 mL

1. Place cream cheese in a large bowl; microwave at Medium for 1 minute to soften. Stir well. Stir in yogurt, chicken, green onions, tomatoes and cilantro.
2. Spread about ½ cup (125 mL) of the chicken mixture down center of each tortilla and roll up. Arrange tortillas in single layer, seam-side down, in prepared baking dish. Spread each tortilla with salsa and sprinkle with cheese. Bake for 30 to 35 minutes or until heated through. Sprinkle with extra chopped cilantro, if desired.

Microwave Method

1. Do not sprinkle with the cheese. Cover dish with waxed paper; microwave at Medium-High for 7 to 9 minutes or until heated through. Sprinkle with cheese; microwave at High for 1 minute or until cheese melts.

SERVES 4

Ever since I devised these yummy tacos, I walk right on by the prepackaged taco mixes and shells in supermarkets. Once the meat is browned, it takes no time to add the beans and seasonings to make the tasty filling. Aside from being lower in fat, I find pitas make much better containers than taco shells, which tend to crumble when you bite into them and cause the filling to spill out.

TIP

To heat pitas, wrap in foil and place in a 350°F (180°C) oven for 15 to 20 minutes. Or wrap four at a time in paper towels and microwave at High for 1 to 1½ minutes.

VARIATION

Sloppy Joe Pitas

Increase beef to 1 lb (500 g). Omit beans and add 1 can (7½ oz/ 213 mL) tomato sauce; cook 3 minutes more or until sauce is slightly thickened.

Taco Pitas

8 oz	lean ground beef	250 g
1	small onion, finely chopped	1
1	large clove garlic, minced	1
2 tsp	chili powder	10 mL
2 tsp	all-purpose flour	10 mL
½ tsp	dried oregano leaves	2 mL
½ tsp	ground cumin	2 mL
Pinch	cayenne pepper	Pinch
½ cup	beef stock	125 mL
1	can (19 oz/540 mL) pinto, black or red kidney beans, drained and rinsed	1
6	7-inch (18 cm) pitas, halved to form pockets, warmed	6
	Salsa, shredded lettuce, tomato wedges, pepper strips, shredded mozzarella or cheddar cheese	

1. In a large nonstick skillet over medium-high heat, cook beef, breaking up with the back of a wooden spoon, for 4 minutes or until no longer pink.
2. Reduce heat to medium. Add onion, garlic, chili powder, flour, oregano, cumin and cayenne pepper. Cook, stirring often, for 5 minutes or until onions are softened.
3. Pour in stock; cook, stirring, until slightly thickened. Stir in beans; cook 2 minutes more or until heated through.
4. Spoon ¼ cup (50 mL) of the mixture into pita pockets; top with salsa, lettuce, tomato, pepper and cheese.

MAKES 4 BURRITOS

Forget forks and knives when serving this tasty pick-up sandwich that has all the appeal of a traditional breakfast of ham and scrambled eggs.

Scrambled Eggs and Ham Burritos

Preheat oven to 350°F (180°C)
Baking sheet

4	large 9-inch (23 cm) flour tortillas	4
1 cup	shredded Cheddar cheese	250 mL
6	eggs	6
1 tbsp	milk	15 mL
1/4 tsp	salt	1 mL
Pinch	freshly ground black pepper	Pinch
2 tsp	butter	10 mL
1/2 cup	diced smoked ham	125 mL
2	green onions, sliced	2
1/3 cup	mild or medium salsa	75 mL

1. Place tortillas on cookie sheet; sprinkle with cheese. Place in oven for 5 minutes or until cheese melts.
2. Meanwhile, in a bowl, beat together eggs, milk, salt and pepper. In a large nonstick skillet, melt butter over medium heat; cook ham and green onions, stirring, for 1 minute or until onion is softened. Add eggs; cook, stirring often, for about 2 minutes or until eggs are just set.
3. Spoon egg mixture along bottom third of tortillas; top with salsa. Fold 1-inch (2.5 cm) of right and left sides of tortilla over filling, starting from the bottom and roll up tortillas around filling. Serve immediately.

MAKES 8 BURRITOS

Mexican dishes are a big hit with teens — and their parents. It makes a nourishing snack or supper. For a meat version, add strips of ham, cooked turkey or chicken.

TIP

Make a batch of burritos, wrap each in a paper towel, then in plastic wrap. Keep handy in the fridge ready to microwave for school lunches or after-school snacks. Remove plastic wrap before microwaving.

Black Bean Vegetable Burritos

1 tbsp	vegetable oil	15 mL
3	green onions, chopped	3
1	large clove garlic, minced	1
1 cup	diced zucchini	250 mL
1	red or green bell pepper, chopped	1
1 tsp	dried oregano leaves	5 mL
1 tsp	ground cumin	5 mL
1	can (19 oz/540 mL) black beans or kidney beans, drained and rinsed	1
8	large 9-inch (23 cm) flour tortillas, preferably whole wheat	8
1 cup	shredded mozzarella or Cheddar cheese	250 mL
1 cup	mild or medium salsa	250 mL
$\frac{1}{2}$ cup	sour cream	125 mL

1. In a large nonstick skillet, heat oil over medium heat. Add green onions, garlic, zucchini, bell pepper, oregano and cumin; cook, stirring, for 5 minutes or until vegetables are tender-crisp. Stir in beans; cook 1 to 2 minutes or until heated through.
2. Spoon $\frac{1}{4}$ cup (50 mL) of the bean mixture down the middle of each tortilla. Top each with 2 tbsp (25 mL) shredded cheese, 2 tbsp (25 mL) salsa and 1 tbsp (15 mL) sour cream. Roll to enclose filling. Wrap each burrito in a paper towel. Place four at a time on a plate; microwave at Medium-High for 3 to 4 minutes or until heated through. To heat a single burrito, microwave at Medium-High for 1 minute.

SERVES 8

Who doesn't love this fragrant accompaniment to a steaming bowl of pasta or tossed salad greens?

Herbed Garlic Bread

Preheat oven to 350°F (180°C)

½ cup	butter, softened	125 mL
2	cloves garlic, minced	2
⅓ cup	freshly grated Parmesan cheese	75 mL
2 tbsp	finely chopped fresh parsley	25 mL
¼ tsp	dried basil leaves	1 mL
¼ tsp	dried oregano leaves	1 mL
2 tsp	fresh lemon juice	10 mL
1	large loaf French or Italian bread, cut into ¾-inch (2 cm) thick slices	1

1. In a bowl, cream together butter, garlic, Parmesan, parsley, basil, oregano and lemon juice.
2. Spread butter mixture on one side of bread slices; reassemble into loaf shape and wrap loaf tightly in foil.
3. Bake in preheated oven for 20 minutes or until heated through.

SERVES 6

Nothing beats a delicious egg dish like this frittata for a special occasion breakfast or brunch, or for an easy supper dish. A frittata is an Italian version of an omelette. Unlike its finicky cousin, which needs careful flipping and turning, a frittata doesn't require any major cooking skills other than stirring — so it's almost impossible to ruin this dish.

TIP

Bake or microwave 2 large potatoes the day before and refrigerate so cubes keep their shape during cooking.

VARIATION

Bacon and Potato Frittata

Instead of ham, add 6 bacon slices, cooked until crisp and crumbled, to egg mixture.

Ham and Potato Frittata

Preheat oven to 375°F (190°C)

2 tbsp	butter	25 mL
1	small onion, finely chopped	1
2 cups	peeled cooked potatoes, cut into ½-inch (1 cm) cubes	500 mL
1	small red bell pepper, finely diced (optional)	1
¾ cup	diced smoked ham (about 4 oz/125 g)	175 mL
	Salt and freshly ground black pepper	
8	eggs	8
2 tbsp	milk	25 mL
2 tbsp	finely chopped fresh parsley	25 mL
1 cup	shredded Cheddar, Edam or Havarti cheese	250 mL

1. In a large nonstick skillet, melt butter over medium-high heat. Add onion, potatoes, red pepper and ham; cook, stirring often, for 5 minutes or until vegetables are tender. Reduce heat to medium-low.
2. Meanwhile, in a large bowl, beat together eggs, milk and parsley; season with salt and pepper. Pour over potato mixture in skillet; cook, stirring gently, for about 1 minute, or until eggs start to set. (The eggs will appear semi-scrambled.) Stir in cheese.
3. If skillet handle is not ovenproof, wrap in double layer of foil to shield it from oven heat. Place skillet in preheated oven for 15 to 20 minutes or until eggs are just set in center. Let cool 5 minutes. Turn out onto large serving plate and cut into wedges.

SERVES 6

You can always count on eggs for an economical meal. This oven-baked crustless quiche is perfect for brunch or an easy supper, served with juicy sliced tomatoes and good bread.

TIP

Wrap zucchini in a clean dry kitchen towel to remove excess moisture.

Crustless Zucchini Quiche

Preheat oven to 325°F (160°C)
10-inch (25 cm) pie plate or quiche dish, buttered

1 tbsp	butter	15 mL
3 cups	grated zucchini (unpeeled), squeezed dry	750 mL
4	green onions, chopped	4
1	red bell pepper, diced	1
6	eggs	6
3/4 cup	shredded Cheddar or Fontina cheese	175 mL
1/2 cup	soft fresh bread crumbs	125 mL
1/4 tsp	salt	1 mL
1/4 tsp	freshly ground black pepper	1 mL

1. In a large nonstick skillet, melt butter over medium-high heat. Add zucchini, green onions and red pepper; cook, stirring often, for 5 minutes or until softened. Let cool slightly.
2. In a large bowl, beat eggs; stir in zucchini mixture, cheese, bread crumbs, salt and pepper. Pour into pie plate. Bake for 35 to 40 minutes or until set in center.

SERVES 6

This ever-popular egg pie with bacon bits is an instant problem solver when you're wondering what to make for a do-ahead brunch or special lunch.

Quiche Lorraine

Preheat oven to 425°F (220°C)
9-inch (23 cm) pie plate or quiche dish

	Pastry for single crust 9-inch (23 cm) pie (see recipe, page 351)	
8	slices bacon, cooked crisp and crumbled	8
1 cup	shredded Swiss Gruyère cheese	250 mL
2 tbsp	finely chopped green onions	25 mL
3	eggs	3
1½ cups	half-and-half (10%) cream	375 mL
½ tsp	salt	2 mL
Pinch	freshly grated nutmeg	Pinch

1. On a lightly floured surface, roll out pastry into a 12-inch (30 cm) round. Roll pastry loosely around rolling pin; unroll into pie plate. Trim edge leaving a ½-inch (1 cm) overhang; turn pastry edge under and crimp edge. Prick with a fork. Line with a sheet of parchment paper or foil; fill with dried beans or pie weights.
2. Bake on middle rack in preheated oven for 10 minutes or until edges are set. Remove pie weights and bake 5 minutes more or until pastry is light golden. Place on rack to cool. Reduce oven temperature to 350°F (180°C).
3. Sprinkle bacon, cheese and green onions evenly over crust. In a bowl, beat eggs; add cream, salt and nutmeg. Pour over bacon mixture. Bake in oven for 30 to 35 minutes or until set in center. Let stand for 10 minutes before cutting.

SERVES 2 TO 3

Versatile mushrooms star in this terrific dish that's perfect to serve for brunch or a light supper.

TIPS

Use a variety of white and exotic mushrooms such as shiitake, portobello and oyster.

Herbed soft goat cheese can replace the cream cheese, if desired.

Cheese and Mushroom Oven Omelette

Preheat oven to 350°F (180°C)
Well-buttered 9- or 10-inch (23 or 25 cm) pie plate, sprinkled with 1 tbsp (15 mL) fine dry bread crumbs

4	eggs, separated	4
2 tbsp	milk	25 mL
	Salt and freshly ground black pepper	
1 tbsp	butter	15 mL
3 cups	sliced assorted mushrooms	750 mL
3	green onions, chopped	3
1/4 cup	light or herb cream cheese	50 mL
1/3 cup	shredded Cheddar cheese	75 mL
2 oz	smoked ham, cut into thin strips, or 3 slices bacon, cooked crisp and crumbled	60 g

1. In a small bowl, beat egg yolks with milk; season with salt and pepper. In a bowl, using an electric mixer, beat egg whites until stiff peaks form. Slowly beat in yolk mixture on low speed until blended into egg whites. Pour into prepared pie plate. Bake for 15 minutes or until just set in the center.
2. Meanwhile, in a large nonstick skillet, melt butter over medium-high heat. Cook mushrooms and green onions, stirring, for 5 minutes or until tender and liquid is evaporated. Remove from heat; stir in cream cheese until smooth.
3. Spoon evenly over omelette; sprinkle with cheese and ham. Bake for 8 minutes more or until cheese is melted.

Dilled Salmon and Egg Salad on Pumpernickel (page 73) ➢

Main Dishes

← Quick Bistro-Style Steak (page 98)

SERVES 4

Dressed up with wine, garlic and herbs, this steak recipe becomes a special dish when you're entertaining friends.

TIPS

Serve with Roasted Garlic Potatoes (see recipe, page 248).

Herbes de Provence is a blend of French herbs that often includes thyme, rosemary, basil and sage. If you can't find this blend in your supermarket, substitute a generous pinch of each of these herbs.

Quick Bistro-Style Steak

4	boneless striploin steaks, each 6 oz (175 g)	4
1/2 tsp	coarsely ground black pepper	2 mL
2 tsp	olive oil	10 mL
2 tsp	butter	10 mL
	Salt	
1/4 cup	finely chopped shallots	50 mL
1	large clove garlic, finely chopped	1
1/4 tsp	dried herbes de Provence (see Tip, left)	1 mL
1/3 cup	red wine or additional beef stock	75 mL
1/2 cup	beef stock	125 mL
1 tbsp	Dijon mustard	15 mL
2 tbsp	chopped fresh parsley	25 mL

1. Remove steaks from refrigerator 30 minutes before cooking. Season with pepper.
2. Heat a large heavy skillet over medium heat until hot; add oil and butter. Increase heat to high; brown steaks about 1 minute on each side. Reduce heat to medium; cook to desired degree of doneness. Transfer to a heated serving platter; season with salt and keep warm.
3. Add shallots, garlic and herbes to skillet; cook, stirring, for 1 minute. Stir in red wine; cook, scraping up any brown bits from bottom of pan, until liquid has almost evaporated.
4. Stir in stock, mustard and parsley; season with salt and pepper to taste. Cook, stirring, until slightly reduced. Spoon sauce over steaks. Serve immediately.

SERVES 6

Here's my favorite way to prepare beef on the barbecue. Flank steak is economical, easy to marinate ahead, and leftovers make great-tasting sandwiches.

TIP

Flank steak becomes more tender the longer it's marinated. Thick-cut round steak can also be prepared in the same way.

Easy Asian Flank Steak

Preheat barbecue grill or broiler

1/4 cup	hoisin sauce	50 mL
2 tbsp	soy sauce	25 mL
2 tbsp	fresh lime juice	25 mL
1 tbsp	vegetable oil	15 mL
4	cloves garlic, minced	4
2 tsp	Oriental chili paste or 1 tsp (5 mL) hot pepper flakes	10 mL
1 1/2 lbs	flank steak	750 g

1. In a shallow glass dish, whisk together hoisin sauce, soy sauce, lime juice, oil, garlic and chili paste; add steak, turning to coat both sides with marinade. Refrigerate, covered, at least 8 hours or up to 24 hours. Remove meat from refrigerator 30 minutes before cooking.

2. Reserving the marinade, place steak on a greased grill over medium-high heat. Cook, basting often with marinade, for 7 to 8 minutes per side or until medium-rare. (Alternately, place steak on foil-lined baking sheet; broil 4 inches (10 cm) below preheated broiler for 7 to 8 minutes on each side.) Transfer to cutting board, cover loosely with foil; let stand for 5 minutes. Thinly slice at right angles to the grain of meat.

SERVES 4

Here's a fast stir-fry that doesn't require a lot of chopping. Serve with steamed rice, cooked rice vermicelli or a string pasta such as linguine.

VARIATION

Substitute boneless chicken breast or pork tenderloin for the beef.

Beef and Broccoli Stir-Fry

1 lb	lean boneless sirloin steak, cut into thin strips	500 g
2 tbsp	hoisin sauce	25 mL
2	cloves garlic, minced	2
1 tbsp	minced fresh gingerroot	15 mL
1 tsp	grated orange zest	5 mL
1/2 cup	orange juice	125 mL
3 tbsp	soy sauce	45 mL
2 tsp	cornstarch	10 mL
1/4 tsp	hot pepper flakes	1 mL
1 tbsp	vegetable oil	15 mL
6 cups	small broccoli florets and peeled chopped stems (about 1 large bunch)	1.5 L
4	green onions, chopped	4

1. In a bowl, toss beef strips with hoisin sauce, garlic and ginger. Let marinate at room temperature for 15 minutes. (Cover and refrigerate if preparing ahead.) In a glass measuring cup, combine orange zest and juice, soy sauce, cornstarch and hot pepper flakes.
2. In a large nonstick skillet, heat oil over high heat; cook beef, stirring, for 2 minutes or until no longer pink. Transfer to a plate.
3. Add broccoli and soy sauce mixture to skillet; reduce heat to medium, cover and cook for 2 to 3 minutes or until broccoli is tender-crisp. Add beef strips with any accumulated juices and green onions; cook, stirring, for 1 minute or until heated through.

SERVES 6

When growing up, Sunday dinner in my home was often a standing rib roast seasoned simply with salt and pepper and served with pan gravy. This recipe moves it up a notch with the addition of a thyme-pepper rub and red wine to enhance the gravy.

Sunday Roast Beef with Wine Gravy

Preheat oven to 450°F (230°C)
Roasting pan

4 lbs	standing rib roast	2 kg
1	large clove garlic, cut in small slivers	1
2 tbsp	Dijon mustard	25 mL
1 tsp	dried thyme leaves	5 mL
1/2 tsp	salt	2 mL
1 tsp	coarsely ground black pepper	5 mL

WINE GRAVY

1/2 cup	red wine	125 mL
1 1/2 cups	beef stock	375 mL
1 tbsp	cornstarch	15 mL
2 tbsp	water	25 mL
1 tbsp	Worcestershire sauce	15 mL
	Salt and freshly ground black pepper	

1. Make small slits in roast and insert garlic slivers. Let roast stand for 1 hour. In a bowl, combine mustard, thyme, salt and pepper. Spread over roast.

2. Place rib-side down in shallow roasting pan. Roast in oven for 15 minutes; reduce heat to 350°F (180°C) and continue to roast for 1 1/4 to 1 1/2 hours or until meat thermometer registers 140°F (60°C) for medium rare. Transfer to carving board, covered loosely with foil, for 15 minutes.

3. Wine Gravy: Skim fat from drippings in pan. Place over medium heat; add wine. Cook, scraping up brown bits from bottom, until reduced by half. Stir in beef stock; strain sauce through a fine sieve into a saucepan. Bring to a boil; cook for 5 minutes or until slightly reduced.

4. In a small bowl, blend cornstarch with water and Worcestershire sauce. Add to pan, stirring constantly, until sauce boils and thickens. Season with salt and pepper to taste. Cut beef into thin slices and accompany with sauce.

SERVES 4

I feel like it's a special occasion when I have a roast chicken in the oven. It conjures up a homey smell and feel. In my opinion, it's one of the most satisfying dishes on earth. Here I place herbs and seasonings under the bird's skin to produce a succulent, flavorful chicken. Slow roasting with lots of garlic creates a wonderful aroma — yet, surprisingly, imparts only a subtle flavor to the gravy.

Thyme-Roasted Chicken with Garlic Gravy

Preheat oven to 325°F (160°C)
Roasting pan with rack

1	chicken (about 3½ lbs/1.75 kg)	1
10	cloves garlic, peeled	10
1 tsp	dried thyme leaves	5 mL
¼ tsp	salt	1 mL
¼ tsp	freshly ground black pepper	1 mL
1⅓ cups	chicken stock, divided (approx.)	325 mL
½ cup	white wine or additional chicken stock	125 mL
1 tbsp	all-purpose flour	15 mL

1. Remove giblets and neck from chicken. Rinse and pat chicken dry inside and out. Place 2 cloves garlic inside cavity. Starting at cavity opening, gently lift skin and rub thyme, salt and pepper over breasts and legs. Tie legs together with string; tuck wings under back.
2. Add remaining garlic, ⅔ cup (150 mL) chicken stock and wine to roasting pan; place chicken, breast side up, on rack in pan.
3. Roast in preheated oven, basting every 30 minutes, adding additional stock if pan juices evaporate, for 1¾ to 2 hours or until pan juices run clear when chicken is pierced and meat thermometer inserted in thigh registers 185°F (85°C).
4. Transfer to a platter; tent with foil and let stand for 10 minutes before carving. Meanwhile, strain pan juices into measure, pressing down firmly to mash garlic into juices; skim off fat. Add enough of remaining stock to make ¾ cup (175 mL).
5. In a small saucepan, stir together 2 tbsp (25 mL) of pan juices and flour; cook, stirring, over medium heat for 1 minute. Gradually whisk in remaining pan juices; cook, stirring, until boiling and thickened. Serve with chicken.

SERVES 4

Who has time to wait around for a chicken to roast when you're in a hurry? I take an hour off the roasting time by doing two things: I cut the bird open along the backbone, place it flat on the broiler pan and then boost the oven temperature. The result? A golden, succulent bird in half the time.

One-Hour Roast Chicken with Sage and Garlic

Preheat oven to 400°F (200°C)
Broiler pan, greased

1	chicken (about 3½ lbs/1.75 kg)	1
1 tbsp	butter, softened	15 mL
2	cloves garlic, minced	2
1 tbsp	minced fresh sage or 1 tsp (5 mL) dried sage leaves	15 mL
1½ tsp	grated lemon zest	7 mL
½ tsp	salt	2 mL
½ tsp	freshly ground black pepper	2 mL
2 tsp	olive oil	10 mL
¼ tsp	paprika	1 mL

1. Remove giblets and neck from chicken. Rinse and pat chicken dry inside and out with paper towels. Using heavy-duty kitchen scissors, cut chicken open along backbone; press down on breast bone to flatten slightly and arrange skin-side up on rack of a broiler pan.
2. In a bowl, blend butter with garlic, sage, lemon zest, salt and pepper. Gently lift breast skin; using a knife or spatula, spread butter mixture under skin to coat breasts and part of legs. Press down on outside skin to smooth and spread butter mixture.
3. In a small bowl, combine olive oil and paprika; brush over chicken.
4. Roast chicken for 1 hour or until juices run clear and a meat thermometer inserted in the thickest part of the thigh registers 185°F (85°C). Transfer chicken to a platter. Tent with foil; let rest 5 minutes before carving.

SERVES 4

A breeze to prepare, this easy-to-assemble dish is elegant enough to serve to company. The herb and lemon butter tucked under the skins keeps the chicken moist and I love the way it imparts a wonderful flavor to the vegetables layered on the bottom.

TIPS

Make extra batches of rosemary butter, shape into small logs, wrap in plastic and store in the freezer. Cut into slices and use to tuck under the breast skins of whole roasting chickens or Cornish hens, or to top grilled meats.

If you purchased whole breasts with backs on, cut away back bone using poultry shears.

Rosemary Chicken Breasts with Layered Potatoes and Onions

Preheat oven to 375°F (190°C)
13-by 9-inch (3 L) shallow baking dish, greased

3	medium potatoes (about 1 lb/500 g)	3
2	small sweet potatoes (about 1 lb/500 g)	2
1	medium onion	1
1 tsp	dried rosemary, crumbled	5 mL
	Salt and freshly ground black pepper	
4	chicken breasts, bone-in with skin	4

ROSEMARY BUTTER

2 tbsp	butter	25 mL
1	large clove garlic, minced	1
1 tsp	grated lemon zest	5 mL
1 tsp	dried rosemary, crumbled	5 mL
1/4 tsp	salt	1 mL
1/4 tsp	freshly ground black pepper	1 mL

1. Peel potatoes, sweet potatoes and onion; cut into very thin slices. Layer vegetables in prepared baking dish. Season with rosemary, salt and pepper.
2. Place chicken breasts, skin-side up, on work surface. Remove any fat deposits under skins. Press down on breast bone to flatten slightly.
3. Rosemary Butter: In a small bowl, mash together butter, garlic, lemon zest, rosemary, salt and pepper. Divide into four portions.
4. Carefully loosen the breast skins and tuck rosemary butter under skins, patting to distribute evenly.
5. Arrange chicken on top of vegetables in baking dish. Cover with sheet of greased foil; roast in preheated oven for 45 minutes. Uncover and roast 25 to 30 minutes more or until vegetables are tender and chicken is nicely colored.

SERVES 4

Kids love simple dishes like this one, with its straightforward flavors. And this chicken dish is simple enough that even young cooks can make it.

TIP

This recipe also works well with a whole cut-up chicken or bone-in chicken breasts. With its tang of lemon and sweetness of honey, this dish is sure to become a family favorite.

Just-For-Kids Honey Lemon Chicken

Preheat oven to 350°F (180°C)
13-by 9-inch (3 L) baking dish

4	chicken legs, skinned	4
2 tbsp	liquid honey	25 mL
2 tsp	grated lemon zest	10 mL
1 tsp	fresh lemon juice	5 mL
1	large clove garlic, minced	1
1/4 tsp	salt	1 mL
1/4 tsp	freshly ground black pepper	1 mL

1. Arrange chicken in baking dish. In a bowl, combine honey, lemon zest, lemon juice, garlic, salt and pepper; spoon over chicken.

2. Bake in oven, basting once, for 45 to 55 minutes or until juices run clear when chicken is pierced.

SERVES 4

Boneless chicken breasts are a staple in my weekly grocery cart. Everyone needs an all-purpose chicken dish to whip up on the spur of the moment. This is one of mine. It's a breeze to cook and always a hit with my family. Serve alongside noodles or rice. Add a salad and you've got dinner ready in 30 minutes.

TIP

Vary the flavors by using different herbs such as tarragon or herbes de Provence.

My Favorite Chicken Dish

4	skinless, boneless chicken breasts	4
2 tbsp	all-purpose flour	25 mL
1/2 tsp	salt	2 mL
1/2 tsp	freshly ground black pepper	2 mL
1 tbsp	butter	15 mL
1/2 cup	chicken stock	125 mL
1/2 cup	orange juice or mixture of juice and part dry white wine	125 mL
1	large clove garlic, finely chopped	1
1/2 tsp	dried Italian herbs or basil leaves	2 mL
1/4 tsp	granulated sugar	1 mL
1 tbsp	chopped fresh parsley or chives	15 mL

1. On a cutting board using a sharp knife, cut each breast lengthwise into two thin pieces. Place flour in a shallow bowl; season with salt and pepper. Coat chicken in flour mixture, shaking off excess.
2. Heat a large nonstick skillet over medium-high heat. Add butter; when foamy, add chicken pieces. Cook 2 minutes per side or until lightly browned. Transfer to a plate.
3. Reduce heat to medium; add stock, orange juice, garlic, Italian herbs and sugar to skillet. Bring to a boil; cook for 1 minute or until slightly reduced. Season sauce with salt and pepper to taste. Return chicken to skillet; reduce heat, cover and simmer for 5 minutes or until no longer pink inside and sauce is slightly thickened. Serve sprinkled with parsley.

SERVES 4

What a relief to know when you come home frazzled from a day at work, you can count on these tasty chicken fingers stashed away in your freezer. Round out the meal with rice and a steamed vegetable, such as broccoli, for a dinner that's on the table in 30 minutes.

TIPS

Buy boneless chicken breasts when they're featured as a supermarket special and make batches of chicken fingers to freeze ahead. Use fresh (not defrosted) chicken breasts; prepare recipe as directed, placing unbaked strips on a rack set on baking sheet. Freeze until firm; transfer to a storage container. Can be frozen for up to two months. No need to defrost before baking.

You can also make extra batches of the crumb mixture and store in the freezer.

Instead of boneless chicken breasts, prepare skinless chicken drumsticks in the same way but bake in a 375°F (190°C) oven for 35 to 40 minutes or until tender.

Yummy Parmesan Chicken Fingers

Preheat oven to 400°F (200°C)
Baking sheet, with greased rack

1/2 cup	finely crushed soda cracker crumbs (about 16 crackers)	125 mL
1/3 cup	freshly grated Parmesan cheese	75 mL
1/2 tsp	dried basil leaves	2 mL
1/2 tsp	dried marjoram leaves	2 mL
1/2 tsp	paprika	2 mL
1/2 tsp	salt	2 mL
1/4 tsp	freshly ground black pepper	1 mL
4	skinless, boneless chicken breasts	4
1	egg	1
2 tbsp	butter	25 mL
1	clove garlic, minced	1

1. In a food processor, combine cracker crumbs, Parmesan cheese, basil, marjoram, paprika, salt and pepper. Process to make fine crumbs. Place in a shallow bowl.
2. Cut chicken breasts into four strips each. In a bowl, beat egg; add chicken strips. Using a fork, dip chicken strips in crumb mixture until evenly coated. Arrange on greased rack set on baking sheet. In small bowl, microwave butter and garlic at High for 45 seconds or until melted. Brush chicken strips with melted butter.
3. Bake in preheated oven for 15 minutes or until no longer pink in center. (If frozen, bake for up to 25 minutes.)

SERVES 6

This popular chicken dish does double duty served warm as a family-pleasing supper or served cold when tucked into a picnic hamper or bagged lunch.

TIP

Make extras of the seasoned crumb mixture and keep in the freezer to coat boneless strips of chicken breasts or fish fillets for a quick supper.

Cornmeal-Crumbed Chicken Drumsticks

Preheat oven to 350°F (180°C)
Baking sheet, lined with greased foil

1/2 cup	sour cream	125 mL
1 tbsp	fresh lemon juice	15 mL
1	large clove garlic, minced	1
1 tsp	salt	5 mL
1/4 tsp	freshly ground black pepper	1 mL
12	chicken drumsticks, skins removed	12

CRUMB COATING

1/3 cup	cornmeal	75 mL
1/3 cup	fine dry bread crumbs	75 mL
1/3 cup	freshly grated Parmesan cheese	75 mL
2 tbsp	minced fresh parsley	25 mL
1 tsp	dried basil leaves	5 mL
1/2 tsp	dried thyme leaves	2 mL
1/2 tsp	paprika	2 mL
1/4 cup	melted butter	50 mL

1. In a bowl, combine sour cream, lemon juice, garlic, salt and pepper. Add drumsticks; stir to coat well. Cover and let marinate in the refrigerator for 2 hours or overnight.

2. Crumb Coating: In a large heavy plastic bag, combine cornmeal, bread crumbs, Parmesan cheese, parsley, basil, thyme and paprika. Add drumsticks in batches and shake to coat well in crumb mixture. Place on prepared baking sheet. Brush drumsticks lightly with melted butter.

3. Bake in oven for 40 to 45 minutes or until drumsticks are golden and no longer pink when cut into at the bone. If serving cold, transfer to a rack to cool. Place in a covered container and refrigerate.

SERVES 4

In the time it takes to cook rice or pasta, this streamlined dish is ready to serve.

Chicken Curry with Red Peppers

1 cup	chicken stock	250 mL
2 tsp	cornstarch	10 mL
1/4 tsp	salt	1 mL
4 tsp	vegetable oil, divided	20 mL
1 lb	skinless, boneless chicken breasts, cut into thin strips	500 g
2	cloves garlic, minced	2
1 tbsp	minced fresh gingerroot	15 mL
1 tbsp	mild curry paste or powder	15 mL
2	large red bell peppers, cut into thin strips	2
4	green onions, sliced	4

1. In a liquid glass measure, combine stock, cornstarch and salt; set aside.
2. In a large nonstick skillet, heat 2 tsp (10 mL) oil over medium-high heat; cook chicken, stirring often, for 5 minutes or until no longer pink inside. Transfer to a plate.
3. Reduce heat to medium; add remaining oil; cook garlic, ginger and curry paste; cook, stirring, for 1 minute. Add peppers; cook, stirring, for 2 minutes. Stir reserved stock mixture and pour into skillet; bring to a boil. Cook, stirring, until thickened. Add chicken and green onions; cook, stirring, for 2 minutes or until heated through.

SERVES 8 TO 10, PLUS LEFTOVERS

Turkey always has the place of honor when my family and friends gathers for holiday meals. It's perfect when serving a crowd. It's economical, too, and everyone loves it. Best of all are the leftovers that get wrapped and placed in the fridge for hearty sandwiches the next day — or even later that night.

TIPS

See Turkey Tips, page 112

VARIATION

Sausage-Apple Stuffing

Cook 1 lb (500 g) bulk sausage meat in a large skillet over medium-high heat, breaking up with back of spoon, until no longer pink; drain off fat. Add 2 peeled, finely chopped apples; combine with bread stuffing mixture.

Roast Turkey with Sage-Bread Stuffing

Preheat oven to 325°F (160°C)
12-cup (3 L) casserole dish, greased
Shallow roasting pan or broiler pan, with greased rack

STUFFING

1⁄3 cup	butter	75 mL
2 cups	chopped onions	500 mL
2 cups	chopped celery	500 mL
8 oz	mushrooms, chopped	250 g
4	cloves garlic, minced	4
1 tbsp	dried rubbed sage	15 mL
1 tsp	dried thyme leaves	5 mL
1 tsp	dried marjoram leaves	5 mL
1 tsp	salt	5 mL
1⁄2 tsp	freshly ground black pepper	2 mL
12 cups	white or whole bread cubes, toasted on baking sheet in 350°F (180°C) oven for 15 minutes	3 L
1⁄2 cup	chopped fresh parsley	125 mL
1 cup	turkey stock (approx.)	250 mL

TURKEY

1	turkey (about 12 to 14 lbs/6 to 7 kg)	1
2 tbsp	melted butter	25 mL
6	cloves garlic, unpeeled	6
1	large onion, cut into 8 wedges	1
2	carrots, cut into chunks	2
1	large stalk celery, cut into chunks	1
1 tsp	dried rosemary leaves, crumbled	5 mL
1⁄2 tsp	dried thyme leaves	2 mL
1⁄2 tsp	dried marjoram leaves	2 mL
	Salt and freshly ground black pepper	

GRAVY

1⁄4 cup	all-purpose flour	50 mL
1⁄2 cup	white wine or additional stock	125 mL
3 cups	turkey gravy stock	750 mL

TURKEY GRAVY STOCK

Pat neck and giblets dry. (Do not use liver.) In a large saucepan, heat 1 tbsp (15 mL) vegetable oil over medium-high heat; cook neck and giblets, stirring, for 8 minutes or until nicely browned. Add 1 each chopped onion, carrot and celery stalk including leaves along with 1 tsp (5 mL) dried thyme; cook, stirring, for 3 minutes or until vegetables are lightly colored. Add 1 cup (250 mL) white wine, if desired. Stir in 6 cups (1.5 L) water; season lightly with salt and pepper. Bring to a boil, cover and simmer over medium-low heat, for 3 hours. Strain stock through cheesecloth-lined or fine sieve; discard solids. Makes about 4 cups (1 L) stock

1. Stuffing: In a large skillet, melt butter over medium heat; cook onions, celery, mushrooms, garlic, sage, thyme, marjoram, salt and pepper, stirring often, for 15 minutes or until tender.
2. In a large bowl, combine onion mixture, bread cubes and parsley. Spoon into casserole dish.
3. To bake, add enough turkey stock to moisten stuffing and toss. (If you plan to stuff the bird, omit stock.) Cover with lid or foil and place in oven for the last hour of roasting turkey, uncovering for last 30 minutes to brown and crisp the top.
4. Turkey: Remove neck and giblets from bird; reserve to make stock. Rinse turkey with cold water; pat dry. Secure legs by tying with string or tuck under skin around the tail; fold wings back and secure neck skin with skewer.
5. Place turkey, breast side up, on rack in roasting pan. Brush bird with melted butter. Lightly crush garlic with side of knife; scatter garlic, onion, carrots and celery in pan. Season turkey and vegetables with rosemary, thyme, marjoram, salt and pepper.
6. Insert meat thermometer into thickest part of inner turkey thigh being careful not to touch bone. Roast turkey for 3¼ to 3½ hours; no need to baste. (If turkey starts to brown too quickly, tent bird loosely with heavy-duty foil, shiny side down.) Turkey is done when meat thermometer registers 170°F (80°C) for unstuffed bird; 180°F (82°C) if stuffed.
7. Remove from oven; cover with foil and let stand for 15 minutes for easy carving.
8. Gravy: Skim fat from roasting pan; place over medium heat. Stir in flour; cook, stirring, for 1 minute. Add wine; cook, stirring, until reduced by half. Stir in stock; bring to boil, scraping up brown bits from bottom of pan, until gravy thickens. Strain through a fine sieve into a saucepan, pressing down on vegetables; discard the vegetables. Season gravy with salt and pepper to taste.

TURKEY TIPS

- I prefer to roast a fresh turkey rather than a frozen bird, which is less moist and juicy. To streamline the preparations, I've done away with stuffing the turkey. Instead, the stuffing is packed into a casserole dish and baked in the oven for the last hour of roasting the bird.
- Not sure what size turkey to buy? Estimate 1 lb (500 g) per person.
- Quick defrosting method: Place frozen turkey (in original wrapping) in cold water and change water frequently. Allow 1 hour per pound (2 hours per kg). Once defrosted, cook turkey within two days.
- Wash hands well before and after handling turkey. Wash and disinfect work surface and utensils with hot soapy water and dry thoroughly.
- Cook turkey thoroughly. Never slow roast at low temperatures or partially cook a bird, then continue roasting later on in day or next day.
- Roast in a 325°F (160°C) oven until a meat thermometer, inserted in the thickest portion of inner thigh, reaches an internal temperature of 170°F (80°C) for unstuffed bird; 180°F (82°C) for stuffed bird.
- Chill leftovers promptly. Do not leave cooked turkey at room temperature for more than 2 hours. Place cooked turkey meat in a casserole or wrap in foil or plastic and refrigerate immediately. Leftovers will keep in fridge for up to four days or freeze for one month.

WHOLE TURKEY ROASTING TIMES

Today's leaner turkeys take less time to cook than in the past. Don't rely on outdated information from old cookbooks and recipes. Here are newly revised roasting times:
Cooking time (hours) in 325°F (160°C) oven

Weight	*Stuffed*	*Unstuffed*
6 to 8 lbs (3 to 3.5 kg)	3 to 3¼	2½ to 2¾
8 to 10 lbs (3.5 to 4.5 kg)	3¼ to 3½	2¾ to 3
10 to 12 lbs (4.5 to 5.5 kg)	3½ to 3¾	3 to 3¼
12 to 16 lbs (5.5 to 7 kg)	3¾ to 4	3¼ to 3½
16 to 22 lbs (7 to 10 kg)	4 to 4½	3½ to 4

SERVES 4

This recipe will make you want to roast a turkey just so you have some leftovers on hand. But, if time does not permit, buy a roasted chicken from the deli section of the supermarket and use the diced meat in this no-fuss dish.

TIP

Mango chutney is called for in this recipe, but any type, whether store-bought or homemade can be used; add according to taste. Serve over basmati rice and sprinkle with chopped cilantro, if desired.

Quick Turkey Curry

2 tsp	vegetable oil	10 mL
1	small onion, chopped	1
1	large clove garlic, minced	1
2 tsp	minced fresh gingerroot	10 mL
1	apple, peeled and chopped	1
1/2 cup	finely diced celery	125 mL
2 tsp	mild curry paste or powder	10 mL
1 tbsp	all-purpose flour	15 mL
1 1/3 cups	chicken stock	325 mL
3 tbsp	mango chutney	45 mL
2 cups	diced cooked turkey or chicken	500 mL
1/4 cup	raisins	50 mL
	Salt and freshly ground black pepper	

1. In a large nonstick skillet, heat oil over medium heat. Add onion, garlic, ginger, apple, celery and curry paste; cook, stirring, for 5 minutes or until softened.

2. Blend in flour; add chicken stock and chutney. Cook, stirring, until sauce comes to a boil and thickens. Stir in turkey and raisins; season with salt and pepper to taste. Cook for 3 minutes or until heated through.

SERVES 8

Lamb is often my first choice when planning a special dinner. It's always a crowd pleaser. I love the heavenly aroma of garlic and rosemary in this recipe — it fills my house and makes an especially warm welcome for friends as they come through the door.

TIPS

Take the lamb out of the fridge about 30 minutes before roasting.

Choose potatoes that are the same size so they roast evenly.

If you don't want to open a bottle of white wine, a good substitute is dry white vermouth. Keep a bottle handy in the cupboard for those recipes that call for white wine.

Rosemary Roast Lamb with New Potatoes

Preheat oven to 350°F (180°C)
Large shallow roasting pan, greased

1	leg of lamb (about 5 to 6 lbs/2.5 to 3 kg)	1
8	cloves garlic	8
	Grated zest and juice of 1 lemon	
2 tbsp	olive oil	25 mL
2 tbsp	chopped fresh rosemary or 1 tbsp (15 mL) dried rosemary, crumbled	25 mL
½ tsp	salt	2 mL
½ tsp	freshly ground black pepper	2 mL
12	whole new potatoes, scrubbed (about 3 lbs/1.5 kg)	12
1 tbsp	all-purpose flour	15 mL
½ cup	white wine	125 mL
1 cup	chicken stock	250 mL

1. Cut 6 cloves garlic into 8 to 10 slivers each. Using the tip of a knife, cut shallow slits all over lamb and insert a garlic sliver into each.
2. Finely chop remaining 2 garlic cloves. In a bowl, combine garlic, lemon zest and juice, oil, rosemary, salt and pepper. Place lamb in prepared roasting pan; surround with potatoes. Brush lamb and potatoes generously with lemon-garlic mixture. Insert meat thermometer into thickest part of leg.
3. Roast in preheated oven for about 1½ hours, turning potatoes over halfway through roasting, until meat thermometer registers 135°F (57°C) for medium-rare. (For medium, remove the potatoes and continue to roast lamb for 15 to 20 minutes more or to your liking.)

4. Remove lamb to a platter; tent with foil and let rest 10 minutes before carving. Transfer potatoes to a dish; keep warm.
5. Skim fat in pan; place over medium heat. Stir in flour and cook, stirring, until lightly colored. Pour in wine; cook, scraping up any brown bits until wine is reduced by half. Stir in stock; bring to a boil, stirring, until thickened. Strain through a fine sieve into a warm sauceboat.
6. Carve the lamb. Arrange slices on serving plate and moisten with some of the sauce; surround with roasted potatoes. Serve with remaining sauce.

SERVES 8

I love the way the sweetness of dried fruit accents the delicate taste of pork in this recipe. And when you stuff the loin with a fruit and spice mixture, you ensure that the meat will be extra moist and flavorful.

TIP

It may appear that you have too much stuffing when you first tie the pork. But once all the strings are in place, it's easy to enclose the meat completely around the fruit mixture.

Company Pork Roast with Fruit Stuffing

Preheat oven to 350°F (180°C)
Roasting pan, with greased rack

STUFFING

1 tbsp	butter	15 mL
1/3 cup	chopped green onions	75 mL
1 tsp	ground cumin	5 mL
1 tsp	mild curry paste or powder	5 mL
1	egg	1
1 cup	chopped mixed dried fruits, such as apricots, prunes, apples, cranberries	250 mL
1/2 cup	soft fresh bread crumbs	125 mL
1 tsp	finely grated orange zest	5 mL
	Salt and freshly ground black pepper	

PORK ROAST

3 lbs	boneless pork loin roast	1.5 kg
2 tsp	vegetable oil	10 mL
1	large clove garlic, minced	1
1 tsp	dried sage leaves	5 mL
1/2 tsp	dried thyme leaves	2 mL

GRAVY

1 tbsp	all-purpose flour	15 mL
1/2 cup	white wine or chicken stock	125 mL
3/4 cup	chicken stock	175 mL

1. In a small skillet, melt butter over medium heat. Add green onions, cumin and curry paste; cook, stirring, for 2 minutes or until softened.

2. In a bowl, beat egg; add onion mixture, dried fruits, bread crumbs and orange zest; season with salt and pepper.

3. Pork Roast: Remove strings from pork roast; unfold roast and trim excess fat. Place pork roast, bone-side up, on work surface. Cover with plastic wrap and pound using a meat mallet to flatten slightly. Season with salt and pepper; spread stuffing down center of meat. Roll the pork around the stuffing and tie securely at six intervals with butcher's string.
4. Place roast on rack in roasting pan. In a small bowl, combine oil, garlic, sage and thyme; spread over pork roast and season with salt and pepper.
5. Roast in preheated oven for 1½ to 1¾ hours or until meat thermometer registers 160°F (70°C).
6. Transfer roast to cutting board; tent with foil and let stand for 10 minutes before carving.
7. Gravy: Drain fat from pan. Place over medium heat; sprinkle with flour. Cook, stirring, for 1 minute or until lightly colored. Add wine; cook until partially reduced. Add stock and bring to a boil, scraping any brown bits from bottom of pan. Season with salt and pepper to taste. Strain sauce through a fine sieve into a warm sauceboat. Cut pork into thick slices and serve accompanied with gravy.

SERVES 4

Sweet potato or winter squash can replace the rutabaga in this mellow ginger-and-spice-infused dish.

TIP

This hearty casserole can be refrigerated, tightly covered, for up to two days.

Pork Chop Bake with Rutabaga and Apples

Preheat oven to 350°F (180°C)
13-by 9-inch (3 L) baking dish

1	rutabaga (1 ½ lbs/750 g)	1
¼ cup	all-purpose flour	50 mL
1 lb	thin boneless pork loin chops, trimmed (about 6)	500 g
2 tbsp	vegetable oil, divided	25 mL
2	large apples, peeled, cored and sliced	2
1	onion, halved lengthwise, sliced into thin wedges	1
2 tbsp	minced fresh gingerroot	25 mL
1 tsp	ground cumin	5 mL
1 tsp	ground coriander	5 mL
1 tsp	salt	5 mL
¼ tsp	freshly ground black pepper	1 mL
¼ tsp	ground cinnamon	1 mL
¼ tsp	freshly grated nutmeg	1 mL
1 cup	apple juice	250 mL
1 tbsp	packed brown sugar	15 mL

1. Peel and quarter rutabaga; cut into ¼-inch (0.5 cm) slices; layer in baking dish.
2. Place flour in a heavy plastic bag; shake pork in batches in flour to coat, shaking off excess; reserve remaining flour.
3. In a large nonstick skillet, heat 1 tbsp (15 mL) oil over medium-high heat; brown pork lightly on both sides. Arrange over rutabaga; top with apple slices.

4. Add remaining oil to skillet; reduce heat to medium. Add onion, ginger, cumin, coriander, salt, pepper, cinnamon and nutmeg; cook, stirring, for 3 minutes, or until onion is softened. Sprinkle with reserved flour. Add apple juice and brown sugar; bring to a boil. Pour over apples in baking dish.
5. Cover and bake in oven for 1 hour or until rutabaga is tender.

SERVES 4

Simple and tasty — this is my favorite way to cook fast-fry pork chops. Serve with rice and steamed broccoli.

Pork Chops with Honey and Thyme

1/2 cup	chicken stock	125 mL
1 tbsp	liquid honey	15 mL
1 tbsp	cider vinegar	15 mL
1 tsp	cornstarch	5 mL
1 lb	thin boneless pork chops, trimmed (about 6)	500 g
1 tbsp	vegetable oil	15 mL
	Salt and freshly ground black pepper	
3	green onions, sliced	3
1/2 tsp	dried thyme leaves	2 mL

1. In a bowl, combine stock, honey, vinegar and cornstarch. Set aside.
2. Blot pork chops dry with paper towels. In a large nonstick skillet, heat oil over high heat; cook pork for 1 to 2 minutes per side, or until lightly browned. Season with salt and pepper. Transfer to a plate.
3. Reduce heat to medium. Stir in green onions and thyme; cook, stirring for 30 seconds. Stir reserved chicken stock mixture and add to skillet; cook, stirring, for 1 minute or until sauce boils and thickens. Return pork and any juices to skillet; cover and cook for 2 minutes or until pork is no longer pink in center. Season sauce, if necessary, with additional salt and pepper to taste.

SERVES 8 TO 10, PLUS LEFTOVERS

The orange and lemon zest adds a wonderful flavor to the ham as well as a terrific garnish.

TIP

You will need the zest from about two oranges and two lemons.

Baked Ham with Citrus-Mustard Glaze

Preheat oven to 325°F (160°C)

1	bone-in smoked ham (about 8 lbs/4 kg)	1
2 tbsp	coarsely grated orange zest	25 mL
2 tbsp	coarsely grated lemon zest	25 mL
1/2 cup	citrus marmalade	125 mL
1/4 cup	maple syrup	50 mL
1/4 cup	white wine vinegar	50 mL
2 tbsp	orange juice	25 mL
2 tsp	dry mustard	10 mL
1 cup	chicken stock (approx.)	250 mL
1 tsp	cornstarch	5 mL

1. Remove skin and trim fat from ham leaving a 1/4-inch (0.5 cm) thick layer. Score the fat to make a diamond pattern. Place ham in a shallow roasting pan and bake, uncovered, for 1 1/4 hours. Drain off any fat in pan.
2. In a small saucepan of boiling water, blanch orange and lemon zest for 1 minute to remove bitterness. Drain and reserve.
3. In a food processor, purée marmalade, maple syrup, vinegar, orange juice and mustard until smooth. Transfer to a bowl.
4. Pour glaze over ham and sprinkle with zests. Bake, basting every 15 minutes, for about 45 minutes or until nicely glazed and meat thermometer registers 140°F (60°C). (Add a small amount of stock to bottom of pan if glaze begins to brown.) Transfer ham to a warm platter, cover loosely with foil and let rest for 15 minutes before carving.
5. Place roasting pan on stovetop over medium heat. Blend stock and cornstarch until smooth; pour into pan; cook, stirring until sauce boils and is slightly thickened.
6. Cut ham into slices and serve accompanied with sauce.

SERVES 4

"You've got to put your rib recipe in your cookbook", advised my son, whose favorite dinner request is a plate of these succulent ribs. So here it is. And since the only way to eat ribs is with your fingers, be sure to have plenty of napkins handy.

TIPS

Ribs are great on the barbecue, too. Partially cook ribs in oven for 45 minutes as directed in recipe. Complete cooking on grill over medium-low flame, basting often with the sauce.

Supermarket shelves boast a large assortment of hot sauces — some quite mild, others having a fiery kick — so experiment with various sauces available and add according to taste.

Zesty Barbecued Spareribs

Preheat oven to 375°F (190°C)
Shallow roasting pan or broiler pan, with rack

3 to 4 lbs	pork spareribs	1.5 to 2 kg
	Salt and freshly ground black pepper	
1 cup	prepared chili sauce or ketchup	250 mL
1/2 cup	liquid honey	125 mL
1	small onion, finely chopped	1
2	cloves garlic, minced	2
2 tbsp	Worcestershire sauce	25 mL
2 tbsp	fresh lemon juice	25 mL
1 tbsp	Dijon mustard	15 mL
1 tsp	hot pepper sauce or to taste	5 mL
1	lemon, cut into wedges	1

1. Place ribs on rack in roasting pan; season with salt and pepper. Cover with foil. Roast in preheated oven for 45 minutes.
2. In a small saucepan, combine chili sauce, honey, onion, garlic, Worcestershire sauce, lemon juice, mustard and hot pepper sauce. Bring to a boil; reduce heat and simmer, stirring occasionally, for 10 to 15 minutes or until slightly thickened.
3. Remove foil; brush ribs generously on both sides with sauce. Roast, uncovered, for 45 minutes, brushing generously every 15 minutes with the sauce, until spareribs are nicely glazed and tender.
4. Cut into serving portions; serve with any remaining sauce and lemon wedges.

SERVES 4
MAKES 4 CUPS (1 L) SAUCE

There are plenty of store-bought barbecue sauces, but none compares to the versatility and popularity of this lip-smackin' sauce. It has a spicy kick to it, but for those who crave it really hot, add more hot pepper flakes or your favorite hot sauce. Don't limit the sauce to just ribs; it's also terrific with other grill favorites, such as burgers, pork chops and kabobs, or try it on chicken wings and legs. This makes a big batch; store extra sauce in a covered container in the refrigerator for up to one month. Or, freeze it.

Tex-Mex Barbecued Spareribs

Preheat barbecue grill or oven to 375°F (190°C)

3 lbs	pork spareribs	1.5 kg
2 cups	Tex-Mex Barbecue sauce (see recipe below)	500 mL

1. Cut ribs into serving-size pieces. Place in Dutch oven or large saucepan of boiling salted water; reduce heat, cover and simmer, for 40 minutes or until tender. Drain.
2. Place ribs on greased grill over medium heat; cook, turning and basting often with sauce, for 15 to 20 minutes or until glazed and tender. Or, place ribs on foil-lined baking sheet. Generously brush both sides of ribs with sauce. Roast, uncovered, brushing often with sauce, for 25 to 30 minutes or until glazed and tender.

Tex-Mex Barbecue Sauce

1	bottle (12 oz/341 mL) beer	1
2 cups	bottled chili sauce or ketchup	500 mL
1/2 cup	cider vinegar	125 mL
1/2 cup	packed brown sugar	125 mL
1/4 cup	Worcestershire sauce	50 mL
2	medium onions, finely chopped	2
4	large cloves garlic, minced	4
2 tbsp	chili powder	25 mL
1 tbsp	dried oregano leaves	15 mL
1 tsp	hot pepper flakes	5 mL

1. In a large saucepan, combine beer, chili sauce, cider vinegar, brown sugar, Worcestershire sauce, onions, garlic, chili powder, oregano and hot pepper flakes. Bring to a boil; reduce heat and simmer, partially covered, stirring occasionally, for 25 minutes or until thickened.

SERVES 4

Tender milk-fed veal is preferred over grain-fed in this classic pan-fried recipe with flavorful herbs. Schnitzel is typically served with French fries, but you could also serve with a salad of vibrant mesclun or watercress greens.

TIP

Make sure cutlets are thin; if necessary pound meat thin between sheets of plastic wrap using a meat mallet or rolling pin.

Herb Wiener Schnitzel

1 lb	thin veal or turkey cutlets (8 cutlets)	500 g
1/2 tsp	salt	2 mL
1/2 tsp	freshly ground black pepper	2 mL
1 cup	plain dry bread crumbs	250 mL
1/3 cup	lightly packed fresh parsley	75 mL
3/4 tsp	dried herbes de Provence or thyme leaves (see Tip, page 98)	4 mL
1/3 cup	all-purpose flour	75 mL
2	eggs, beaten	2
2 tbsp	butter, divided	25 mL
2 tbsp	vegetable oil, divided (approx.)	25 mL
	Lemon wedges	

1. Blot veal dry with paper towels. Season with salt and pepper.

2. In a food processor, process bread crumbs, parsley and herbes de Provence.

3. Place flour, beaten eggs and bread crumb mixture in three separate shallow bowls. Just before cooking, dredge veal in flour, shaking off excess; dip in egg and then coat well in bread crumb mixture.

4. In a large nonstick skillet, heat 1 tbsp (15 mL) each butter and oil over medium-high heat. Cook veal in batches, adding more butter and oil as needed and wiping skillet clean with paper towels between batches, for 1 1/2 minutes per side or until golden. Transfer to a baking sheet; place in warm oven while cooking remaining schnitzel. Serve accompanied with lemon wedges.

SERVES 4

We've somehow forgotten this delicious classic preparation — and it's worth considering again. Together, the golden red paprika and tangy sour cream bring out the best in tender veal and meaty mushrooms.

TIP

Fettuccine or broad egg noodles make a delicious companion to this creamy veal in mushroom sauce.

Veal Paprikash

2 tbsp	vegetable oil, divided	25 mL
1 lb	grain-fed veal scallops or boneless beef sirloin, cut into thin strips	500 g
4 cups	quartered mushrooms (about 12 oz/375 g)	1 L
1	large onion, halved lengthwise and thinly sliced	1
2	cloves garlic, minced	2
4 tsp	paprika	20 mL
1/2 tsp	dried marjoram leaves	2 mL
1/2 tsp	salt	2 mL
1/4 tsp	freshly ground black pepper	1 mL
1 tbsp	all-purpose flour	15 mL
3/4 cup	chicken stock	175 mL
1/2 cup	sour cream	125 mL
	Salt and freshly ground black pepper	

1. In a large nonstick skillet, heat 1 tbsp (15 mL) oil over high heat; stir-fry veal in two batches, each for 3 minutes or until browned but still pink inside. Transfer to a plate along with pan juices; keep warm.
2. Reduce heat to medium. Add remaining oil. Add mushrooms, onion, garlic, paprika, marjoram, salt and pepper; cook, stirring often, for 7 minutes or until lightly colored.
3. Sprinkle mushroom mixture with flour; pour in stock. Cook, stirring, for 2 minutes or until thickened. Stir in sour cream. Return veal and accumulated juices to pan; cook 1 minute more or until heated through. Adjust seasoning with salt and pepper to taste; serve immediately.

SERVES 6 TO 8

You will be delighted by the tantalizing aromas of rosemary and garlic wafting through your kitchen whenever you prepare this distinctive roast — ideal for a Sunday or other special occasion.

TIP

Pancetta is unsmoked Italian bacon that is available in supermarket deli counters.

Tuscan Roast Veal with Rosemary and White Wine

Preheat oven to 350°F (180°C)
Roasting pan

2 oz	pancetta, finely diced, or bacon (see Tip, left)	60 g
1/4 cup	finely chopped fresh parsley	50 mL
2	cloves garlic, minced	2
1 tsp	grated lemon zest	5 mL
	Salt and freshly ground black pepper	
3 lbs	leg of veal roast, well trimmed, tied	1.5 kg
2 tbsp	olive oil	25 mL
1 tbsp	chopped fresh rosemary or 1 1/2 tsp (7 mL) dried rosemary, crumbled	15 mL
1 cup	dry white wine, divided	250 mL
1 cup	chicken or veal stock, divided	250 mL

1. In a bowl, combine pancetta, parsley, garlic and zest; season with salt and pepper. Stuff into cavity of roast, as evenly as possible. (Prepare earlier in the day and refrigerate to allow flavors to penetrate veal.)
2. Place veal in pan. Brush with oil; season with rosemary, salt and pepper. Place in oven and roast, uncovered, for 30 minutes. Add 1/2 cup (125 mL) each wine and stock to roasting pan. Tent loosely with foil and continue to roast for 1 1/2 hours more, adding more wine and stock to the pan as necessary, until meat thermometer registers 170°F (80°C).
3. Transfer meat to serving platter and keep warm. Pour remaining wine and stock into roasting pan and place on stovetop over high heat. Bring to a boil, scraping up any brown bits from bottom of pan. Strain into a saucepan and boil until partially reduced. Slice veal into slices and drizzle with some of the pan juices. Serve remainder in a sauceboat.

SERVES 4

This easy-to-make saucy veal is one of my all-time favorite dishes to serve when I'm entertaining. Delicious served with noodles and a green vegetable such as asparagus.

TIP

If you prefer a cream sauce, stir in ¼ cup (50 mL) whipping (35%) cream at end of cooking and heat through.

Veal Scaloppini with Marsala

1 lb	thin veal or pork cutlets	500 g
½ tsp	salt	2 mL
¼ tsp	freshly ground black pepper	1 mL
¼ cup	all-purpose flour	50 mL
1 tbsp	butter, divided	15 mL
1 tbsp	olive oil, divided	15 mL
⅓ cup	minced shallots	75 mL
¾ lb	assorted mushrooms, such as shiitake, oyster and button mushrooms, sliced	375 g
1 tbsp	chopped fresh thyme or 1 tsp (5 mL) dried thyme leaves	15 mL
½ cup	dry Marsala or white wine	125 mL
½ cup	chicken stock	125 mL

1. Blot veal dry with paper towels. Season with salt and pepper; dredge in flour, shaking off excess.
2. In a large nonstick skillet, heat 1½ tsp (7 mL) each butter and oil over high heat; cook veal in batches, adding more butter and oil as needed, for 1 minute per side or until lightly browned. Transfer to a plate.
3. Reduce heat to medium; cook shallots, mushrooms and thyme, stirring, for 5 minutes or until softened. Add Marsala and stock; cook for 2 minutes or until slightly reduced. Return veal to skillet. Cook for 2 to 3 minutes, turning occasionally, until heated through and coated in sauce. Adjust seasoning with salt and pepper to taste.

SERVES 4

Fresh gingerroot gives such a sparkling flavor to salmon — or any fish, for that matter. Substituting dried ground ginger just doesn't come close to imparting the same crisp taste as fresh gingerroot, which is available in most supermarkets and produce stores.

TIPS

To store gingerroot, peel it, place in glass jar and add white wine or sherry to cover. As an added bonus, you can use the ginger-infused wine or sherry to flavor other fish or chicken dishes, or stir-fries.

One of the best uses for the microwave in my kitchen is for quickly cooking fish such as this salmon. Arrange fish and sauce in a shallow baking dish and cover with microwave-safe plastic wrap; turn back one corner to vent. Microwave at Medium for 4 minutes. Turn fish over and re-cover; microwave at Medium for 3 to 5 minutes more or until salmon turns opaque.

This fish dish is also great to cook on the barbecue.

Salmon with Lemon-Ginger Sauce

Preheat oven to 425°F (220°C)
Shallow baking dish

4	salmon fillets, each 5 oz (150 g)	4
MARINADE		
2	green onions	2
1 1/2 tsp	minced fresh gingerroot	7 mL
1	clove garlic, minced	1
2 tbsp	soy sauce	25 mL
1 tbsp	fresh lemon juice	15 mL
1 tsp	grated lemon zest	5 mL
1 tsp	granulated sugar	5 mL
1 tsp	sesame oil	5 mL

1. Place salmon fillets in a single layer in baking dish.
2. Marinade: Chop green onions; set aside chopped green tops for garnish. In a bowl, combine white part of green onions, ginger, garlic, soy sauce, lemon juice and zest, sugar and sesame oil. Pour marinade over salmon; let stand at room temperature for 15 minutes or in the refrigerator for up to 1 hour.
3. Bake, uncovered, in preheated oven for 13 to 15 minutes or until salmon turns opaque. Arrange on serving plates, spoon sauce over and sprinkle with reserved green onion tops.

Yummy Parmesan Chicken Fingers (page 107) ➢
Overleaf: Zesty Barbecued Spareribs (page 122)

SERVES 4

What to do with fresh cod from the market and ripe tomatoes plucked from your garden? Add some briny olives and pungent capers, and make this delicious fish dish that bursts with the sunny flavors of the Mediterranean.

TIP

Don't skimp on the olive oil — it's what gives this dish its distinct character and flavor.

Cod Provençal

Preheat oven to 425°F (220°C)
Shallow baking dish

1¼ lbs	cod or halibut, cut into 4 pieces	625 g
	Salt and freshly ground black pepper	
2	ripe tomatoes, diced	2
2	green onions, sliced	2
1	clove garlic, minced	1
¼ cup	Kalamata olives, rinsed, cut into slivers	50 mL
2 tbsp	chopped fresh parsley or basil leaves	25 mL
1 tbsp	capers, drained and rinsed	15 mL
Pinch	hot pepper flakes (optional)	Pinch
2 tbsp	olive oil	25 mL

1. Arrange cod in a single layer in baking dish. Season with salt and pepper.
2. In a bowl, combine tomatoes, green onions, garlic, olives, parsley, capers and hot pepper flakes, if using; season with salt and pepper. Spoon tomato-olive mixture over fish fillets; drizzle with oil.
3. Bake in preheated oven for 15 to 20 minutes or until fish flakes when tested with a fork. Serve in warmed wide shallow bowls and spoon pan juices over top.

< Old-Fashioned Beef Stew (page 134)

SERVES 4

No trip to the fish market is required to make this quick main-course dish. Packaged frozen fish fillets work just fine. And here's an extra bonus — even with a small amount of light cream added, this dish is low in fat.

TIP

To defrost package of frozen fish fillets (see Tip, page 132).

Cod with Mushrooms and Tomato

Preheat oven to 375°F (190°C)
8-inch (2 L) square baking dish

1	package (14 oz/400 g) frozen cod, sole, turbot or haddock fillets, defrosted	1
	Salt and freshly ground black pepper	
1 1/2 cups	sliced mushrooms	375 mL
1	large tomato, seeded and diced	1
2	green onions, sliced	2
2 tbsp	chopped fresh dill or parsley	25 mL
1/3 cup	dry white wine or fish stock	75 mL
1 tbsp	cornstarch	15 mL
1/3 cup	half-and-half (10%) cream	75 mL

1. Arrange fish fillets in a single layer in baking dish; season with salt and pepper. Layer with mushrooms, tomato, green onions and dill. Pour wine over top. Bake for 20 to 25 minutes or until fish is opaque and flakes when tested with a fork.
2. Remove from oven; carefully pour juices from dish into small saucepan. (Place a large plate or lid over dish.) Return fish to turned-off oven to keep warm.
3. In a bowl, blend cornstarch with 2 tbsp (25 mL) cold water; stir in cream. Add to saucepan. Place over medium heat; cook, whisking, until sauce comes to a boil and thickens. Season with salt and pepper to taste. (Sauce will be thick.) Pour over fish and serve.

SERVES 4

Want to wow your guests? Put this on your menu. Tender sole fillets with vibrant red pepper stuffing marry well in a light wine and cream sauce. It makes an attractive fish dish that never fails to impress.

TIP

In the past, fish dishes were adorned with silky rich sauces loaded with cream and butter. Adding only a small amount of whipping cream still gives this sauce its luxurious and creamy appeal, but keeps the calorie count way down.

Stuffed Sole

Preheat oven to 425°F (220°C)
8-inch (2 L) square baking dish

1 tbsp	butter	15 mL
¼ cup	chopped green onions	50 mL
1 cup	chopped mushrooms	250 mL
1	red bell pepper, cut into very thin 1-inch (2.5 cm) strips	1
1 tsp	dried tarragon	5 mL
	Salt and white pepper	
8	small sole fillets (about 1½ pounds/750 g)	8
⅓ cup	white wine or fish stock	75 mL
2 tsp	cornstarch	10 mL
⅓ cup	whipping (35%) cream	75 mL

1. In a nonstick skillet, heat butter over medium heat. Add green onions, mushrooms, pepper and tarragon; cook, stirring, for 3 minutes or until softened. Let cool.
2. Lay sole fillets, skinned side down, on work surface with smaller tapered ends closest to you; season with salt and pepper. Spoon a generous tablespoonful (15 mL) on bottom ends of fillets. Roll up and place fillets seam-side down in baking dish. Pour wine over top. (Recipe can be prepared up to this point earlier in day, then covered and refrigerated.)
3. To bake, cover with lid or foil; place in preheated oven for 16 to 20 minutes or until fish turns opaque.
4. Using a slotted spoon, remove fillets and arrange on serving plate; cover and keep warm.
5. Strain fish juices through a fine sieve into a medium saucepan; bring to a boil over high heat and reduce to about ½ cup (125 mL). In a bowl, blend cornstarch with 1 tbsp (15 mL) cold water; stir in cream. Pour into saucepan, whisking constantly, until sauce comes to a boil and thickens. Adjust seasoning with salt and pepper to taste. Spoon sauce over fish and serve.

SERVES 3 TO 4

This easy oven method is my preferred way to cook white fish fillets, such as sole, haddock or turbot. As much as I like to quickly fry a crumb-coated fillet in a skillet on the stovetop, only one or two can fit comfortably in the pan at one time. Hence the speed and practicality of cooking all the fillets at once by the oven method. Increase time accordingly for thicker fillets.

TIP

To defrost package of frozen fish fillets, remove package wrapping; place fish on plate. Microwave at Medium for 3 minutes. Shield ends with thin strips of foil to prevent them from cooking before the rest of the fish has defrosted. Microwave at Defrost for 3 minutes more or until fish separates into fillets. Let stand for 10 minutes to complete defrosting. Pat dry with paper towels to absorb excess moisture.

Crispy Almond Baked Fish

Preheat oven to 425°F (220°C)
Baking sheet

1/2 cup	soft fresh bread crumbs	125 mL
1/3 cup	sliced blanched almonds	75 mL
1/2 tsp	dried tarragon or basil leaves	2 mL
1/2 tsp	grated orange or lemon zest	2 mL
1 lb	fish fillets, such as sole, haddock or turbot	500 g
2 tbsp	butter, melted	25 mL
	Salt and freshly ground black pepper	
	Lemon wedges	

1. In a food processor, combine bread crumbs, almonds, tarragon and orange zest. Process, using on-off turns, until almonds are finely chopped.
2. Wrap fish in paper towels to absorb excess moisture. Brush baking sheet with some of the melted butter. Arrange fillets on sheet in single layer. Brush tops with remaining butter; season with salt and pepper. Sprinkle crumb mixture over fish and pat lightly.
3. Bake in preheated oven for 8 to 10 minutes or until fish flakes when tested with a fork. (Time depends on thickness of fish; increase time accordingly.) Serve with lemon wedges.

Stews, Pot Roasts and One-Pot Simmers

SERVES 4 TO 6

What's more comforting than a satisfying stew? You start feeling good the minute you set this one-pot dish to simmer on the stovetop. As the herb-infused aroma wafts through your kitchen the good feeling grows. The first forkful confirms that this stew is comfort food at its best. What's more, it can comfort you all over again the next day with easy-to-reheat leftovers. Delicious served with crusty bread to mop up the flavorful sauce.

TIP

A word about parsley. Use either the curly leaf variety or the more strongly flavored flat-leaf type. Wash well in plenty of water to remove dirt; dry parsley in a salad spinner or wrap in clean towel. The drier the parsley, the longer it lasts in your refrigerator. Wrap in paper towels, then in a plastic bag and refrigerate. To save time, every few weeks I finely chop a few bunches of parsley, pack into a container and freeze. Though not suitable for fresh salads, the frozen parsley is perfect to add to soups, stews, meat loaves and casseroles.

Old-Fashioned Beef Stew

1/4 cup	all-purpose flour	50 mL
1 tsp	salt	5 mL
1/2 tsp	freshly ground black pepper	2 mL
1 1/2 lbs	stewing beef, cut into 1 1/2-inch (4 cm) cubes	750 g
2 tbsp	vegetable oil (approx.), divided	25 mL
2	medium onions, chopped	2
3	cloves garlic, finely chopped	3
1 tsp	dried thyme leaves	5 mL
1 tsp	dried marjoram leaves	5 mL
1	bay leaf	1
1 cup	red wine or additional beef stock	250 mL
3 tbsp	tomato paste	45 mL
3 cups	beef stock (approx.)	750 mL
5	carrots	5
2	stalks celery	2
4 to 5	potatoes (about 1 1/2 lbs/750 g)	4 to 5
12 oz	green beans	375 g
1/4 cup	chopped fresh parsley (see Tip, left)	50 mL

1. Combine flour, salt and pepper in a heavy plastic bag. In batches, add beef to flour mixture and toss to coat. Transfer to a plate. Reserve remaining flour mixture.
2. In a Dutch oven or large saucepan, heat 1 tbsp (15 mL) oil over medium-high heat; cook beef in batches, adding more oil as needed, until browned all over. Transfer to a plate.
3. Reduce heat to medium-low. Add onions, garlic, thyme, marjoram, bay leaf and remaining flour to pan; cook, stirring, for 4 minutes or until softened. Add wine and tomato paste; cook, stirring, to scrape up brown bits. Return beef and any accumulated juices to pan; pour in stock.

4. Bring to a boil, stirring, until slightly thickened. Reduce heat, cover and simmer over medium-low heat, stirring occasionally, for 1 hour.
5. Meanwhile, peel carrots and halve lengthwise. Cut carrots and celery into 1½-inch (4 cm) chunks. Peel potatoes and quarter. Add vegetables to pan. Cover and simmer for 30 minutes.
6. Trim ends of beans and cut into 2-inch (5 cm) lengths. Stir into stew mixture, adding more stock if necessary, until vegetables are just covered. Cover and simmer for 30 minutes more or until vegetables are tender. Remove bay leaf and stir in parsley. Adjust seasoning with salt and pepper to taste.

SERVES 4

Stews are very convenient for reheating and freezing, so they can be a real time saver. Keep stew in a covered container in the refrigerator for up to three days. Or, double the recipe and freeze half for another meal.

VARIATION

Substitute 1 large fennel bulb for the celery, if desired. Trim top from fennel; cut in half lengthwise and remove core. Cut into strips.

Rosemary Beef Ragout

4 tsp	olive oil, divided	20 mL
1 lb	stewing beef, cut into 1-inch (2.5 cm) cubes	500 g
2	large onions, chopped	2
3	cloves garlic, finely chopped	3
1½ tsp	dried rosemary, crumbled	7 mL
2 tbsp	balsamic or red wine vinegar	25 mL
2 tbsp	all-purpose flour	25 mL
2½ cups	beef stock	625 mL
2 tbsp	tomato paste	25 mL
½ tsp	salt	2 mL
½ tsp	freshly ground black pepper	2 mL
12 oz	peeled baby carrots	375 g
3	stalks celery, thickly cut	3

1. In a Dutch oven or large saucepan, heat 2 tsp (10 mL) oil over high heat. Brown beef in batches; transfer to a plate.
2. Add remaining oil to pan. Reduce heat to medium and add onions, garlic and rosemary; cook, stirring, for 3 minutes, or until softened. Add vinegar; cook until almost evaporated. Sprinkle with flour. Add stock, tomato paste, salt and pepper. Bring to a boil; cook, stirring, until slightly thickened.
3. Return meat and accumulated juices to pan; reduce heat, cover and simmer for 1¼ hours. Add carrots and celery; simmer, covered, for 30 minutes or until beef and vegetables are tender.

SERVES 6 TO 8

Guinness, a dark Irish beer, adds a rich intense flavor to this simple beef stew that benefits from being made a day ahead.

TIP

Instead of Guinness, substitute another dark beer such as stout or dark ale. If the beer you use is only available in 12 oz (341 mL) bottles or cans, add an extra ½ cup (125 mL) beef stock to the stew.

Irish Beef Stew

2 tbsp	vegetable oil (approx.), divided	25 mL
3 lbs	lean stewing beef, cut into 1½-inch (4 cm) cubes	1.5 kg
2	large onions, thinly sliced	2
3	cloves garlic, finely chopped	3
1 tbsp	chopped fresh thyme or 1 tsp (5 mL) dried thyme leaves	15 mL
1	large bay leaf	1
1 tsp	salt	5 mL
½ tsp	freshly ground black pepper	2 mL
2 tbsp	all-purpose flour	25 mL
1	can (16 oz/440 mL) pub draft Guinness	1
½ cup	beef stock	125 mL
2 tbsp	chopped fresh parsley	25 mL

1. In a Dutch oven or large saucepan, heat 1 tbsp (15 mL) oil over high heat. Cook beef in batches for 3 to 5 minutes, adding more oil as needed, until browned on all sides. Transfer to a plate as meat browns.
2. Reduce heat to medium; cook onions, garlic, thyme, bay leaf, salt and pepper, stirring often, for 5 minutes or until softened. Stir in flour; add beef including juices, beer and stock to pan.
3. Bring to a boil over high heat; reduce heat, cover and simmer for 1½ hours. Remove lid; simmer for 30 minutes more until beef is very tender. Adjust seasoning with salt and pepper to taste; remove bay leaf. Sprinkle with parsley before serving.

SERVES 8

When I was growing up, pot roasts were a staple in my house. I can remember coming home from school to the tantalizing smell of a roast slowly braising in the oven. This recipe features a richly colored sauce from caramelized onions and a subtle sweet-sour taste from the beer and brown sugar. It's delicious served with creamy mashed potatoes or egg noodles.

TIP

Use a light-colored beer, or an amber one, such as pale ale. For a robust-flavored stew, try a dark beer, such as porter or stout.

Pot Roast with Beer and Caramelized Onions

Preheat oven to 325°F (160°C)

1	beef pot roast, such as cross-rib, rump or brisket (about 3 to 4 lbs/1.5 to 2 kg)	1
¼ cup	all-purpose flour	50 mL
2 tbsp	vegetable oil (approx.), divided	25 mL
4	medium onions, halved lengthwise and thinly sliced (about 1¼ lbs/625 g)	4
2 tbsp	packed brown sugar	25 mL
2	bay leaves	2
1 tsp	salt	5 mL
½ tsp	ground cinnamon	2 mL
½ tsp	ground ginger	2 mL
½ tsp	freshly ground black pepper	2 mL
3	large cloves garlic, finely chopped	3
2 tbsp	balsamic vinegar	25 mL
1	bottle (12 oz/341 mL) beer	1
1	can (7½ oz/213 mL) tomato sauce	1
1½ lbs	carrots (about 8)	750 g
1	small rutabaga (about 1 lb/500 g)	1

1. On a large plate, roll meat in flour to coat. Shake off excess; reserve.
2. In a Dutch oven or large saucepan, heat 1 tbsp (15 mL) oil over medium-high heat. Brown meat on all sides, about 6 minutes. Transfer to a plate.
3. Reduce heat to medium. Add remaining oil to Dutch oven. Add onions, brown sugar, bay leaves, salt, cinnamon, ginger and pepper; cook, stirring often, for 12 to 15 minutes or until onions are softened and nicely colored. (Add more oil, if needed, to prevent onions from burning.)

4. Add reserved flour and garlic; cook, stirring, for 30 seconds. Add vinegar; cook until evaporated. Pour in beer and tomato sauce; bring to a boil, stirring, until thickened. Return meat and accumulated juices to pan. Cover and roast in preheated oven for 2 hours.
5. Meanwhile, peel carrots and rutabaga; cut into 2-by ½-inch (5 by 1 cm) strips. Add to beef. Cover and cook 1 to 1½ hours more or until meat is tender.
6. Remove roast from pan; cut into thin slices. Arrange on serving platter; surround with vegetables. Skim any fat from sauce; remove bay leaves and spoon some sauce over meat and pour the rest into a warmed sauceboat to serve on the side.

SERVES 6 TO 8

This homey standby always provides me with welcome leftovers for later in the week or even to have stashed away in the freezer for an easy supper.

TIP

Pot roast always tastes better the next day; let cool, cover and refrigerate. Also freezes well.

Country Pot Roast

Preheat oven to 350°F (180°C)

1	boneless beef pot roast, such as rump or brisket (about 3 to 4 lbs/1.5 to 2 kg)	1
1/4 cup	all-purpose flour	50 mL
2 tbsp	olive oil	25 mL
1	large onion, chopped	1
3	cloves garlic, finely chopped	3
1 1/2 tsp	dried oregano leaves	7 mL
1	bay leaf	1
1 tsp	salt	5 mL
1/2 tsp	freshly ground black pepper	2 mL
1/4 cup	red wine vinegar	50 mL
1	can (19 oz/540 mL) stewed tomatoes, including juice	1
1/2 cup	beef stock	125 mL
2 tbsp	fancy molasses or brown sugar	25 mL

1. Pat roast dry with paper towels. Place flour on a plate and coat beef with flour; reserve remaining flour on plate.
2. In a Dutch oven or large saucepan, heat oil over medium-high heat and brown roast on all sides, about 6 minutes. Transfer to plate.
3. Reduce heat to medium; cook onion, garlic, oregano, bay leaf, salt and pepper, stirring, for 3 minutes, or until lightly colored. Add vinegar; scrap up brown bits from bottom of pan. Stir remaining flour into pan; add tomatoes with juice, stock and molasses. Bring to a boil; return beef to pan. Cover and place in oven; braise for 2 1/2 to 3 hours or until meat is fork-tender.
4. Cut beef into slices and arrange on a platter. Discard bay leaf and purée sauce in a food processor or blender until smooth. Spoon some of the sauce over meat; transfer rest to a gravy boat. Serve with mashed potatoes.

SERVES 4 TO 6

When it comes to favorite recipes, these slowly braised short ribs in a rich herb-orange flavored sauce served with lots of creamy mashed potatoes are the quintessence of comfort food.

TIP

For maximum flavor, braise meat the day ahead. Let cool, cover and refrigerate. Skim fat before reheating.

Braised Beef Short Ribs

3 lbs	boneless beef short ribs	1.5 kg
2 tbsp	olive oil, divided	25 mL
2	onions, chopped	2
3	cloves garlic, finely chopped	3
1 tsp	dried rosemary or thyme leaves, crumbled	5 mL
1 tsp	salt	5 mL
½ tsp	freshly ground black pepper	2 mL
1 ½ cups	beef stock (approx.)	375 mL
1 cup	canned tomatoes, including juice, chopped	250 mL
2 tbsp	Worcestershire sauce	25 mL
3	strips orange peel (3-inch/8 cm in length)	3

1. Pat short ribs dry with paper towels. In a Dutch oven or large saucepan, heat 1 tbsp (15 mL) oil over medium-high heat; brown short ribs in batches, adding more oil as needed, until nicely browned on all sides. Transfer to a plate.
2. Reduce heat to medium; cook onions, garlic, rosemary, salt and pepper, stirring often, for 5 minutes or until softened.
3. Add stock, tomatoes with juice, Worcestershire sauce and orange peel. Return beef and accumulated juices to pan; bring to a boil. Cover and reduce heat; simmer for 2 hours, adding additional stock to keep beef covered while braising, until beef is fork-tender.

SERVES 4

The rich flavors of this classic Italian dish come from the slow braising of the succulent veal shanks. While not essential, the addition of the gremolata adds a fragrant seasoning to fork-tender veal. Serve with rice or polenta.

Osso Buco

4	thick veal shanks	4
2 tbsp	all-purpose flour	25 mL
2 tbsp	butter	25 mL
1	onion, chopped	1
2	large cloves garlic, finely chopped	2
2	small carrots, peeled and diced	2
1	stalk celery, finely chopped	1
2 tsp	chopped fresh rosemary or thyme leaves or 1 tsp (5 mL) dried rosemary or thyme leaves	10 mL
3/4 tsp	salt	4 mL
1/2 tsp	freshly ground black pepper	2 mL
1/2 cup	white wine	125 mL
3/4 cup	chicken stock (approx.)	175 mL
2 tbsp	tomato paste	25 mL

GREMOLATA (OPTIONAL)

1/4 cup	chopped fresh parsley	50 mL
2 tsp	grated lemon zest	10 mL
1	clove garlic, minced	1

1. Pat veal shanks dry with paper towel. Place flour on a plate; coat veal in the flour, shaking off excess.

2. In a Dutch oven or large saucepan, heat butter over medium-high heat; brown veal on all sides. Transfer to a plate and set aside.

3. Add onion, garlic, carrots, celery, rosemary, salt and pepper to pan; cook, stirring for 3 minutes until lightly colored. Stir in wine, scrapping up brown bits from bottom of pan; add stock and tomato paste. Return veal to pan; bring to a boil. Reduce heat; cover and simmer, adding more stock if needed, for 1 1/4 to 1 1/2 hours or until veal is very tender.

4. Gremolata: In a small bowl, combine parsley, lemon zest and garlic. Transfer veal to a serving platter; spoon sauce over top. Sprinkle with gremolata and serve.

SERVES 6

Richly flavored braised meats like veal are always a welcome choice for a family meal. I make them in advance, since their flavor improves when refrigerated and reheated the next day. Serve this simple dish with noodles or creamy mashed potatoes.

TIP

To brown meat without having to add a lot of oil, pat meat dry with paper towels before cooking. Add a bit of the oil to the pan and heat until hot but not smoking. Add a small amount of the meat at a time until nicely colored; remove. Add a bit more oil to pan if necessary and reheat before adding next batch of meat.

Veal Braised with Onions

2 tbsp	olive oil, divided	25 mL
2 lbs	lean stewing veal, cut into 3/4-inch (2 cm) cubes	1 kg
2	large onions, chopped	2
2	cloves garlic, finely chopped	2
2 tbsp	all-purpose flour	25 mL
1 1/2 cups	chicken stock	375 mL
1/2 cup	dry white wine or additional stock	125 mL
2 tbsp	tomato paste	25 mL
1 tsp	salt	5 mL
1/2 tsp	freshly ground black pepper	2 mL
1/4 cup	chopped fresh parsley	50 mL
1 tsp	grated lemon zest	5 mL

1. In a Dutch oven or large saucepan, heat 1 tbsp (15 mL) oil over high heat; brown veal in batches. Transfer to a plate.
2. Reduce heat to medium; add remaining oil. Cook onions and garlic, stirring, for 5 minutes or until lightly colored. Blend in flour; stir in stock, wine and tomato paste. Add veal along with accumulated juices; season with salt and pepper. Bring to a boil.
3. Reduce heat, cover and simmer, stirring occasionally, for 50 minutes. Stir in parsley and lemon zest; cook, covered, for 10 minutes or until veal is tender.

SERVES 8

I like to make this delicious comfort stew ahead and have it tucked away in the freezer ready for company. Adding the peppers at the end of cooking helps keep their shape and lends a slightly smoky taste that lingers in your memory long after the last bite.

TIP

Use a combination of green, red and yellow peppers for maximum color effect.

VARIATION

Beef can be substituted for the veal.

Veal Ragout with Sweet Peppers

3 lbs	lean stewing veal, cut into 1-inch (2.5 cm) cubes	1.5 kg
2 tbsp	all-purpose flour	25 mL
4 tbsp	olive oil (approx.), divided	60 mL
1	Spanish onion, chopped (about 1 lb/500 g)	1
4	large cloves garlic, finely chopped	4
1 tsp	dried thyme leaves	5 mL
1 tsp	paprika	5 mL
1	bay leaf	1
1 tsp	salt	5 mL
½ tsp	freshly ground black pepper	2 mL
1 cup	red wine or beef stock	250 mL
4	tomatoes, chopped	4
4	bell peppers (any color), cubed	4
⅓ cup	chopped fresh parsley	75 mL

1. In a bowl, toss veal cubes with flour until well-coated. In a Dutch oven or large heavy saucepan, heat 1 tbsp (15 mL) oil over high heat. In small batches, add veal and cook until nicely browned on all sides, adding more oil as needed. Remove and set aside.
2. Reduce heat to medium. Add 1 tbsp (15 mL) more oil. Add onion, garlic, thyme, paprika, bay leaf, salt and pepper; cook, stirring often, for 5 minutes or until softened.
3. Add wine and bring to a boil. Stir in veal along with accumulated juices; add tomatoes. Bring to boil; reduce heat to medium-low and simmer, covered, for 1¼ to 1½ hours or until veal is tender. (The recipe can be prepared to this point up to 48 hours ahead, then covered and refrigerated — or freeze for up to three months. Before reheating, let defrost in fridge overnight. Bring to a boil; cover and simmer for 20 minutes or until veal is thoroughly heated.)

4. Shortly before serving, heat 1 tbsp (15 mL) oil in a large nonstick skillet over high heat; cook pepper cubes, stirring, for 2 to 3 minutes or until lightly colored. Reduce heat to medium-low, cover and simmer for 8 to 10 minutes or until tender-crisp.
5. Add peppers to veal; stir in parsley and simmer for 5 minutes to let the flavors blend. Adjust seasoning with salt and pepper to taste. Remove bay leaf.

SERVES 4

This rustic dish is perfect with a glass of red wine on a wind-down Friday night. Do give the fennel a try; when raw, this vegetable has an assertive anise taste. However, when cooked, it's much more mellow and inviting.

VARIATION

Instead of fennel, use about 3 cups (750 mL) shredded cabbage.

One-Pot Italian Sausages Braised with Potatoes

1 lb	mild or hot Italian sausages	500 g
2 tbsp	water (approx.)	25 mL
1 tbsp	olive oil	15 mL
1	large onion, halved lengthwise, sliced	1
1	large bulb fennel, trimmed, cored and cut into strips	1
2	cloves garlic, finely chopped	2
1 tsp	dried oregano leaves	5 mL
4	medium potatoes, peeled and cubed (about $1\frac{1}{2}$ lbs/750 g)	4
1	can (14 oz/398 mL) tomatoes, including juice, chopped	1
$\frac{1}{2}$ cup	beef stock	125 mL
$\frac{1}{2}$ tsp	salt	2 mL
$\frac{1}{4}$ tsp	freshly ground black pepper	1 mL
2 tbsp	chopped fresh parsley	25 mL

1. With a fork, prick sausages all over and place in large saucepan over medium-high heat. Add water and cook, turning often and adding more water as needed (to prevent sausages from sticking), for 10 to 12 minutes or until browned and no longer pink in center. Transfer to a cutting board. Let cool slightly; cut into slices.
2. Drain fat from pan; add oil, onion, fennel, garlic and oregano; cook, stirring, for 3 minutes or until softened. Add potatoes, tomatoes with juice, stock, salt and pepper; bring to a boil. Reduce heat, cover and cook for 15 minutes or until potatoes are almost tender. Return sausage to pan; cover and cook for 8 minutes or until potatoes are tender. Sprinkle with parsley.

SERVES 6

Here's a soothing dish to serve for casual get-togethers. This stew requires no more preparation time than a stir-fry or one-pot dish. Cutting the meat into smaller pieces also shortens the cooking time.

VARIATION

Lean stewing beef can be substituted for the pork. For a vegetarian dish, replace meat with cubes of firm tofu. Add along with kidney beans.

Make-Ahead Southwestern Pork Stew

4 tsp	olive oil, divided	20 mL
1 lb	lean stewing pork, cut into ¾-inch (2 cm) cubes	500 g
2	medium onions, chopped	2
3	cloves garlic, finely chopped	3
4 tsp	chili powder	20 mL
1½ tsp	dried oregano leaves	7 mL
1 tsp	ground cumin	5 mL
¾ tsp	salt	4 mL
½ tsp	hot pepper flakes	2 mL
3 tbsp	all-purpose flour	45 mL
2 cups	beef or chicken stock	500 mL
1	can (28 oz/796 mL) tomatoes, including juice, chopped	1
2	bell peppers (assorted colors), cubed	2
2 cups	frozen corn kernels	500 mL
1	can (19 oz/540 mL) kidney beans or black beans, drained and rinsed	1
	Chopped cilantro (optional)	

1. In a Dutch oven or large saucepan, heat 2 tsp (10 mL) oil over high heat; brown pork in batches. Transfer to a plate. Add remaining oil to pan; reduce heat to medium. Add onions, garlic, chili powder, oregano, cumin, salt and hot pepper flakes; cook, stirring, for 2 minutes or until softened.
2. Sprinkle with flour; stir in stock and tomatoes with juice. Bring to a boil, stirring until thickened. Return pork and accumulated juices to pan; reduce heat, cover and simmer for 1 hour or until meat is tender.
3. Add bell peppers, corn and kidney beans; simmer, covered, for 15 minutes or until vegetables are tender. Garnish with chopped cilantro, if desired.

SERVES 4 TO 5

To survive the 6 o'clock weeknight rush, batch-cook stews and sauce-based meals on weekends and keep in fridge for up to three days or freeze for easy reheating. When you breeze through the door at night, you simply have to decide whether you'll serve the stew with pasta or rice — and dinner's on the table.

TIP

Sun-dried tomatoes sold dry in packages are more economical than those packed in oil. To reconstitute, place in a bowl and cover with boiling water. Or cover with cold water and microwave at High for 2 minutes or until just boiling. Let stand for 10 minutes or until softened; drain and chop.

Everyone's Favorite Chicken Cacciatore

3 tbsp	all-purpose flour	45 mL
1/2 tsp	salt	2 mL
1/2 tsp	freshly ground black pepper	2 mL
2 lbs	skinless chicken thighs (about 10)	1 kg
2 tbsp	olive oil, divided	25 mL
1	small onion, chopped	1
2	cloves garlic, finely chopped	2
3 cups	sliced mushrooms	750 mL
1/2 cup	white wine or chicken stock	125 mL
1	can (19 oz/540 mL) tomatoes, including juice, chopped	1
1/3 cup	chopped sun-dried tomatoes	75 mL
1/4 cup	chopped fresh basil leaves or parsley or a mixture of both	50 mL

1. In a heavy plastic bag, shake together flour, salt and pepper. In batches, toss chicken to coat, shaking off excess.
2. In a Dutch oven or large saucepan, heat 1 tbsp (15 mL) oil over medium-high heat. Brown chicken on all sides. Transfer to a plate. Add remaining oil; cook onion, garlic and mushrooms, stirring, for 5 minutes or until softened.
3. Add wine; return chicken and any juices to pan along with tomatoes with juice and sun-dried tomatoes. Bring to a boil; reduce heat, cover and simmer for 35 minutes or until chicken is tender. Stir in basil; season with salt and pepper to taste.

SERVES 4

Even if you don't have a lot of time to spend in the kitchen, you can rustle up a great-tasting stew using boneless chicken thighs and convenient frozen vegetables. This satisfying dish does away with browning the chicken. You'll save time but not lose any flavor. Serve over noodles.

TIP

Use 5 cups (1.25 L) fresh vegetables instead of frozen, if you wish. Cut them into bite-size pieces. For slower-cooking vegetables, such as carrots and celery, add them along with the chicken. For faster-cooking ones, such as broccoli and zucchini, add in the last 10 minutes of cooking.

Streamlined Chicken and Vegetable Stew

1 tbsp	butter	15 mL
1	large onion, chopped	1
2	cloves garlic, finely chopped	2
1 tsp	dried Italian herbs or fines herbes	5 mL
1 lb	skinless, boneless chicken thighs cut into 1-inch (2.5 cm) cubes (about 8)	500 g
3 tbsp	all-purpose flour	45 mL
2 cups	chicken stock	500 mL
1	package (1 lb/500 g) frozen mixed vegetables	1
	Salt and freshly ground black pepper	

1. In a Dutch oven or large saucepan, melt butter over medium heat. Add onion, garlic and Italian herbs; cook, stirring, for 4 minutes or until lightly colored.
2. In a bowl, toss chicken with flour until well-coated. Add to pan along with any remaining flour; stir in chicken stock. Bring to a boil and cook, stirring, until sauce thickens. Reduce heat, cover and simmer, stirring occasionally, for 20 minutes.
3. Add frozen vegetables; return to a boil. Season with salt and pepper to taste. Reduce heat, cover and simmer for 10 minutes or until chicken and vegetables are tender.

SERVES 6

Some dishes never lose their appeal — like this old-fashioned favorite, which is perfect to make on a lazy Sunday afternoon. It requires a little time to prepare, but once the creamy chicken mixture and its golden biscuit crust is bubbling away in the oven, you'll be glad you made the effort. And so will your family.

TIPS

I've chosen a biscuit crust to make this a cobbler, but you can cover the savory chicken filling with your favorite pie pastry or frozen puff pastry to make a pot pie. Or you can omit the topping altogether and serve over rice or noodles.

The chicken-vegetable mixture without the crust freezes well for up to three months.

Fines herbes, available in the spice section of your grocery store, contains dried parsley, chives, tarragon and chervil. You can also use an Italian herb mix of basil, oregano and marjoram.

Chicken-Vegetable Cobbler

Preheat oven to 400°F (200°C)
12-cup (3 L) deep casserole dish

2 lbs	chicken legs, with thighs, skin and excess fat removed	1 kg
3½ cups	water	850 mL
1 tsp	salt	5 mL
	Freshly ground black pepper	
1	bay leaf	1
2 tbsp	butter	25 mL
2 cups	quartered mushrooms	500 mL
1	medium onion, chopped	1
1	large clove garlic, minced	1
2 tsp	dried fines herbes or dried basil leaves	10 mL
⅓ cup	all-purpose flour	75 mL
3	carrots, peeled and sliced	3
2	stalks celery, chopped	2
½ cup	whipping (35%) cream or table (18%) cream	125 mL
1 cup	frozen peas	250 mL
¼ cup	chopped fresh parsley	50 mL
	Cheddar Biscuit Crust (see recipe right)	

1. In a large saucepan, combine chicken, water, salt, pepper and bay leaf. Bring to a boil; reduce heat to medium-low, cover and simmer for 1 hour. Let stand until chicken is cool enough to handle. Pull chicken meat from bones; cut into bite-size pieces. Strain stock, skim off any fat; there should be 2½ cups (625 mL) of stock. Add water, if necessary. Discard bay leaf. Set aside.
2. In a large saucepan, melt butter over medium heat; cook mushrooms, onion, garlic and fines herbes, stirring often, for 5 minutes or until softened.

3. Blend flour with small amount of stock until smooth; add rest of stock. Stir into mushroom mixture; bring to a boil, stirring, until thickened and smooth.
4. Add carrots and celery; cover and simmer over low heat, stirring occasionally, for 15 minutes or until vegetables are just tender.
5. Add chicken, cream, peas and parsley; season with additional salt and pepper to taste. Heat through. Spoon hot chicken mixture into casserole dish.
6. Meanwhile, make Cheddar Biscuit Crust (see recipe below). Roll out on lightly floured board to make a circle large enough to cover casserole. Arrange on top of hot chicken mixture. (If making chicken mixture ahead, cover and refrigerate; microwave at Medium-High, or reheat in saucepan on stovetop until piping hot before topping with crust.)
7. Bake in preheated oven for about 25 to 30 minutes or until crust is golden and filling is bubbly.

Cheddar Biscuit Crust

1 1/3 cups	all-purpose flour	325 mL
2 tsp	baking powder	10 mL
1/2 tsp	baking soda	2 mL
1/4 tsp	salt	1 mL
1/2 cup	shredded Cheddar cheese	125 mL
1/2 cup	buttermilk	125 mL
1/4 cup	butter, melted	50 mL

1. In a bowl, combine flour, baking powder, baking soda and salt. Add cheese. Combine buttermilk and butter; stir into flour mixture to make a soft dough.

SERVES 4

Economical chicken thighs make a comforting weeknight supper. Here they star in a full-bodied stew with chunks of wholesome sweet potatoes. It's equally good when made with a winter squash, such as butternut, instead.

TIPS

Replace sweet potatoes, if desired, with 4 potatoes, peeled and cubed, and 4 sliced carrots.

To prepare ahead, cover and refrigerate for up to three days or freeze for up to one month.

Chicken and Sweet Potato Stew

3 tbsp	all-purpose flour	45 mL
1 tsp	salt	5 mL
½ tsp	freshly ground black pepper	2 mL
2 lbs	skinless chicken thighs (10 thighs)	1 kg
2 tbsp	vegetable oil, divided	25 mL
1	large onion, chopped	1
2	cloves garlic, finely chopped	2
1½ tsp	mild curry paste or powder	7 mL
1 tsp	dried thyme leaves	5 mL
½ tsp	dried marjoram leaves	2 mL
1½ cups	chicken stock	375 mL
3	sweet potatoes (about 2 lbs/1 kg)	3
¼ cup	chopped fresh parsley	50 mL

1. In a heavy plastic bag, shake together flour, salt and pepper. In batches, add chicken; shake to coat.
2. In a Dutch oven or large saucepan, heat 1 tbsp (15 mL) oil over medium-high heat; brown chicken on all sides. Transfer to a plate.
3. Add remaining oil to pan; reduce heat to medium. Cook onion, garlic, curry paste, thyme and marjoram, stirring, for 5 minutes or until softened.
4. Add stock; bring to boil. Return chicken and any juices to pan; cover and simmer for 20 minutes. Peel and quarter sweet potatoes; cut into 2-inch (5 cm) chunks. Add to pan; simmer, covered, for 20 minutes or until tender. Stir in parsley.

FREEZING AND REHEATING SOUPS AND CASSEROLES

- Label and date containers and casseroles before refrigerating or freezing.
- Meat- and chicken-based soups, stews and casseroles can be kept safely for up to three days in the refrigerator; vegetable-based dishes can be kept refrigerated for five days.
- To reheat, place in saucepan over medium heat, stirring occasionally, until piping hot; or place in covered casserole and bake in 350°F (180°C) oven for 30 to 45 minutes or until piping hot; or microwave, covered with lid or microwave-safe plastic wrap, at Medium-High for 9 to 15 minutes, stirring occasionally, or until heated through to center. For single servings, microwave, covered, at Medium-High for 3 to 5 minutes.
- Stews, soups and casseroles can be frozen for up to three months. Defrost in refrigerator overnight and reheat as directed above.

SERVES 6

Looking for a winning dish to serve for a buffet or potluck? Look no further than this pastry-topped chicken pie with lots of tasty mushrooms.

TIP

To make ahead, let chicken mixture cool. Cover and refrigerate for up to one day. Reheat filling until piping hot. Place in baking dish; top with pastry.

Company Chicken Mushroom Pot Pie

Preheat oven to 400°F (200°C)
8-cup (2 L) shallow casserole dish

3 tbsp	butter, divided	45 mL
6	large skinless, boneless chicken breasts, cut into $\frac{3}{4}$-inch (2 cm) cubes	6
12 oz	shiitake or cremini mushrooms, sliced	375 g
$\frac{1}{4}$ cup	finely chopped shallots	50 mL
1	large clove garlic, minced	1
2 tsp	finely chopped fresh thyme or $\frac{3}{4}$ tsp (4 mL) dried thyme leaves	10 mL
1 tsp	salt	5 mL
$\frac{1}{4}$ tsp	freshly ground black pepper	1 mL
$\frac{1}{2}$ cup	dry white wine or additional chicken stock	125 mL
3 tbsp	all-purpose flour	45 mL
$\frac{1}{2}$ cup	chicken stock, divided	125 mL
$\frac{1}{2}$ cup	whipping (35%) cream	125 mL
2 tbsp	chopped fresh parsley or chives	25 mL
	Pastry for single-crust 9-inch (23 cm) pie (see recipe, page 351)	
1	egg, lightly beaten	1

1. In a Dutch oven or large saucepan, heat 1 tbsp (15 mL) butter over medium-high heat; brown half the chicken. Transfer to a bowl. Add 1 tbsp (15 mL) butter to pan; brown remaining chicken. Transfer to a bowl.

2. Add remaining butter to pan; add mushrooms, shallots, garlic, thyme, salt and pepper. Cook, stirring, for 3 minutes or until mushrooms are softened. Add wine; bring to a boil. Cook for 3 minutes or until slightly reduced.

3. In a bowl, blend flour with ¼ cup (50 mL) stock to make a smooth paste; stir in remaining stock. Stir into pan; cook until sauce boils and thickens. Return chicken and any juices to pan. Stir in cream; bring to a boil. Reduce heat, cover and simmer for 5 minutes or until chicken is just tender. Stir in parsley and transfer to baking dish.

4. On a lightly floured surface, roll out pastry slightly larger than size of baking dish and fit over filling. Trim edge leaving a ½-inch (1 cm) overhang; turn under and seal to edge of dish. Cut slits for steam vents. Lightly brush with egg. Bake in oven for 25 to 30 minutes or until filling is bubbly and pastry is golden.

SERVES 6

Oregano-scented tomato sauce with a burst of heat from hot pepper flakes is the perfect foil for buttery lima beans and lamb.

TIP

Stew can be cooked ahead and stored in a tightly covered container in the refrigerator for up to three days or frozen for up to one month.

Greek Lamb and Bean Stew

Preheat oven to 350°F (180°C)

2 cups	dried large lima beans	500 mL
2 tbsp	olive oil, divided	25 mL
1 lb	lean boneless lamb, cut into 1-inch (2.5 cm) pieces	500 g
1	Spanish onion (1 lb/500 g), chopped	1
4	cloves garlic, finely chopped	4
1 tbsp	dried oregano leaves	15 mL
½ tsp	hot pepper flakes	2 mL
1	can (19 oz/540 mL) tomatoes, including juice, chopped	1
1 tsp	salt	5 mL
½ tsp	freshly ground black pepper	2 mL
1	each large red and green bell pepper, seeded and cubed	1
½ cup	Kalamata olives	125 mL
¼ cup	chopped fresh parsley	50 mL

1. Sort and rinse beans. In a large saucepan, bring beans and 8 cups (2 L) cold water to a boil; cover and cook for 15 minutes. Drain and return to pot. Add 8 cups (2 L) water: bring to a boil. Reduce heat and simmer, partially covered, for 45 minutes or until tender. Drain.
2. Meanwhile, in a Dutch oven or large saucepan, heat 1 tbsp (15 mL) oil over high heat; brown lamb, in batches if necessary. Transfer to a plate. Add remaining oil to pan; reduce heat to medium.
3. Add onion, garlic, oregano and hot pepper flakes; cook, stirring, for 5 minutes or until softened. Return meat to pan along with any juices. Add tomatoes with juice, salt and pepper; bring to boil. Reduce heat, cover and simmer for 45 minutes.
4. Add beans, red and green peppers, olives and about ½ cup (125 mL) water to make a sauce-like consistency. Cover and bake in oven for 40 minutes or until lamb is tender. Stir in parsley.

SERVES 6

Sometimes you crave a dish that explodes with spicy flavors. The ginger and hot pepper flakes used here will satisfy that craving — and soothe your soul, too. I like to serve this spice-infused stew with basmati rice.

TIPS

To cook basmati rice, rinse 1½ cups (375 mL) rice in several changes of cold water. Place in bowl; add cold water to cover. Let soak 15 minutes; drain. In a saucepan bring 2¼ cups (550 mL) water and 1 tbsp (15 mL) oil to a boil; add rice and 1 tsp (5 mL) salt. Return to boil, reduce heat to low and simmer, covered, for 10 minutes. Remove and let stand, covered, for 5 minutes. Uncover and fluff with a fork.

Buy a 3-lb (1.5 kg) leg of lamb or shoulder roast to get 1-½ lbs (750 g) boneless lamb.

VARIATION

Beef can be substituted for the lamb; increase cooking time to 1½ hours or until meat is tender.

Spicy Lamb Stew

2 tbsp	vegetable oil (approx.), divided	25 mL
1½ lbs	lean boneless lamb, cut into 1-inch (2.5 cm) cubes	750 g
1	large onion, chopped	1
2	cloves garlic, finely chopped	2
1 tbsp	minced fresh gingerroot	15 mL
1 tsp	ground cumin	5 mL
1 tsp	ground coriander	5 mL
½ tsp	ground cinnamon	2 mL
½ tsp	salt	2 mL
¼ tsp	hot pepper flakes or more to taste	1 mL
Pinch	ground cloves	Pinch
1 tbsp	all-purpose flour	15 mL
½ cup	plain yogurt	125 mL
1	large tomato, chopped	1
½ cup	lamb or chicken stock	125 mL
¼ cup	chopped fresh cilantro or parsley	50 mL

1. In a large saucepan, heat 1 tbsp (15 mL) oil over medium-high heat; cook lamb in batches, adding more oil as needed, until browned on all sides. Remove from pan and set aside.
2. Reduce heat to medium. Add onion, garlic, ginger, cumin, coriander, cinnamon, salt, hot pepper flakes and cloves; cook, stirring, for 2 minutes or until softened.
3. Sprinkle with flour; stir in yogurt. Cook for 1 minute or until thickened. Add lamb with any accumulated juices, tomato and stock; bring to a boil. Reduce heat and simmer, covered, for 45 minutes or until lamb is tender. Sprinkle with cilantro or parsley before serving.

SERVES 4 AS A MAIN COURSE OR 6 AS A STARTER

Do you pine for the days when elegant luncheons were in fashion? Here's a special dish reminiscent of days gone by, when ladies in white gloves lunched ever so elegantly on richly flavored seafood sauces served in puff pastry shells. You could serve this dish the same way, or serve it over rice, or toss with pasta.

TIPS

Cooked lobster can replace part of the shellfish.

For a less expensive version, omit scallops and shrimp; increase the amount of sole, haddock or cod to 1½ lbs (750 g).

The moisture content of fresh and frozen seafood differs and may result in the finished sauce being too thick or too thin. To eliminate this problem, poach the uncooked seafood first in wine and stock.

Seafood Supreme

1 cup	fish or chicken stock (approx.)	250 mL
½ cup	dry white wine or vermouth	125 mL
8 oz	sole or other white fish, cut into 1-inch (2.5 cm) cubes	250 g
8 oz	small scallops	250 g
8 oz	small cooked, peeled shrimp	250 g
3 tbsp	butter	45 mL
⅓ cup	finely chopped green onions	75 mL
¾ cup	diced red bell pepper	175 mL
¼ cup	all-purpose flour	50 mL
½ cup	whipping (35%) cream	125 mL
	Salt and ground white pepper	
2 tbsp	chopped fresh dill or parsley	25 mL

1. In a saucepan, bring stock and wine to a boil over medium heat. Add sole cubes; poach 2 minutes (start timing when fish is added to stock). Add scallops; poach 1 to 2 minutes more or until seafood is opaque. Remove using a slotted spoon; place in a bowl along with shrimp and set aside.
2. Strain stock into glass measure; there should be 2 cups (500 mL). Add water, if necessary; reserve.
3. In a saucepan, melt butter over medium heat. Add green onions and red peppers; cook, stirring, for 3 minutes or until softened. Blend in flour; pour in reserved stock mixture. Bring to a boil, stirring, until sauce is very thick and smooth. Stir in cream; bring to a boil.
4. Just before serving, add seafood and heat through. Season with salt and white pepper to taste; stir in dill. Serve immediately.

SERVES 4

Gingerroot adds a sparking flavor to this low-cal stew. Serve steaming bowls with chunks of crusty whole-grain bread. It's a complete meal!

TIP

Instead of fish, add $1\frac{1}{2}$ cups (375 mL) small cooked shrimp.

Easy Curried Fish Stew

1 tbsp	vegetable oil	15 mL
1	small onion, finely chopped	1
1 tbsp	minced fresh gingerroot	15 mL
2 tsp	mild curry paste or powder	10 mL
2 cups	diced peeled potatoes	500 mL
$1\frac{1}{2}$ cups	thinly sliced carrots	375 mL
$2\frac{1}{4}$ cups	fish or chicken stock	550 mL
1 tbsp	cornstarch	15 mL
	Salt and freshly ground black pepper	
$1\frac{1}{2}$ cups	snow peas, ends trimmed, halved	375 mL
1 lb	fish fillets, cut into chunks	500 g

1. In a large saucepan, heat oil over medium heat. Add onion, ginger and curry paste; cook, stirring, for 2 minutes or until softened. Add potatoes, carrots and fish stock. Bring to a boil; reduce heat, cover and simmer for 10 to 12 minutes or until vegetables are just tender.

2. In a bowl, blend cornstarch with 2 tbsp (25 mL) water. Add to stew and cook, stirring, until thickened. Season with salt and pepper to taste. Stir in snow peas and fish; cover and cook for 2 to 3 minutes or until snow peas are tender-crisp and fish is opaque.

SERVES 6 TO 8

Jambalaya is the perfect party dish. A one-pot wonder originating from New Orleans, it pleases all palates with its piquant flavors and mix of chicken, sausage and shrimp. Set this dish on the table and watch it disappear.

TIP

Try not to stir the jambalaya or the rice will turn sticky.

If using chicken thighs with the bone in, increase cooking time by 5 to 10 minutes.

VARIATION

Try replacing the sausage with 8 oz (250 g) cubed smoked ham.

Jambalaya

Preheat oven to 350°F (180°C)
12-cup (3 L) baking dish or ovenproof serving dish

2 tbsp	olive oil	25 mL
1 1/2 lbs	skinless, boneless chicken thighs (about 12)	750 g
8 oz	andouille, chorizo or other smoked sausage, thinly sliced	250 g
1	large onion, chopped	1
3	cloves garlic, finely chopped	3
2	stalks celery, diced	2
2	bell peppers, any color, diced	2
1 tsp	dried thyme leaves	5 mL
1 tsp	paprika	5 mL
1/2 tsp	salt	2 mL
1/4 tsp	ground allspice	1 mL
1/4 tsp	cayenne pepper	1 mL
1 1/2 cups	long-grain rice	375 mL
1	can (14 oz/398 mL) tomatoes, including juice, chopped	1
1 3/4 cups	chicken stock	425 mL
8 oz	medium raw shrimp, in the shell	250 g
1/3 cup	chopped fresh parsley	75 mL
3	green onions, finely chopped	3

1. In a Dutch oven, heat oil over medium-high heat. Add chicken and cook for 5 minutes or until browned on both sides. Transfer to a plate.
2. Add sausage, onion, garlic, celery, peppers, thyme, paprika, salt, allspice and cayenne; cook, stirring often, for 5 minutes or until vegetables are softened. Return chicken to dish along with accumulated juices.
3. Stir in rice, tomatoes with juice and stock; bring to a boil. Transfer to baking dish. Cover and bake in preheated oven for 30 minutes or until rice and chicken are just tender.
4. Stir in shrimp, parsley and green onions; cover and bake for 5 to 8 minutes more or until shrimp turns pink.

One-Pot Italian Sausages Braised with Potatoes (page 146)

Overleaf: Thyme-Roasted Chicken with Garlic Gravy (page 102) ➢

A Pound of Ground

Chicken-Vegetable Cobbler (page 150)

SERVES 6

I could make this juicy meat loaf with garlic mashed potatoes every week and never hear a complaint from my family that it's served too often.

TIPS

I like to use oatmeal as a binder, since it gives a coarser texture to the meat loaf (bread crumbs produce a finer one). Use whichever binder you prefer.

I always double the recipe and wrap the extra cooked meat loaf in plastic wrap, then in foil, for the freezer. Defrost overnight in the fridge. To reheat, cut into slices and place in saucepan. Moisten with about ½ cup (125 mL) beef stock; set over medium heat until piping hot. Or place meat loaf and stock in casserole dish and microwave at Medium until heated through.

Best-Ever Meat Loaf

Preheat oven to 350°F (180°C)
9-by 5-inch (2 L) loaf pan

1 tbsp	vegetable oil	15 mL
1	medium onion, chopped	1
2	cloves garlic, minced	2
1 tsp	dried basil leaves	5 mL
1 tsp	dried marjoram leaves	5 mL
¾ tsp	salt	4 mL
¼ tsp	freshly ground black pepper	1 mL
1	egg	1
¼ cup	chili sauce or ketchup	50 mL
1 tbsp	Worcestershire sauce	15 mL
2 tbsp	chopped fresh parsley	25 mL
1½ lbs	lean ground beef	750 g
¾ cup	quick-cooking rolled oats or ½ cup (125 mL) dry bread crumbs	175 mL

1. In a large nonstick skillet, heat oil over medium heat. Add onion, garlic, basil, marjoram, salt and pepper; cook, stirring, for 3 minutes or until softened. (Or place in microwave-safe bowl; microwave, covered, at High for 3 minutes.) Let cool slightly.
2. In a large bowl, beat egg; stir in onion mixture, chili sauce, Worcestershire sauce and parsley. Crumble beef over mixture and sprinkle with rolled oats. Using a wooden spoon, gently mix until evenly combined.
3. Press mixture lightly into loaf pan. Bake in preheated oven for 1 hour or until meat thermometer registers 170°F (80°C). Let stand for 5 minutes. Drain pan juices; turn out onto a plate and cut into thick slices.

SERVES 6

Ground meats are one of the best supermarket buys for budget-trimming meals. I serve this family favorite meat loaf accompanied with fluffy mashed potatoes and glazed carrots for a delicious, economical supper.

VARIATION

Mini Veal Meat Loaves

Divide into 12 balls; lightly press into muffin cups. Bake at 400°F (200°C) for 20 minutes or until no longer pink in center. Drain off juice.

Veal Meat Loaf

Preheat oven to 350°F (180°C)
9-by 5-inch (2 L) loaf pan

1 tbsp	olive oil	15 mL
1	onion, finely chopped	1
1	large clove garlic, finely chopped	1
½ tsp	dried thyme or marjoram leaves	2 mL
1 tsp	salt	5 mL
¼ tsp	freshly ground black pepper	1 mL
1	egg	1
¼ cup	chicken stock	50 mL
1 tsp	grated lemon zest	5 mL
½ cup	dry seasoned bread crumbs	125 mL
2 tbsp	finely chopped fresh parsley	25 mL
1½ lbs	lean ground veal or chicken	750 g

1. In a large nonstick skillet, heat oil over medium heat; cook onion, garlic, thyme, salt and pepper, stirring often, for 3 minutes or until softened. Let cool slightly.
2. In a bowl, beat together egg, stock and lemon zest. Stir in onion mixture, bread crumbs, parsley and veal. Using a wooden spoon, gently mix until evenly combined.
3. Press mixture lightly into loaf pan. Bake in preheated oven for 1 hour or until meat thermometer registers 170°F (80°C). Let stand for 5 minutes. Drain pan juices; turn out onto a plate a cut into thick slices.

SERVES 6

Instead of ketchup, serve salsa with this oregano and cumin-flavored meat loaf.

VARIATION

Instead of all beef, use ¾ lb (375 g) each ground pork and ground beef, if desired.

Southwest Meat Loaf

Preheat oven to 350°F (180°C)
9-by 5-inch (2 L) loaf pan

1 tbsp	olive oil	15 mL
1	small green bell pepper, finely chopped	1
2	jalapeño peppers, minced (optional)	2
1	onion, finely chopped	1
2	cloves garlic, finely chopped	2
1 tsp	dried oregano leaves	5 mL
1 tsp	ground cumin	5 mL
1 tsp	salt	5 mL
¼ tsp	freshly ground black pepper	1 mL
1	egg	1
2 tsp	Dijon mustard	10 mL
1 cup	soft fresh bread crumbs	250 mL
1½ lbs	lean ground beef	750 g

1. In a large nonstick skillet, heat oil over medium heat; cook green pepper, jalapeño peppers, if using, onion, garlic, oregano, cumin, salt and pepper, stirring often, for 5 minutes or until softened. Let cool slightly.
2. In a bowl, beat egg and mustard. Stir in vegetable mixture, bread crumbs and beef. Using a wooden spoon, gently mix until evenly combined.
3. Press mixture lightly into loaf pan. Bake in preheated oven for 1 hour or until meat thermometer registers 170°F (80°C). Let stand for 5 minutes. Drain pan juices; turn out onto a plate and cut into thick slices.

SERVES 4 TO 5

Everyone loves meat loaf and mashed potatoes. Here's a creative way to prepare this favorite combo.

TIP

Make a double batch of meat loaf. Press into two pie plates; bake according to recipe until no longer pink in center. Top one meat loaf with mashed potatoes; let the other one cool, wrap well and freeze for another meal.

Meat Loaf and Mashed Potato Pie

Preheat oven to 375°F (190°C)
Deep 9- or 10-inch (23 or 25 cm) pie plate, greased

MASHED POTATO TOPPING

6	medium Russet or Yukon Gold potatoes, peeled and cubed (about 2 lbs/1 kg)	6
½ cup	sour cream	125 mL
	Salt and freshly ground black pepper	

MEAT LOAF

1	egg	1
¼ cup	chili sauce or ketchup	50 mL
¼ cup	minced onion	50 mL
1	clove garlic, minced	1
1 tsp	Worcestershire sauce	5 mL
½ tsp	salt	2 mL
¼ tsp	freshly ground black pepper	1 mL
¼ cup	dry seasoned bread crumbs	50 mL
1 lb	lean ground beef or veal	500 g
½ cup	shredded Cheddar cheese	125 mL

1. Mashed Potato Topping: In a large saucepan, cook potatoes in boiling salted water until tender. Drain well and return to saucepan; place over low heat for 1 minute to dry. Mash using potato masher or electric mixer at low speed until smooth. Beat in sour cream; season with salt and pepper to taste. Keep warm over low heat.
2. Meat Loaf: In a bowl, beat egg; stir in chili sauce, onion, garlic, Worcestershire sauce, salt and pepper. Mix in bread crumbs and beef. Press evenly in pie plate. Bake for 25 to 30 minutes or until no longer pink in center; drain juice.
3. Spread mashed potatoes over meat; sprinkle with cheese. (Can be prepared up to one day ahead; cover and refrigerate.) Bake for 20 to 25 minutes or until cheese is melted. (Bake 10 minutes longer, if refrigerated.)

SERVES 6

Mushrooms add a depth of flavor to this dish and help cut down on the amount of meat used. When my children were young and didn't like the sight of mushrooms in their favorite supper dish, I would finely chop the mushrooms in a food processor and they never knew the difference.

Shepherd's Pie

Preheat oven to 375°F (190°C)
Shallow 12-by 8-inch (2.5 L) baking dish

MASHED POTATO TOPPING

6	potatoes, peeled and cubed (about 2 lbs/1 kg)	6
3/4 cup	milk or buttermilk	175 mL

MEAT LAYER

1 lb	lean ground beef or veal	500 g
8 oz	mushrooms, sliced or chopped	250 g
1	medium onion, finely chopped	1
2	cloves garlic, minced	2
1/2 tsp	dried thyme leaves	2 mL
1/2 tsp	dried marjoram leaves	2 mL
3 tbsp	all-purpose flour	45 mL
1 1/2 cups	beef stock	375 mL
2 tbsp	tomato paste (see Tip, page 173)	25 mL
2 tsp	Worcestershire sauce	10 mL
	Salt and freshly ground black pepper	
1	can (12 oz/341 mL) corn kernels, drained	1

BREAD CRUMB TOPPING

2 tbsp	dry bread crumbs	25 mL
2 tbsp	freshly grated Parmesan cheese	25 mL
1/4 tsp	paprika	1 mL

1. Mashed Potato Topping: In a large saucepan of boiling salted water, cook potatoes until tender. Drain and mash using a potato masher or electric mixer; beat in milk until smooth. Season with salt and pepper to taste.

2. Meat Layer: In a large nonstick skillet, cook beef over medium-high heat, breaking up with a wooden spoon, for 5 minutes or until no longer pink.

3. Reduce heat to medium. Add mushrooms, onion, garlic, thyme and marjoram; cook, stirring often, for 5 minutes or until softened. Sprinkle with flour; stir in stock, tomato paste and Worcestershire sauce. Bring to a boil; reduce heat and simmer, covered, for 8 minutes. Season with salt, if necessary, and pepper to taste.
4. Spread meat mixture in baking dish; layer with corn. Place small spoonfuls of mashed potatoes over corn and spread evenly.(The recipe can be prepared up to this point earlier in the day or the day before, then covered and refrigerated.)
5. Bread Crumb Topping: In a small bowl, combine bread crumbs, Parmesan and paprika; sprinkle over top of shepherd's pie.
6. Bake in preheated oven for 25 to 30 minutes (40 minutes, if refrigerated) or until filling is bubbly.

SERVES 6 TO 8

You won't be able to resist this old-standby with new-fashioned Italian flavors. The garlic is slowly roasted in olive oil and imparts a sweet mellow flavor to the mashed potato and bean topping.

TIP

To make ahead, prepare dish, cover and refrigerate up to one day; increase baking time by 10 minutes.

Italian Shepherd's Pie

Preheat oven to 350°F (180°C)
13-by 9-inch (3 L) casserole dish, greased

GARLIC MASHED POTATOES AND BEANS

6	large Russet potatoes, peeled and cubed (about 3 lbs/1.5 kg)	6
2 tbsp	olive oil	25 mL
8	cloves garlic, thinly sliced	8
1	can (19 oz/540 mL) white kidney beans, drained and rinsed	1
1/4 cup	chopped fresh parsley	50 mL

MEAT LAYER

1 1/2 lbs	lean ground beef, veal or chicken	750 g
1	large onion, finely chopped	1
3	cloves garlic, finely chopped	3
2 cups	diced carrots	500 mL
1 cup	chopped celery	250 mL
2 tsp	dried basil leaves	10 mL
1 1/2 tsp	dried oregano leaves	7 mL
3/4 tsp	salt	4 mL
1/4 tsp	hot pepper flakes	1 mL
1	can (28 oz/796 mL) plum tomatoes including juice	1
1/4 cup	tomato paste	50 mL

BREAD CRUMB TOPPING

2 tbsp	freshly grated Parmesan cheese	25 mL
2 tbsp	fine dry bread crumbs	25 mL

1. Garlic Mashed Potatoes and Beans: In a large saucepan of boiling salted water, cook potatoes for 20 minutes or until tender.

2. Meanwhile, in a small saucepan over low heat, combine oil and garlic. Cook, stirring occasionally, for 5 to 7 minutes or until garlic is tender but not browned.

3. Drain potatoes, reserving $\frac{1}{2}$ cup (125 mL) cooking liquid. Using an electric mixer, mash potatoes until smooth; mash in beans and garlic mixture, adding enough of the cooking liquid to make a smooth purée. Stir in parsley.
4. In a Dutch oven or large saucepan over medium-high heat, cook beef, breaking up with a wooden spoon, for 7 minutes or until no longer pink. Reduce heat to medium; add onion, garlic, carrots, celery, basil, oregano, salt and hot pepper flakes. Cook, stirring, for 5 minutes or until vegetables are softened.
5. In a food processor, purée tomatoes with juice. Stir into beef mixture with tomato paste; bring to a boil. Reduce heat to medium-low, cover and simmer, stirring occasionally, for 20 minutes or until vegetables are tender. Spread in prepared baking dish. Spoon potato mixture evenly over meat layer.
6. Bread Crumb Topping: In a small bowl, combine Parmesan cheese and bread crumbs; sprinkle over top. Bake in oven for 40 to 45 minutes or until bubbly and top is golden.

SERVES 6

There are many versions of Quebec's famous meat pie. This exceptional one from my friend Helene Laurendeau is drawn from both her mother and mother-in-law's recipes. These, in turn, came from the late Jehane Benoit, the doyenne of French Canadian cooking. Helene often prepares individual meat pies for easy serving when her family gathers for Christmas dinner.

TIP

Unbaked meat pies freeze well for up to two months. Let defrost in refrigerator overnight before baking.

Tourtière

Preheat oven to 425°F (220°C)
9-inch (23 cm) pie plate, lightly greased

	Pastry for double crust 9-inch (23 cm) pie (see recipe right)	
1 lb	lean ground pork	500 g
8 oz	lean ground veal	250 g
1	large onion, finely chopped	1
2	cloves garlic, minced	2
1/2 tsp	dried thyme leaves	2 mL
1/2 tsp	dried savory leaves	2 mL
3/4 tsp	salt	4 mL
1/4 tsp	ground allspice	1 mL
1/4 tsp	ground cloves	1 mL
1/4 tsp	freshly ground black pepper	1 mL
3/4 cup	beef stock or water	175 mL
1/3 cup	fine dry bread crumbs	75 mL
1	egg yolk	1

1. In a Dutch oven or large saucepan over medium-high heat, cook pork and veal, breaking up with a wooden spoon, for 5 minutes. Add onion, garlic, thyme, savory, salt, allspice, cloves and pepper; cook, stirring often, for 5 minutes.
2. Add stock; bring to a boil. Reduce heat; partially cover and simmer, stirring occasionally, for 20 minutes or until most of liquid has evaporated. Remove from heat. Stir in bread crumbs to absorb excess moisture; let cool, then refrigerate until chilled.
3. On a lightly floured surface, roll out half the pastry into a 12-inch (30 cm) round. Line prepared pie plate with pastry. Trim edges. Spoon filling into pie shell. Cover with top pastry; trim edges, crimp to seal and cut steam vents. In a small bowl, beat egg yolk with 2 tsp (10 mL) water. Brush pastry with egg wash.
4. Bake pie in preheated oven for 15 minutes; reduce heat to 375°F (190°C) and bake for 25 to 30 minutes more or until pastry is golden.

All-Purpose Double Crust Pie Pastry

Makes enough pastry for 9-inch (23 cm) double crust pie

1/2 cup	cold butter, cubed	125 mL
1/4 cup	shortening	50 mL
2 cups	all-purpose flour	500 mL
1/4 tsp	salt	1 mL
5 tbsp	cold water (approx.)	75 mL

1. Place butter and shortening on a plate; place in freezer for 20 minutes or until firm. Cut into small bits.
2. In a food processor, combine flour and salt. Add butter and shortening; process to make fine crumbs. Transfer mixture to a bowl; sprinkle with enough water to hold pastry together. Gather dough into a ball.
3. Divide dough in two. Shape each piece into a 5-inch (13 cm) disc; wrap in plastic wrap. Refrigerate for 1 hour before using.

MAKES 4 BURGERS

If burgers are starting to become mundane, put some excitement in those patties. Instead of cheese on top of the burger, put shredded cheese right in the ground meat mixture for moist burgers with a twist. Mama would be pleased.

TIP

For an easy vegetable topping, cut green or red bell peppers and a large red onion into rounds, brush lightly with olive oil and grill alongside burgers.

Mama's Italian Cheeseburgers

Preheat barbecue, greased

1/4 cup	tomato pasta sauce	50 mL
1/4 cup	grated or minced onion	50 mL
1	clove garlic, minced	1
1/4 tsp	dried basil or oregano leaves	1 mL
1/4 tsp	salt	1 mL
1/4 tsp	freshly ground black pepper	1 mL
3/4 cup	shredded mozzarella or Fontina cheese	175 mL
1/3 cup	dry seasoned bread crumbs	75 mL
1 lb	lean ground beef	500 g
4	hamburger buns, split and lightly toasted	4

1. In a bowl, combine tomato pasta sauce, onion, garlic, basil, salt and pepper. Stir in cheese and bread crumbs; mix in beef. Shape into four 3/4-inch (2 cm) thick patties.

2. Place on greased grill over medium-high heat; cook, turning once, for 6 to 7 minutes on each side, or until no longer pink in center. Serve in buns.

SERVES 4

Here's a satisfying meat loaf-like dish with a tasty gravy that's wonderful accompanied by creamy mashed potatoes. Peel the potatoes and start them cooking on the stovetop before you begin preparing the patties so both will be ready at about the same time.

TIP

Unless you're using expensive tomato paste from a tube, you can freeze leftover tomato paste. Put tablespoons (15 mL) of leftover canned tomato paste on a waxed paper-lined plate or in ice-cube trays; freeze until firm. Transfer to a small freezer bag and have handy in the freezer to add to recipes.

Salisbury Steak

1	egg	1
2 tbsp	fine dry bread crumbs	25 mL
1	small onion, minced	1
1 tbsp	Worcestershire sauce	15 mL
1/2 tsp	salt	2 mL
1/4 tsp	freshly ground black pepper	1 mL
1 lb	lean ground beef	500 g
2 tsp	vegetable oil	10 mL
1 1/2 cups	chopped mushrooms	375 mL
1	clove garlic, minced	1
1/4 tsp	dried thyme or marjoram leaves	1 mL
1 tbsp	all-purpose flour	15 mL
1 cup	beef stock	250 mL
1 tbsp	tomato paste	15 mL

1. In a bowl, beat egg; stir in bread crumbs, half the onion, half the Worcestershire sauce, salt and pepper; mix in ground beef. Form into four patties, each 4 inches (10 cm) in diameter.
2. In a large nonstick skillet, heat oil over medium-high heat; brown patties, about 2 minutes on each side. Transfer to a plate. Add remaining onion, mushrooms, garlic and thyme to skillet; cook, stirring, for 2 minutes or until softened.
3. Sprinkle with flour; stir in remaining Worcestershire sauce, beef stock and tomato paste. Cook, stirring, for 1 minute or until thickened. Return patties to skillet; reduce heat, cover and simmer, turning once, for 10 minutes or until patties are no longer pink in center.

MAKES 48 MEATBALLS

We often think of meatballs with spaghetti, but they are equally delicious in a variety of sauces such as Sweet-and-Sour and Spicy Black Bean (see recipes following).

TIPS

To freeze meatballs, place in a single layer on a baking sheet until frozen then transfer to a covered container or freezer bag. To quickly reheat, place the frozen meatballs in a casserole dish, cover and microwave at Medium until defrosted.

For Spaghetti with Meatballs, see recipe, page 203.

Basic Meatballs

Preheat oven to 400°F (200°C)
Baking sheets

1	large egg	1
2 tbsp	water	25 mL
1/3 cup	fine dry bread crumbs	75 mL
1/3 cup	minced green onions	75 mL
1	clove garlic, minced	1
3/4 tsp	salt	4 mL
1/2 tsp	freshly ground black pepper	2 mL
1 1/2 lbs	lean ground beef	750 g

1. In a large bowl, beat egg with water; stir in bread crumbs, green onions, garlic, salt and pepper. Mix in beef.
2. Form by tablespoonfuls (15 mL) into balls; arrange on baking sheets. Bake for 15 minutes or until browned and no longer pink inside. Drain on paper towels.

SERVES 6

Take advantage of supermarket specials for lean ground beef and cook batches of meatballs ahead. Freeze them for this quick dish.

Everyone's Favorite Sweet-and-Sour Meatballs

1	can (14 oz/398 mL) pineapple chunks	1
1/4 cup	packed brown sugar	50 mL
1/4 cup	rice vinegar	50 mL
1/4 cup	soy sauce	50 mL
4 tsp	cornstarch	20 mL
48	Basic meatballs (see recipe, page 174)	48

1. Drain pineapple chucks and reserve. Measure pineapple juice; add enough water to make 1 cup (250 mL).
2. In a large saucepan, combine pineapple juice, brown sugar, vinegar, soy sauce and cornstarch. Place over medium heat, stirring, until sauce comes to a boil and thickens.
3. Stir in meatballs and pineapple chunks; cook for 3 to 5 minutes or until piping hot.

SERVES 6

It takes only a few minutes to assemble the spicy-sweet sauce for these winning meatballs.

Meatballs in Spicy Black Bean Sauce

1/2 cup	orange juice	125 mL
1/2 cup	water	125 mL
1/4 cup	packed brown sugar	50 mL
1/4 cup	rice vinegar	50 mL
2 tbsp	black bean sauce	25 mL
2 tbsp	soy sauce	25 mL
1 tbsp	cornstarch	15 mL
2 tsp	minced fresh gingerroot	10 mL
1/2 tsp	chili paste or hot pepper sauce	2 mL
2 tbsp	chopped green onion tops	25 mL
48	Basic Meatballs (see recipe, page 174)	48

1. In a large saucepan, combine orange juice, water, brown sugar, rice vinegar, black bean sauce, soy sauce, cornstarch, ginger and chili paste. Cook over medium heat, stirring, for 3 minutes or until sauce boils and thickens.

2. Add meatballs and stir to coat; cook for 2 minutes or until hot. Transfer to serving bowl; sprinkle with green onion tops.

SERVES 4

Leftover pasta in the fridge is perfect for this pizza-like supper dish that's especially appealing to the younger set.

TIP

It's easy to turn this recipe into a vegetarian dish — just omit the meat. Broccoli can be replaced by zucchini, bell peppers or whatever vegetables you have on hand.

Kids' Favorite Spaghetti Pie

Preheat oven to 350°F (180°C)
9- or 10-inch (23 or 25 cm) glass pie plate, greased

8 oz	mild or hot Italian sausages, casings removed, or lean ground beef	250 g
2 cups	sliced mushrooms	500 mL
1	small onion, chopped	1
1	large clove garlic, finely chopped	1
1½ tsp	dried oregano leaves	7 mL
2 cups	tomato pasta sauce	500 mL
2 cups	small broccoli florets	500 mL
3 cups	cooked spaghetti or other string pasta (6 oz/175 g uncooked)	750 mL
1½ cups	shredded mozzarella cheese	375 mL

1. In a medium saucepan over medium-high heat, cook sausage meat, breaking up with a wooden spoon, for 4 minutes or until no longer pink. Drain in sieve to remove any fat. Return to saucepan. Add mushrooms, onion, garlic, and oregano; cook, stirring, for 3 minutes or until vegetables are softened. Add tomato pasta sauce; cover and simmer for 10 minutes.
2. Rinse broccoli; place in a covered casserole dish. Microwave at High for 2 to 2½ minutes or until bright green and almost tender. Rinse under cold water to chill; drain.
3. Arrange spaghetti in pie plate. Spread with meat sauce; top with broccoli and sprinkle with cheese. Bake for 25 to 30 minutes or until cheese is melted. Cut into wedges and serve.

SERVES 4

No need to buy pricey packaged dinner mixes when it's easy to create your own. It's just a matter of using pantry staples already in your cupboard. In about the time it takes to fix an accompanying salad, this dish is ready to set on the table.

TIP

Use your own homemade tomato sauce (see Big-Batch Tomato Sauce, page 202) or rely on the many top-notch bottled sauces now available in supermarkets to cut down on preparation time.

Beefy Macaroni with Zucchini

1 lb	lean ground beef or turkey	500 g
1	small onion, chopped	1
2	cloves garlic, finely chopped	2
1 tsp	dried basil or oregano leaves	5 mL
1 1/2 cups	tomato pasta sauce	375 mL
1 1/2 cups	chicken or beef stock (approx.)	375 mL
1 cup	elbow macaroni	250 mL
2	medium zucchini, cut into 1/2-inch (1 cm) cubes	2

1. In a large nonstick skillet over medium-high heat, cook beef, breaking up with a wooden spoon, for 5 minutes or until no longer pink. Add onion, garlic and basil; cook, stirring, for 2 minutes.
2. Add tomato pasta sauce and stock; bring to a boil. Stir in pasta; reduce heat, cover and cook for 2 minutes.
3. Stir in zucchini; cook, covered, stirring occasionally, adding more stock if needed, for 5 to 7 minutes or until pasta and zucchini are tender.

SERVES 6

Here's a pasta dish with all the appeal of cabbage rolls, but is far easier to whip up for dinner. Its sweet-sour accent is a welcome departure from traditional pasta sauces and a good match for the cabbage.

TIP

The dish can be made a day ahead and reheated; it also freezes well. As a time-saver, buy packaged shredded cabbage in the produce department.

Beefy Macaroni with Cabbage

1 lb	lean ground beef	500 g
1	large onion, chopped	1
2	large cloves garlic, minced	2
½ tsp	fennel seeds	2 mL
8 cups	shredded cabbage (1 lb/500 g package)	2 L
2 tbsp	red wine vinegar	25 mL
2 tbsp	packed brown sugar	25 mL
1	can (28 oz/796 mL) stewed tomatoes, including juice	1
1 tsp	salt	5 mL
½ tsp	freshly ground black pepper	2 mL
2 cups	elbow macaroni	500 mL

1. In a Dutch oven or large saucepan over medium-high heat, cook beef, breaking up with a wooden spoon, for 5 minutes or until no longer pink.
2. Add onion, garlic and fennel seeds; cook, stirring often, for 3 minutes or until onion is softened. Stir in cabbage, vinegar and brown sugar; cook, stirring often, for 3 minutes or until cabbage is wilted. Stir in stewed tomatoes with juice, salt and pepper. Bring to a boil; reduce heat, cover and simmer for 5 minutes or until cabbage is tender.
3. Meanwhile, cook pasta in a large pot of boiling salted water until tender but firm. Drain well. Stir into cabbage mixture; cook for 2 minutes or until piping hot.

SERVES 4

Economical ground meats provide versatile options for the harried cook. Serve this tasty ground chicken dish with a salad or green vegetable such as broccoli. Dinner is ready in about 30 minutes.

TIP

When ground chicken is browned in a skillet, it doesn't turn into a fine crumble like other ground meats. I overcome the problem by placing the cooked chicken in a food processor and chopping it using on-off turns to break up meat lumps.

Chicken Paprika with Noodles

1 lb	lean ground chicken or turkey	500 g
1 tbsp	butter	15 mL
1	medium onion, chopped	1
8 oz	mushrooms, sliced	250 g
1 tbsp	paprika	15 mL
2 tbsp	all-purpose flour	25 mL
1 1/3 cups	chicken stock	325 mL
1/2 cup	sour cream	125 mL
2 tbsp	chopped fresh dill or parsley	25 mL
	Salt and freshly ground black pepper	
8 oz	fettuccine or broad egg noodles	250 g

1. In a large nonstick skillet over medium-high heat, cook chicken, breaking up with a wooden spoon, for 5 minutes or until no longer pink. Remove; drain in sieve to remove any fat and set aside.

2. Melt butter in skillet. Add onion, mushrooms and paprika; cook, stirring often, for 3 minutes or until vegetables are softened.

3. Sprinkle with flour; stir in stock and return chicken to skillet. Bring to a boil; cook, stirring, until thickened. Reduce heat, cover and simmer for 5 minutes. Remove from heat and stir in sour cream (it may curdle if added over the heat) and dill; season with salt and pepper to taste.

4. Cook pasta in a large pot of boiling salted water until tender but firm. Drain well. Return to pot and toss with chicken mixture. Serve immediately.

SERVES 4

Looking for a fast-track dinner? Convenient frozen hash browns come to the rescue along with quick-cooking ground beef for a family-pleasing meal.

TIP

To defrost hash browns, place on a plate lined with paper towels; microwave at High for 3 to 4 minutes, stirring once.

VARIATION

Breakfast Sausage and Potato Hash with Poached Eggs

Substitute breakfast sausage (with casings removed) for the beef. Prepare recipe as directed; omit Worcestershire sauce. Divide mixture among four serving plates and top each with a poached or fried egg.

Beef and Potato Hash

1 lb	lean ground beef	500 g
2 tsp	Worcestershire sauce	10 mL
1 tbsp	vegetable oil	15 mL
1	medium onion, chopped	1
1	green bell pepper, chopped	1
4 cups	frozen hash brown potatoes, defrosted	1 L
	Salt and freshly ground black pepper	

1. In a large nonstick skillet over medium-high heat, cook beef, breaking up with a wooden spoon, for 5 minutes or until no longer pink. Place in sieve to drain any fat; transfer to a bowl. Stir in Worcestershire sauce.

2. Add oil to skillet; cook onion, green pepper and potatoes, stirring often, for 8 to 10 minutes or until potatoes are golden. Add ground beef; season with salt and pepper to taste. Cook for 2 minutes or until heated through.

SERVES 4 TO 6

Looking for an inviting dinner-in-a-dish everyone in the family will enjoy? This hearty chili-flavored beef casserole topped with a tasty cornbread crust fills the bill. I've kept the seasonings tame so it appeals to the sensitive taste buds of young diners, but boost the seasonings if desired.

TIP

Add 1 tsp (5 mL) additional chili powder along with ¼ tsp (1 mL) hot pepper flakes or to taste to the ground beef mixture for a more assertive chili flavor.

Tex-Mex Cobbler

Preheat oven to 400°F (200°C)
10-cup (2.5 L) casserole dish

1 lb	lean ground beef	500 g
1	onion, chopped	1
2	cloves garlic, finely chopped	2
1	large green bell pepper, chopped	1
2 tsp	chili powder	10 mL
1 tsp	dried oregano leaves	5 mL
½ tsp	ground cumin	2 mL
2 tbsp	all-purpose flour	25 mL
1½ cups	beef stock	375 mL
1	can (7½ oz/213 mL) tomato sauce	1
1	can (12 oz/341 mL) corn kernels, drained	1
	Cheddar Cornbread Crust (see recipe, right)	

1. In a large nonstick skillet over medium-high heat, cook beef, breaking up with a wooden spoon, for 5 minutes or until no longer pink.
2. Stir in onion, garlic, green pepper, chili powder, oregano and cumin; cook, stirring, for 4 minutes or until softened.
3. Blend in flour; stir in stock and tomato sauce. Bring to a boil, stirring, until thickened. Reduce heat, cover and simmer for 5 minutes. Stir in corn; cook for 2 minutes or until piping hot. Spoon into casserole dish.
4. Meanwhile, make Cheddar Cornbread Crust (see recipe right). Spoon over beef mixture in an even layer. Bake for 20 to 25 minutes or until top is light golden and filling is bubbly.

Cheddar Cornbread Crust

2/3 cup	all-purpose flour	150 mL
1/2 cup	cornmeal	125 mL
1 1/2 tsp	granulated sugar	7 mL
1 1/2 tsp	baking powder	7 mL
1/4 tsp	salt	1 mL
1/2 cup	shredded Cheddar cheese	125 mL
1	egg	1
2/3 cup	milk	150 mL

1. In a bowl, combine flour, cornmeal, sugar, baking powder and salt; mix in cheese. In another bowl, beat together egg and milk. Stir into dry ingredients to make a smooth batter.

SERVES 4

Some days you just don't have time to think about what's for supper. Rather than getting takeout, here's an easy dish that counts on convenient frozen vegetables to get dinner on the table in 20 minutes.

TIP

Cook extra rice ahead and keep it handy in the fridge. Or use instant rice prepared according to package directions.

Speedy Beef and Vegetable Fried Rice

1 lb	lean ground beef	500 g
3	green onions, sliced	3
1	large clove garlic, minced	1
2 tsp	minced fresh gingerroot	10 mL
2 cups	cooked rice, preferably basmati	500 mL
4 cups	frozen Oriental mixed vegetables (see Tip, page 149)	1 L
3 tbsp	soy sauce	45 mL

1. In a large nonstick skillet over medium-high heat, cook beef, breaking up with a wooden spoon, for 5 minutes or until no longer pink. Add green onions, garlic and ginger; cook, stirring, for 1 minute. Stir in rice; cook, stirring, for 2 minutes.
2. Add vegetables and soy sauce. Reduce heat to medium, cover and cook, stirring occasionally, (adding 2 tbsp/25 mL water if necessary to prevent from sticking), for 5 minutes or until vegetables are tender.

Microwave Salsa Beef and Rice Casserole

SERVES 4 TO 6

Here's a terrific make-ahead casserole dish that reheats in the microwave in about the same time as it takes to toss a salad and set the table.

10-cup (2.5 L) casserole dish

2 tsp	vegetable oil	10 mL
2	medium zucchini, halved lengthwise, thinly sliced	2
1 ½ cups	fresh, frozen or canned corn kernels	375 mL
1 ½ cups	medium salsa	375 mL
1 lb	lean ground beef	500 g
1	onion, finely chopped	1
2	large cloves garlic, minced	2
4 tsp	chili powder	20 mL
1 tsp	dried oregano leaves	5 mL
1 tsp	salt	5 mL
½ tsp	freshly ground black pepper	2 mL
3 cups	cooked white or brown rice (see Tip, left)	750 mL
1 cup	shredded Cheddar cheese	250 mL

1. In a large nonstick skillet, heat oil over medium-high heat. Add zucchini and cook, stirring, for 3 minutes or until softened. Transfer to a bowl; stir in corn and salsa.
2. Add beef to skillet; cook, breaking up with a wooden spoon, for 5 minutes or until no longer pink. Add onion, garlic, chili powder, oregano, salt and pepper; cook, stirring, for 3 minutes. Stir in rice.
3. In a casserole dish, layer half the beef mixture, then half the vegetable mixture. Repeat layers. Sprinkle with cheese. Cover and microwave at High for 12 to 16 minutes (5 to 7 minutes longer if refrigerated) or until piping hot in center.

TIPS

To oven-bake, cover and place in a 375°F (190°C) oven for 40 minutes; remove cover and bake another 15 to 20 minutes or until center is piping hot and cheese is golden.

To cook rice, bring 2 cups (500 mL) water to a boil in a medium saucepan; add 1 cup (250 mL) white long-grain rice and ½ tsp (2 mL) salt. Return to a boil; reduce heat to low, cover and simmer for 20 minutes. If using brown rice, increase water to 2½ cups (625 mL) and increase cooking time to 40 to 45 minutes. Makes 3 cups (750 mL) rice.

VARIATION

Replace half or all the beef with Italian sausages. Remove casings and brown sausage meat; drain well.

SERVES 4

This homey dish is a great way to take advantage of the economical vegetables on display at country farm markets in the fall.

Rice and Beef-Stuffed Peppers

Preheat oven to 350°F (180°C)
13-by 9-inch (3 L) baking dish

4	large green or red bell peppers	4
8 oz	lean ground beef	250 g
8 oz	hot or mild Italian sausages, casing removed	250 g
2 tsp	olive oil	10 mL
4	green onions, sliced	4
2	cloves garlic, finely chopped	2
1 tsp	dried basil leaves	5 mL
2	large tomatoes, peeled, seeded and diced	2
1 cup	fresh or frozen corn kernels	250 mL
3/4 tsp	salt	4 mL
1/2 tsp	freshly ground black pepper	2 mL
1 1/2 cups	cooked rice	375 mL
1 cup	shredded mozzarella cheese	250 mL
1/3 cup	freshly grated Parmesan cheese	75 mL
1/2 cup	chicken stock	125 mL

1. Cut peppers in half lengthwise. Remove seeds and membranes. In a large pot of boiling salted water, blanch peppers for 5 minutes; drain and place cut-side down on rack to cool.
2. In a large nonstick skillet, cook beef and sausage over medium-high heat, breaking up with a wooden spoon, for 5 to 7 minutes or until no longer pink. Drain in sieve to remove fat; set aside.

3. Add oil to skillet; cook green onion, garlic and basil, stirring, for 2 minutes or until softened. Stir in tomatoes, corn, salt and pepper; cook, stirring, for 3 to 5 minutes or until corn is tender. Stir in rice and ground beef; cook, stirring, for 3 minutes or until heated through.
4. In a bowl, combine mozzarella and Parmesan cheeses. Stir half of the cheese into rice mixture. Arrange peppers, cut-side up in casserole dish. Fill with rice mixture; top with remaining cheese. Pour stock into casserole dish; bake peppers for 30 to 35 minutes or until top is golden and filling is piping hot.

SERVES 4

Serve this one-pot family favorite with warm pita bread along with a cucumber and tomato salad.

Beef and Potato Curry

1 lb	lean ground beef	500 g
1	onion, chopped	1
2	large cloves garlic, finely chopped	2
2 tbsp	tomato paste	25 mL
1 tbsp	mild curry paste or powder	15 mL
1 tbsp	minced fresh gingerroot	15 mL
1/4 tsp	salt	1 mL
4	potatoes, peeled and diced (about 1 1/2 lbs/750 g)	4
2 cups	beef stock	500 mL
1 1/2 cups	frozen peas	375 mL
1/4 cup	chopped fresh cilantro or parsley (optional)	50 mL

1. In a Dutch oven or large saucepan over medium-high heat, cook beef, breaking up with a wooden spoon, for 5 minutes or until no longer pink. Add onion, garlic, tomato paste, curry paste, ginger and salt; cook, stirring, for 5 minutes or until onion is softened.
2. Add potatoes and stock; bring to boil. Reduce heat, cover and simmer for 15 minutes. Stir in peas; cook, covered, for 5 minutes or until potatoes and peas are tender. Stir in cilantro, is using.

SERVES 4 TO 6

Satisfying casseroles like this one are always a welcome choice when planning make-ahead meals for the freezer.

TIPS

Cooked cabbage rolls can be frozen for up to two months.

To easily chop canned tomatoes, run a knife through the tomatoes right in the can.

If inner cabbage leaves are not softened, blanch cabbage again in boiling water to soften leaves.

Stuffed Cabbage Rolls

Preheat oven to 350°F (180°C)
12-cup (3 L) casserole dish

1	medium head green cabbage, cored (about 3 lbs/1.5 kg)	1
4 tsp	vegetable oil	20 mL
1	large onion, finely chopped	1
2	large cloves garlic, finely chopped	2
1 tsp	paprika	5 mL
1½ cups	cooked rice	375 mL
1 lb	lean ground beef	500 g
	Salt and freshly ground black pepper	
1	can (28 oz/796 mL) plum tomatoes, including juice	1
2 tsp	packed brown sugar	10 mL

1. In a large pot of boiling salted water, cook cabbage for 5 to 6 minutes or until leaves are softened. Drain, rinse under cold water, carefully separating 12 leaves. Using a knife, trim coarse veins from cabbage leaves.
2. In a large saucepan, heat oil over medium heat; cook onion, garlic and paprika, stirring, for 5 minutes or until softened. In a bowl, combine half the onion mixture, rice, beef, 1 tsp (5 mL) salt and ½ tsp (2 mL) pepper; mix well.
3. In a food processor, purée tomatoes including juice. Add with brown sugar to onion mixture in saucepan; bring to a boil. Cover and reduce heat; simmer for 15 minutes, stirring occasionally. Season with salt and pepper to taste.
4. Spoon ¼ cup (50 mL) rice mixture onto each cabbage leaf just above stem. Fold ends and sides over filling; roll up. Spoon 1 cup (250 mL) tomato sauce in bottom of Dutch oven or casserole dish. Layer with half the cabbage rolls; pour 1 cup (250 mL) tomato sauce over. Top with remaining cabbage rolls and pour remaining sauce over. Cover and bake for 1 to 1¼ hours or until rolls are tender.

SERVES 6 TO 8

Every cook has a special version of chili. Here's mine — it's meaty and nicely spiced with just the right amount of beans. Not everyone agrees that beans belong in a chili — witness the Texas version dubbed "bowl of red" — but I love the way the beans absorb the spices and rich tomato flavor.

TIP

The flavor of the chili hinges on the quality of chili powder used. Most powders are a blend of dried, ground mild chilies, as well as cumin, oregano, garlic and salt. Read the list of ingredients to be sure you're not buying one with starch and sugar fillers. Chili powder should not be confused with powdered or ground chilies of the cayenne pepper variety.

Amazing Chili

1 1/2 lbs	lean ground beef	750 g
2	onions, chopped	2
3	cloves garlic, finely chopped	3
2	stalks celery, chopped	2
1	large green bell pepper, chopped	1
2 tbsp	chili powder	25 mL
1 1/2 tsp	dried oregano leaves	7 mL
1 1/2 tsp	ground cumin	7 mL
1 tsp	salt	5 mL
1/2 tsp	hot pepper flakes or to taste	2 mL
1	can (28 oz/796 mL) tomatoes, including juice, chopped	1
1 cup	beef stock	250 mL
1	can (19 oz/540 mL) pinto or red kidney beans, drained and rinsed	1
1/4 cup	chopped fresh parsley or cilantro	50 mL

1. In a Dutch oven or large saucepan, cook beef over medium-high heat, breaking up with a wooden spoon, for about 7 minutes or until no longer pink.
2. Reduce heat to medium. Add onions, garlic, celery, green pepper, chili powder, oregano, cumin, salt and hot pepper flakes; cook, stirring often, for 5 minutes or until vegetables are softened.
3. Stir in tomatoes with juice and stock. Bring to a boil; reduce heat, cover and simmer, stirring occasionally, for 1 hour.
4. Add beans and parsley; cover and simmer for 10 minutes more.

SERVES 12

This beanless chili has a hot kick to it so reduce the amount of pepper flakes if you prefer it on the tamer side. Ladle into bowls and have ready shredded Cheddar cheese, sliced green onions, sour cream and chopped cilantro so everyone can choose their fixings. Terrific served with cheddar drop biscuits.

TIP

If you wish to add beans, omit cornmeal; add 2 cans (each 19 oz/ 540 mL) red kidney beans, drained and rinsed, to chili instead.

Dynamite Beanless Chili

3 lbs	lean ground beef	1.5 kg
2 tbsp	olive oil	25 mL
2	large onions, chopped	2
6	cloves garlic, finely chopped	6
5 to 6	jalapeño peppers, minced	5 to 6
3 tbsp	chili powder	45 mL
1 tbsp	dried oregano leaves	15 mL
1 tbsp	ground cumin	15 mL
2	bay leaves	2
2 tsp	salt	10 mL
2 tsp	hot pepper flakes or to taste	10 mL
1	can (28 oz/596 mL) tomatoes, including juice, chopped	1
1	can (10 oz/284 mL) beef broth (undiluted)	1
1	can (5½ oz/142 g) tomato paste	1
3	red or green bell peppers, diced	3
¼ cup	cornmeal	50 mL

1. In a large Dutch oven or stockpot, cook beef over medium-high heat in two batches, breaking up with a wooden spoon, for about 7 minutes or until no longer pink. Transfer to a bowl.
2. Reduce heat to medium; add oil to pan. Cook onions, garlic, jalapeño peppers, chili powder, oregano, cumin, bay leaves, salt and hot pepper flakes, stirring, for 5 minutes or until softened.
3. Return meat to pan; add tomatoes with juice, 2 cups (500 mL) water, broth and tomato paste. Bring to a boil, simmer, covered, for 30 minutes, stirring occasionally. Add peppers; cook for 30 minutes more.
4. In a bowl, stir together ¼ cup (50 mL) water with cornmeal; stir into meat mixture. Cook for 10 minutes or until sauce is thickened. Remove bay leaves before serving.

SERVES 4 TO 6

Here's a streamlined version of chili that's a snap. Make a double batch and have containers stashed away in the freezer for quick microwave meals. Just ladle into bowls and, if desired, top with shredded Monterey Jack cheese. Set out a basket of crusty bread — supper is that easy.

TIP

Add just a pinch of hot pepper flakes for a mild chili; but if you want to turn up the heat, use amount specified in the recipe.

20-Minute Chili

1 lb	lean ground beef or turkey	500 g
1	large onion, chopped	1
2	large cloves garlic, finely chopped	2
1	large green bell pepper, chopped	1
4 tsp	chili powder	20 mL
1 tbsp	all-purpose flour	15 mL
1 tsp	dried basil leaves	5 mL
1 tsp	dried oregano leaves	5 mL
1/2 tsp	hot pepper flakes or to taste	2 mL
2 cups	tomato pasta sauce	500 mL
1 1/3 cups	beef stock	325 mL
1	can (19 oz/540 mL) kidney beans or pinto beans, drained and rinsed	1
	Salt and freshly ground black pepper	

1. In a Dutch oven or large saucepan over medium-high heat, cook beef, breaking up with a wooden spoon, for 5 minutes or until no longer pink.
2. Reduce heat to medium. Add onion, garlic, green pepper, chili powder, flour, basil, oregano and hot pepper flakes; cook, stirring, for 4 minutes or until vegetables are softened.
3. Stir in tomato sauce and stock. Bring to a boil; cook, stirring, until thickened. Add beans; season with salt and pepper to taste. Reduce heat and simmer, covered, for 10 minutes.

Mama's Italian Cheeseburgers (page 172) ➢
Overleaf: Spanish Vegetable Paella (page 225)

Pasta and Grains

continued on next page

Amazing Chili (page 190)

PASTA TIPS

How to Cook Pasta

You can ruin a good pasta dish if you don't cook the pasta properly. The most common error is not using enough water to boil the pasta — with the result that it cooks unevenly and sticks together.

- To cook 1 lb (500 g) of pasta: Using a large pot, bring 16 cups (4 L) of water to a full rolling boil. Add 1 tbsp (15 mL) salt (this is important for flavor) and all the pasta at once. (Do not add oil.) Stir immediately to prevent pasta from sticking. Cover with a lid to return water quickly to full boil. Then uncover and stir occasionally. Taste to see if pasta is al dente, or firm to the bite. Drain immediately. Unless directed otherwise, never rinse pasta — this chills it and removes the coating of starch that helps sauce cling to pasta. Return to pot or place in large warmed serving bowl; add the sauce and toss until well coated. (Never plunk pasta on serving plates and ladle sauce on top.) Serve immediately.

Freezing and Refrigerating Pasta

Here are some general guidelines for making pasta dishes ahead and refrigerating or freezing:

- Make pasta sauces up to two days ahead and refrigerate or freeze for up to two months. If assembling pasta dish ahead: Cook pasta and chill under cold water; drain. Toss cold pasta with cold sauce and spoon into casserole dish. It's best to assemble casserole no more than a few hours ahead to prevent pasta from absorbing too much of the sauce.
- To freeze: Do not add the cheese topping (it goes rubbery when frozen). Cover with plastic wrap, then with foil. Freeze for up to two months. Let defrost in refrigerator overnight. Increase baking time by about 10 minutes.

SERVES 8

Today's store-bought tomato sauces and packaged shredded cheeses ease the making of traditional lasagna. This updated version serves a crowd and replaces ground meat with plenty of healthy vegetables.

TIP

To make ahead, cover and refrigerate for up to two days or overwrap with foil and freeze for up to two months. Let thaw completely in refrigerator for 24 hours.

Roasted Vegetable Lasagna with Spicy Tomato Sauce

Preheat oven to 400°F (200°C)
2 baking sheets
13-by 9-inch (3 L) baking dish, greased

ROASTED VEGETABLES

1	red onion	1
2	small zucchini, diced	2
1	large bulb fennel, diced	1
1	large red bell pepper, diced	1
1 tbsp	dried oregano leaves	15 mL
1/2 tsp	freshly ground black pepper	2 mL
2 tbsp	olive oil	25 mL

CHEESE FILLING

2	eggs	2
1/2 tsp	freshly ground black pepper	2 mL
1 1/2 cups	ricotta cheese	375 mL
1 cup	crumbled feta cheese (about 4 oz/125 g)	250 mL
1/4 cup	chopped fresh parsley	50 mL

PASTA SAUCE

12	lasagna noodles	12
1	jar (26 oz/700 mL) spicy tomato sauce with roasted red peppers	1
1	can (7 1/2 oz/213 mL) tomato sauce	1
1/3 cup	chopped Kalamata olives (optional)	75 mL
1 1/2 cups	shredded mozzarella cheese	375 mL

1. Roasted Vegetables: In a bowl, combine onion, zucchini, fennel, pepper, oregano and pepper; drizzle with oil and toss to coat. Spread on baking sheets. Roast in preheated oven, stirring occasionally, for 20 to 25 minutes or until tender. Remove and set aside. Reduce oven temperature to 350°F (180°C).
2. Cheese Filling: In a bowl, beat eggs and pepper; stir in ricotta, feta and parsley.

3. Meanwhile, in a large pot of boiling salted water, cook noodles for 8 minutes or until almost tender. Drain; chill under cold running water. Arrange in single layer on damp tea towel.
4. In a large bowl, combine bottled and canned tomato sauces; spread ¾ cup (175 mL) sauce in baking dish. Stir roasted vegetables and olives, if using, into remaining tomato sauce.
5. Layer three noodles in baking dish. Spread with ¼ of the vegetable sauce; top with ⅓ of the ricotta mixture. Repeat layers twice. Arrange remaining noodles over top; spread with remaining sauce.
6. Sprinkle top with mozzarella cheese; cover loosely with foil. Bake in 350°F (180°C) oven for 30 minutes; uncover and bake for 20 to 25 minutes more or until bubbly and top is golden. Let stand for 5 minutes before cutting.

SERVES 8

Everyone loves lasagna but who has the time to make it from scratch? Try this uncomplicated version that makes even a non-cook look like a pro in the kitchen. It's also the perfect recipe for young cooks, since there's no chopping involved. Once you assemble the ingredients, it takes a mere 15 minutes to prepare and the lasagna is ready for the oven.

TIP

Lasagna freezes well; cover with plastic wrap then with foil and freeze for up to two months. Let defrost in the refrigerator overnight before baking.

Easy Lasagna

Preheat oven to 350°F (180°C)
13-by 9-inch (3 L) baking dish, lightly greased

2 cups	ricotta cheese	500 mL
2	eggs, beaten	2
1⁄3 cup	freshly grated Parmesan cheese	75 mL
1⁄4 tsp	freshly ground black pepper	1 mL
1⁄4 tsp	freshly grated nutmeg	1 mL
12	precooked lasagna noodles	12
3 cups	spaghetti sauce (homemade or store-bought)	750 mL
2 cups	shredded mozzarella cheese	500 mL

1. In a bowl, combine ricotta, eggs and Parmesan cheese; season with pepper and nutmeg.
2. Depending on thickness of the spaghetti sauce, add about 3⁄4 cup (175 mL) water to thin sauce. (Precooked noodles absorb extra moisture while cooking.)
3. Spoon 1⁄2 cup (125 mL) sauce in bottom of prepared baking dish. Layer with three lasagna noodles. Spread with 3⁄4 cup (175 mL) of the sauce and then 1⁄3 of the ricotta mixture. Repeat with two more layers of noodles, sauce and ricotta cheese. Layer with rest of noodles and top with remaining sauce. Sprinkle with mozzarella cheese.
4. Bake, uncovered, in preheated oven for 45 minutes or until cheese is melted and sauce is bubbly.

SERVES 4 TO 6

As popular today as in the 1950s, classic macaroni and cheese has a lot going for it. It's not hard to make, so why open up a box of the pre-packaged stuff when you can create the real thing in your kitchen?

Best-Ever Macaroni and Cheese

Preheat oven to 375°F (190°C)
8-cup (2 L) deep casserole dish, greased

3 tbsp	butter	45 mL
1/4 cup	all-purpose flour	50 mL
1	bay leaf	1
3 cups	milk	750 mL
1 tbsp	Dijon mustard	15 mL
	Salt and cayenne pepper	
2 cups	shredded Cheddar cheese, preferably aged (about 8 oz/250 g)	500 mL
2 cups	elbow macaroni	500 mL
1 tbsp	butter, melted	15 mL
1 cup	soft fresh bread crumbs	250 mL

1. In a large saucepan, melt butter over medium heat. Blend in flour and add bay leaf; cook, stirring, for 30 seconds. Pour in 1 cup (250 mL) milk, whisking constantly, until mixture comes to a boil and is very thick. Pour in rest of milk in a slow stream, whisking constantly, until sauce comes to a full boil and is smooth. Whisk in mustard.
2. Reduce heat to low; stir in cheese until melted. Remove bay leaf; season with salt and a dash of cayenne pepper to taste. Remove from heat.
3. Meanwhile, in a large pot of boiling salted water, cook macaroni for 8 minutes or until just tender. (Do not overcook; pasta continues to cook in sauce.) Drain well. Stir into cheese sauce until well coated.
4. Spoon into prepared casserole dish. In a bowl, toss 1 tbsp (15 mL) melted butter with bread crumbs; sprinkle over top. Bake in preheated oven for 25 minutes or until bubbly and top is lightly browned.

SERVES 4

Here's another streamlined mac and cheese that's as easy to assemble as the pre-packaged version.

TIPS

For a speedy, meal-in-one dinner add 3 to 4 cups (750 mL to 1 L) small broccoli florets to the pot of boiling pasta for the last 3 minutes of cooking; remove from heat when broccoli is tender-crisp.

To reheat leftovers on the stovetop or in the microwave, stir in additional milk until sauce is creamy.

Easy One-Pot Macaroni and Cheese

2 tbsp	all-purpose flour	25 mL
1 1/2 cups	milk	375 mL
1 1/2 cups	shredded Cheddar cheese	375 mL
1/4 cup	freshly grated Parmesan cheese	50 mL
1 tsp	Dijon mustard	5 mL
	Salt and cayenne pepper	
2 cups	elbow macaroni	500 mL

1. In a large saucepan, whisk flour with 1/4 cup (50 mL) milk to make a smooth paste; stir in remaining milk until smooth. Place over medium heat; cook, stirring, until mixture comes to a boil and thickens. Reduce heat to low; stir in cheeses and mustard. Cook, stirring, until melted. Season with salt and a pinch of cayenne pepper to taste; keep warm.
2. Cook pasta in a large pot of boiling salted water until tender but firm. Drain well; stir into cheese mixture. Cook for 1 minute or until sauce coats the pasta. Serve immediately.

Fettuccine Alfredo

SERVES 6

This luxurious pasta delivers so much pleasure it's worth the calorie splurge once in a while. Serve it on special occasions as a main course or as a starter dish. Delicioso!

1 cup	whipping (35%) cream	250 mL
1 cup	table (18%) cream	250 mL
1/4 cup	butter, softened	50 mL
1 1/2 cups	freshly grated Parmesan cheese	375 mL
1/4 tsp	freshly ground black pepper	1 mL
	Salt and freshly grated nutmeg	
1 lb	fettuccine	500 g
1/4 cup	finely chopped fresh chives, basil or parsley	50 mL

1. In a large saucepan, bring whipping cream and table cream to a boil over medium heat; boil until reduced to about 1 1/2 cups (375 mL). Reduce heat to low; whisk in butter and cheese until sauce is smooth. Add pepper; season with salt and nutmeg to taste. Keep warm.
2. Meanwhile, in a large pot of boiling salted water, cook pasta until tender but still firm. Drain well; return to pot; pour cream sauce over pasta. Sprinkle with herbs; toss well. Serve immediately on warm plates.

TIPS

The creamy flavor of fettuccine Alfredo comes not only from the cream and butter but also from the quality of the Parmesan cheese. You're in for a rich and nutty-sweet treat when you indulge in a morsel of Parmigiano Reggiano or its less-aged (and milder) cousin, Grana Padano. There's just no comparison between authentic Parmesan and the containers of inferior boxed grated cheese found on supermarket shelves.

Like coffee, Parmesan looses its wonderful aromatic flavor and moisture if grated ahead. Choose a wedge in a cheese shop and have it grated for you. Or better still, grate the cheese as you need it.

Store Parmesan wedges wrapped in plastic wrap, then in foil, in the refrigerator; it keeps well for weeks.

MAKES ABOUT 7 CUPS (1.75 L)

Here's an indispensable sauce I always have handy in the freezer to use as a base for my family's favorite pasta dishes. It's a versatile sauce and I've included several ways to serve it.

TIPS

In summer, instead of canned tomatoes, I make this sauce with 5 lbs (2.5 kg) of fresh ripe tomatoes, preferably the plum variety. To prepare, remove tomato cores; cut an X in the bottom of each. Plunge in boiling water for 30 seconds to loosen skins. Chill in cold water; drain. Slip off skins; cut tomatoes in half crosswise and squeeze out seeds. Chop finely.

Instead of dried basil and oregano, replace dried herbs with ⅓ cup (75 mL) chopped fresh basil; add towards end of cooking.

To save time, chop vegetables in the food processor.

Big-Batch Tomato Sauce

2 tbsp	olive oil	25 mL
1	medium onion, finely chopped	1
2	medium carrots, peeled and finely chopped	2
1	stalk celery, including leaves, finely chopped	1
4	cloves garlic, finely chopped	4
1 tbsp	dried basil leaves	15 mL
1½ tsp	dried oregano leaves	7 mL
1 tsp	salt	5 mL
1 tsp	granulated sugar	5 mL
½ tsp	freshly ground black pepper	2 mL
1	bay leaf	1
2	cans (28 oz/796 mL) plum tomatoes, including juice, chopped	2
1	can (5½ oz/156 mL) tomato paste	1
¼ cup	finely chopped fresh parsley	50 mL

1. In a Dutch oven or large saucepan, heat oil over medium-high heat. Add onion, carrots, celery, garlic, basil, oregano, salt, sugar, pepper and bay leaf; cook, stirring often, for 5 minutes or until vegetables are softened.

2. Stir in tomatoes with juice, tomato paste and 1 tomato-paste can of water. Bring to a boil; reduce heat and simmer, partially covered, for 35 to 40 minutes, stirring occasionally, until slightly thickened. Remove bay leaf; stir in parsley. Let cool; pack into containers and refrigerate or freeze.

SERVES 4

This dish is the essence of Italian cooking — comforting, hearty and sure to please.

Spaghetti with Meatballs

3 cups	Big-Batch Tomato Sauce (see recipe, page 202)	750 mL
24	Basic Meatballs (half the recipe, see page 174)	24
½ cup	beef stock	125 mL
12 oz	spaghetti or other string pasta	375 g
½ cup	freshly grated Parmesan cheese	125 mL

1. In a large saucepan, combine tomato sauce, meatballs and stock; bring to a boil. Reduce heat, cover and simmer for 15 minutes.

2. Cook pasta in a large pot of boiling salted water until tender but firm; drain well and toss with sauce. Place in serving bowls and sprinkle with Parmesan cheese.

Spaghetti with Meat Sauce

SERVES 4

Intensely flavored thanks to the addition of red wine — this easy pasta dish suits those nights when you crave something simple but satisfying.

VARIATION

Instead of ground beef, use half veal and half pork or a combination of all three.

12 oz	lean ground beef	375 g
1/2 cup	red wine or beef stock	125 mL
3 cups	Big-Batch Tomato Sauce (see recipe, page 202)	750 mL
	Salt, freshly ground pepper and hot pepper flakes	
12 oz	spaghetti	375 g
1/2 cup	freshly ground Parmesan cheese	125 mL

1. In a large nonstick skillet over medium-high heat, cook beef, breaking up with a wooden spoon, for 5 minutes, or until no longer pink. Add wine; cook until partly reduced.
2. Stir in tomato sauce; season with salt, pepper and hot pepper flakes, to taste. Reduce heat, cover and simmer for 15 minutes.
3. Cook pasta in a large pot of boiling salted water until tender but firm; drain well and toss with sauce. Place in serving bowls and sprinkle with Parmesan cheese.

SERVES 2 AS A MAIN COURSE OR 4 AS A SIDE DISH

Italian restaurants always feature their famous "rosé" sauce tossed with pasta. Here is my rendition of this classic favorite.

Tortellini with Creamy Tomato Sauce

1 1/2 cups	Big-Batch Tomato Sauce (see recipe, page 202)	375 mL
1/2 cup	whipping (35%) cream	125 mL
8 oz	cheese- or meat-stuffed tortellini	250 g

1. In a large saucepan over medium heat, combine tomato sauce and whipping cream; bring to a boil. (Do not substitute light cream as it may curdle). Reduce heat to medium-low and simmer, partially covered, for 5 minutes or until slightly thickened.

2. In a large pot of boiling salted water, cook tortellini until just tender; drain and toss with sauce.

SERVES 8 TO 10

This casual country-style dish — perfect for large potluck dinners — is an easy-make-ahead casserole that's a real crowd pleaser.

TIP

Substitute 1 lb (500 g) mild or hot Italian sausages for half of the chicken called for in this hearty Italian dish. Prick sausages with a fork and cook in a large skillet in 1 tbsp (15 mL) oil, turning often, until cooked through. Cut into slices and add along with browned chicken.

Chicken Penne Bake

Preheat oven to 350°F (180°C)
16-cup (4 L) baking dish, greased

2 tbsp	olive oil, divided	25 mL
2 lbs	skinless, boneless chicken thighs, cut into 1-inch (2.5 cm) pieces	1 kg
2	onions, chopped	2
6	cloves garlic, chopped	6
4 cups	sliced mushrooms	1 L
2 tsp	dried basil leaves	10 mL
2 tsp	dried oregano leaves	10 mL
1 tsp	hot pepper flakes	5 mL
1 tsp	salt	5 mL
1	can (28 oz/796 mL) plum tomatoes, including juice	1
1	can (5½ oz/156 mL) tomato paste	1
1½ cups	chicken stock	375 mL
1	each green and red bell pepper, chopped	1
½ cup	dry-cured black olives	125 mL
½ cup	chopped fresh parsley	125 mL
12 oz	penne or other tube-shaped pasta	375 g
2 cups	shredded mozzarella cheese	500 mL
½ cup	freshly grated Pecorino Romano or Parmesan cheese	125 mL

1. In a Dutch oven or large saucepan, heat 1 tbsp (15 mL) olive oil over medium-high heat; brown chicken in batches. Transfer to a plate.
2. Add remaining oil; cook onions, garlic, mushrooms, basil, oregano, hot pepper flakes and salt, stirring, for 5 minutes or until softened. Return chicken to pan along with accumulated juices.
3. In a food processor, purée tomatoes with juice. Add to chicken mixture with tomato paste and stock. Bring to a boil; reduce heat, cover and cook for 25 minutes. Add peppers and olives; cook, covered, for 10 minutes or until peppers are tender. Stir in parsley. (If making ahead let cool and refrigerate.)

4. In a large pot of boiling salted water, cook pasta until tender but firm; drain. Rinse under cold water to chill; drain well. Stir pasta into sauce. Spoon half into prepared baking dish; sprinkle with half the mozzarella and Romano cheeses. Top with remaining pasta and sprinkle with remaining cheeses. (Can be prepared to this point, covered and refrigerated for up to one day.)
5. Cover and bake in oven for 45 minutes; uncover and bake for 30 minutes more or until piping hot in center and top is golden.

SERVES 6

With leftover cooked chicken or turkey, you can make a wonderful pasta dish that's great for company. To make the dish in advance, cook the sauce, cover and refrigerate. Boil the pasta, rinse under cold water and chill. Combine the cold sauce and pasta up to 4 hours before the dish goes in the oven. (This prevents the pasta from absorbing too much of the sauce.)

VARIATION

This casserole also works well with ham instead of chicken.

Company Chicken Tetrazzini

Preheat oven to 350°F (180°C)
13-by 9-inch (3 L) baking dish, greased

2 tbsp	butter	25 mL
8 oz	mushrooms, sliced	250 g
4	green onions, finely chopped	4
1 tsp	dried basil leaves	5 mL
1/4 cup	all-purpose flour	50 mL
2 cups	chicken or turkey stock	500 mL
1/2 cup	whipping (35%) cream or table (18%) cream	125 mL
1/4 cup	medium-dry sherry	50 mL
2 cups	cubed cooked chicken or turkey	500 mL
2/3 cup	freshly grated Parmesan cheese	150 mL
	Salt and freshly ground black pepper	
8 oz	broad egg noodles	250 g

1. In a large saucepan, melt butter over medium-high heat. Add mushrooms, green onions and basil; cook for 4 minutes or until softened. In a bowl, blend flour with 1/3 cup (75 mL) stock to make a smooth paste; stir in remaining stock. Pour into saucepan; bring to a boil, stirring, until thickened. Add cream, sherry and chicken; cook over medium heat for 2 to 3 minutes or until heated through. Remove from heat. Stir in half the Parmesan cheese; season with salt and pepper to taste.
2. Cook noodles in a large pot of boiling salted water until almost tender but firm. Drain well. Return to pot; add chicken mixture and toss to coat well. Spoon into prepared baking dish. Sprinkle with remaining Parmesan cheese. Bake for 30 to 35 minutes or until heated through. (If refrigerated, cook 10 minutes more or until piping hot in center.)

SERVES 4

Infusing shrimp with pungent hot peppers and garlic then flambéing with vodka as in this winning entertaining dish is sure to illicit raves from your guests.

Fettuccine with Shrimp and Vegetables

3 tbsp	olive oil, divided	45 mL
1 1/2 lbs	large deveined raw shrimp, peeled with tails left on	375 g
2	cloves garlic, finely chopped	2
1/2 tsp	hot pepper flakes or to taste	2 mL
1/3 cup	vodka (optional)	75 mL
2	small red bell peppers, cut into thin strips	2
1	fennel bulb, top trimmed and cut into thin strips	1
1 cup	fish or chicken stock	250 mL
1 cup	whipping (35%) cream	250 mL
1 tbsp	grated orange zest	15 mL
1/2 tsp	salt	2 mL
1/4 tsp	freshly ground black pepper	1 mL
12 oz	fettuccine	375 g
1/3 cup	chopped fresh parsley	75 mL

1. In a large nonstick skillet, heat half the oil over high heat until almost smoking; add shrimp, garlic and hot pepper flakes. Cook, stirring, for 1 to 2 minutes or until shrimp are pink and almost cooked through. Add vodka, if using, and ignite with a match. Cook, shaking skillet, until flames subside. Transfer shrimp and juices to a bowl.
2. Add remaining oil to pan; cook red pepper and fennel strips, stirring, for 2 minutes or until tender-crisp. Transfer to bowl with shrimp.
3. Add stock, cream, zest, salt and pepper to pan; bring to a boil. Reduce heat to medium and boil sauce until reduced by half. Return shrimp and vegetables to skillet and heat through. Season with salt and pepper to taste.
4. In a large pot of boiling salted water, cook pasta until just tender but firm. Drain well. Return to pot. Toss with shrimp and vegetables; sprinkle with parsley.

SERVES 8

This modern rendition of a tuna casserole includes a nutritional boost of broccoli in a creamy basil sauce. To prepare the casserole ahead, make the sauce the day before and refrigerate. Assemble the dish no more than 4 hours ahead to prevent pasta from soaking up the sauce.

TIPS

If fresh basil is unavailable, substitute 2 tsp (10 mL) dried basil leaves and cook with onions.

For a vegetarian version, omit tuna and substitute 1 can (19 oz/540 mL) kidney beans, drained and rinsed.

Creamy Tuna Pasta Bake

Preheat oven to 350°F (180°C)
13-by 9-inch (3 L) baking dish, greased

2 tbsp	butter	25 mL
6	green onions, chopped	6
3	cloves garlic, finely chopped	3
4 cups	sliced mushrooms	1 L
1/2 tsp	salt	2 mL
1/2 tsp	freshly ground black pepper	2 mL
1/3 cup	all-purpose flour	75 mL
2 cups	milk or light (5%) cream	500 mL
1 1/2 cups	chicken stock	375 mL
3	tomatoes, seeded and diced	3
2/3 cup	freshly grated Parmesan cheese	150 mL
1/2 cup	chopped fresh basil	125 mL
12 oz	penne	375 g
4 cups	broccoli florets and chopped peeled stems	1 L
2	cans (each 6 1/2 oz/170 g) flaked tuna, drained	2
1 1/2 cups	soft fresh bread crumbs	375 mL
1 cup	shredded Asiago or mozzarella cheese	250 mL

1. In a Dutch oven or large saucepan, melt butter over medium-high heat. Cook green onions, garlic, mushrooms, salt and pepper, stirring occasionally, for 5 minutes or until softened.
2. In a bowl, whisk flour with 1 cup (250 mL) milk until smooth; add remaining milk. Add to pan along with stock. Bring to a boil, stirring, for 3 minutes or until sauce thickens. Remove from heat. Stir in tomatoes, Parmesan and basil. (Can be prepared to this point, covered and refrigerated for up to one day.)

3. In a large pot of boiling salted water, cook pasta for 7 minutes or until almost tender. Add broccoli; cook for 2 minutes or until broccoli is bright green and crisp, and pasta is just tender. Drain; chill under cold water. Drain well and return to pot. Stir in tuna and sauce. Spread in baking dish. (Casserole can be prepared to this point; cover and refrigerate for up to 4 hours before serving. Increase baking time by 15 minutes.)
4. In a bowl, combine bread crumbs and Asiago cheese; sprinkle over top. Bake in preheated oven for 40 to 45 minutes or until golden and center is piping hot.

SERVES 4 TO 6

This recipe takes an old standby to new heights. What's great, too, is that it keeps well in the fridge for up to two days before baking. Just pop it in the oven when you get home from work for an effortless meal. Serve with a crisp green salad.

TIP

To make ahead, cook noodles, rinse under cold water to chill; drain. Combine cold noodles and cold sauce; spoon into casserole dish, cover and refrigerate. Add crumb topping just before baking to prevent it from getting soggy.

Tuna Noodle Bake with Cheddar Crumb Topping

Preheat oven to 350°F (180°C)
13-by 9-inch (3 L) casserole dish, lightly greased

1 tbsp	butter	15 mL
8 oz	mushrooms, sliced	250 g
¾ cup	chopped green onions	175 mL
2 tbsp	all-purpose flour	25 mL
1	can (10 oz/284 mL) chicken broth, undiluted	1
1 cup	milk	250 mL
4 oz	cream cheese, softened	125 g
1	can (6½ oz/184 g) solid white tuna, drained and flaked	1
1 cup	frozen peas	250 mL
8 oz	broad egg noodles	250 g

CHEDDAR CRUMB TOPPING

½ cup	dry bread crumbs	125 mL
2 tbsp	melted butter	25 mL
1 cup	shredded Cheddar cheese	250 mL

1. In a saucepan, melt butter over medium heat. Add mushrooms and green onions; cook, stirring, for 3 minutes or until softened.
2. Blend in flour; pour in broth and milk. Bring to a boil, stirring constantly, until slightly thickened. Stir in cream cheese until melted. Add tuna and peas; cook 2 minutes more or until heated through. Remove from heat.
3. Cook noodles in a large pot of boiling water until tender but still firm. Drain well. Stir noodles into sauce. Spoon into prepared casserole dish.
4. Cheddar Crumb Topping: In a bowl, toss bread crumbs with melted butter; add Cheddar cheese. Just before baking, sprinkle topping over noodles.
5. Bake in preheated oven for about 30 minutes (10 minutes longer if refrigerated) or until top is golden.

SERVES 6

Vegetarians in your household will request this dish often and come to think of it as a comfort food. Its vibrant combination of Asian flavors tastes terrific and is nourishing, too. Any leftovers make a great next-day lunch.

TIP

Cut vegetables into uniform 2-inch (5 cm) lengths. This colorful pasta dish takes only a few minutes to cook, so have ingredients assembled before you start.

Spicy Noodles with Vegetables and Peanut Sauce

1/4 cup	peanut butter	50 mL
1/3 cup	water	75 mL
2 tbsp	soy sauce	25 mL
2 tbsp	lime juice	25 mL
2 tbsp	packed brown sugar	25 mL
1/4 tsp	hot pepper flakes or to taste	1 mL
1 tbsp	sesame oil	15 mL
2 tbsp	vegetable oil	25 mL
1 tbsp	minced fresh gingerroot	15 mL
2	cloves garlic, minced	2
1	leek, white and light green part only, cleaned and cut into matchstick strips	1
2	small Italian eggplants, cut into thin strips (about 2 cups/500 mL)	2
2	bell peppers (assorted colors), cut into thin strips	2
12 oz	linguine, broken into thirds	375 g
1/2 cup	chopped fresh cilantro or parsley	125 mL

1. In a small saucepan, combine peanut butter, water, soy sauce, lime juice, brown sugar, hot pepper flakes and sesame oil. Stir over medium heat until mixture is warm and smooth. Set aside.
2. In wok or large nonstick skillet, heat oil over high heat. Add ginger, garlic, leek and eggplant; cook, stirring, for 2 minutes. Add peppers; cook, stirring, for 1 minute more or until vegetables are just tender-crisp. Stir in peanut sauce until heated through.
3. Meanwhile, in a large pot of boiling salted water, cook linguine until tender but firm. Drain and return to pot. Toss with vegetables and peanut sauce until well coated; sprinkle with cilantro. Serve warm or at room temperature.

SERVES 8 TO 10

Planning a party — or going to one? This meatless dish is perfect to serve company or take along to a pot luck supper. It makes a large party dish or you can divide it into smaller portions and place into two 8-cup (2 L) baking dishes. Enjoy one now and freeze the other for another delicious meal.

Party Pasta with Mushrooms, Spinach and Tomato

Preheat oven to 350°F (180°C)
16-cup (4 L) baking dish, lightly greased

2 tbsp	butter	25 mL
1	medium onion, finely chopped	1
4	cloves garlic, minced	4
4 cups	sliced mushrooms	1 L
1 tsp	dried basil leaves	5 mL
1 tsp	dried oregano leaves	5 mL
1 tsp	dried marjoram leaves	5 mL
1 tsp	salt	5 mL
1/2 tsp	dried rosemary, crumbled	2 mL
1/2 tsp	freshly ground black pepper	2 mL
1/4 cup	all-purpose flour	50 mL
1 1/2 cups	milk	375 mL
2 cups	half-and-half (10%) cream	500 mL
1	can (28 oz/796 mL) tomatoes, including juice, chopped	1
2	packages (each 10 oz/300 g) fresh or frozen spinach, cooked, squeezed dry and chopped	2
1 lb	bow tie pasta (farfalle)	500 g
2 cups	shredded Fontina or Provolone cheese	500 mL
1/2 cup	freshly grated Parmesan cheese	125 mL

1. In a Dutch oven or large saucepan, melt butter over medium-high heat. Add onion, garlic, mushrooms, basil, oregano, marjoram, salt, rosemary and pepper; cook, stirring often, for 5 minutes or until softened.
2. In a bowl, blend flour with just enough milk to make a smooth paste; stir in remaining milk. Gradually add milk mixture and cream to mushroom mixture, stirring constantly, until sauce comes to a full boil and thickens.

3. Add tomatoes with juice and spinach; cook, stirring often, for 3 to 5 minutes, or until piping hot. Adjust seasoning with salt and pepper to taste. Let sauce cool to room temperature.
4. Meanwhile, cook pasta in a large pot of boiling salted water until tender but firm. Drain well. Return pasta to pot and stir in sauce until coated.
5. Place half the pasta in prepared baking dish. Sprinkle with half the Fontina and half the Parmesan cheese. Layer with rest of pasta and sprinkle with remaining Fontina and Parmesan cheese.
6. Bake, uncovered, in preheated oven for 40 to 45 minutes or until center is piping hot and top is lightly browned. Serve immediately.

SERVES 6

This hearty pasta dish, brimming with chunks of tasty sausage and colorful peppers, makes a delicious feast for any occasion.

VARIATION

Add ⅓ cup (75 mL) small black olives to the sauce along with the parsley for an added dimension of flavor. For a vegetarian version, omit the sausages.

Baked Penne with Italian Sausage and Sweet Peppers

Preheat oven to 350°F (180°C)
13-by 9-inch (3 L) baking dish, lightly greased

2 tbsp	olive oil, divided	25 mL
12 oz	hot or mild Italian sausages	375 g
3	bell peppers (assorted colors)	3
1	large onion, halved lengthwise and thinly sliced	1
2	cloves garlic, finely chopped	2
1 tsp	dried basil leaves	5 mL
1 tsp	dried oregano leaves	5 mL
½ tsp	salt	2 mL
½ tsp	hot pepper flakes or to taste	2 mL
1	can (28 oz/796 mL) plum tomatoes, including juice, chopped	1
¼ cup	chopped oil-packed sun-dried tomatoes (optional)	50 mL
¼ cup	chopped fresh parsley	50 mL
12 oz	penne or other small tube-shaped pasta	375 g
1½ cups	grated Fontina or mozzarella cheese	375 mL
⅓ cup	freshly grated Romano or Parmesan cheese	75 mL

1. Prick skins of sausages with a fork. In a Dutch oven or large saucepan, heat 1 tbsp (15 mL) oil over medium-high heat; cook sausages for 5 minutes or until browned on all sides. (Sausages will not be cooked through.) Remove from pan, cut into slices and reserve.
2. Add remaining oil to pan. Add peppers, onion, garlic, basil, oregano, salt and hot pepper flakes; cook, stirring often, for 7 minutes or until softened.

3. Return sausage slices to pan along with canned tomatoes with juice and sun-dried tomatoes, if using. Bring to a boil; reduce heat to medium-low; cover and simmer, stirring occasionally, for 20 minutes. Stir in parsley. Adjust seasoning with salt, if necessary.

4. Meanwhile, cook pasta in a large pot of boiling salted water until tender but firm. Drain well. Place half of the cooked pasta in prepared baking dish. Pour in half of the sauce. Layer again with remaining pasta and top with remaining sauce.

5. In a bowl, combine Fontina and Romano cheeses; sprinkle over top of casserole. Bake, uncovered, in preheated oven for 30 to 35 minutes or until cheese is melted and lightly colored.

SERVES 4

Here's a popular noodle dish you'll spot on many restaurant menus that is easy to recreate in your home kitchen.

TIP

Other pasta such as angel hair can be substituted. Cook noodles according to package directions before adding to recipe.

Singapore Noodles

6 oz	rice vermicelli	175 g
3 tbsp	soy sauce	45 mL
2 tsp	mild curry paste or powder	10 mL
2 tbsp	vegetable oil, divided	25 mL
1	red or green bell pepper, cut into thin strips	1
5	green onions, sliced	5
2	large cloves garlic, minced	2
3 cups	bean sprouts, rinsed and dried	375 mL
12 oz	cooked, peeled baby shrimp	375 g

1. In a large pot of lightly salted boiling water, cook noodles for 3 minutes. Drain; chill under cold water and drain well. Cut noodles using scissors into 3-inch (8 cm) lengths; set aside.
2. In a small bowl, combine soy sauce and curry paste; set aside.
3. Heat a wok or large nonstick skillet over high heat until very hot; add 1 tbsp (15 mL) oil, tilting wok to coat sides. Stir-fry pepper strips, green onions and garlic for 1 minute. Add bean sprouts and shrimp; stir-fry for 1 to 2 minutes or until vegetables are tender-crisp. Transfer to a bowl.
4. Add remaining oil to wok; when very hot, add noodles and soy sauce mixture. Stir-fry for 1 minute or until heated through. Return vegetable-shrimp mixture to wok and stir-fry for 1 minute more. Serve immediately.

SERVES 4 AS A MAIN COURSE OR 6 AS A SIDE DISH

Even when my pantry is almost empty, chances are I'll have a can of tomatoes and dried pasta on hand to whip up this easy supper dish.

TIP

Improvise if you don't have any fresh herbs by using 1 tsp (5 mL) each dried basil and dried oregano for the fresh basil and parsley.

VARIATION

Quick Creamy Tomato Sauce

Instead of the traditional accompaniment of freshly grated Parmesan cheese, toss hot pasta with 5 oz (150 g) creamy goat cheese, soft Brie or Gorgonzola, rind removed and cut into small pieces.

Spaghetti with Garlic Tomato Sauce

2 tbsp	olive oil	25 mL
3	cloves garlic thinly sliced, then coarsely chopped	3
1/4 tsp	hot pepper flakes	1 mL
1	can (28 oz/796 mL) plum tomatoes, including juice, chopped	1
	Salt and freshly ground black pepper	
Pinch	granulated sugar	Pinch
12 oz	spaghetti	375 g
2 tbsp	chopped fresh parsley	25 mL
2 tbsp	chopped fresh basil or chives	25 mL

1. In a large saucepan, heat oil over medium heat; stir in garlic and hot pepper flakes. Reduce heat to low; cook, stirring, for 1 minute or until garlic is light golden. (Do not let garlic brown or sauce will be bitter.)
2. Add tomatoes with juice; season with salt, pepper and sugar to taste. Bring to a boil, reduce heat and simmer, partially covered, stirring occasionally, for 15 minutes.
3. Cook pasta in a large pot of boiling salted water until tender but firm. Drain well; return to pot. Add tomato sauce, parsley and basil; toss well. Adjust seasoning with salt and pepper. Serve immediately.

SERVES 2 AS A MAIN DISH OR 4 AS A SIDE DISH

I like to use fusilli in this recipe because the sauce clings nicely to the corkscrew-shaped pasta, but feel free to use whatever pasta you have in your pantry.

TIP

You can make this 5-minute pasta sauce the day ahead and refrigerate. Reheat on stovetop or microwave before tossing with hot cooked pasta.

Fast Fusilli with Mushrooms and Peas

2 tsp	butter	10 mL
2 cups	sliced mushrooms	500 mL
2	green onions, sliced	2
4 oz	herb and garlic cream cheese	125 g
1 cup	frozen peas	250 mL
1/2 cup	milk	125 mL
1/3 cup	freshly grated Parmesan cheese	75 mL
8 oz	fusilli, penne or other tube-shaped pasta	250 g
	Salt and freshly ground black pepper	

1. In a large saucepan, melt butter over medium heat. Add mushrooms and green onions; cook, stirring, for 3 minutes or until softened. Add cream cheese, peas, milk and Parmesan; cook, stirring, for 2 minutes or until piping hot.
2. Cook pasta in a large pot of boiling salted water until tender but firm. Drain well. Stir into mushroom mixture; toss to coat well. Season with salt and pepper to taste. Serve immediately.

SERVES 4 AS A STARTER OR SIDE DISH

Toss this luxurious basil and walnut sauce with bow ties or any other interesting pasta shapes and get ready to entertain. It takes only 5 minutes to make and can be prepared a few hours ahead and reheated over low heat just before serving.

Creamy Bow Ties with Basil

1 tbsp	butter	15 mL
4	green onions, sliced	4
2	cloves garlic, finely chopped	2
1/4 cup	finely chopped walnuts	50 mL
1 cup	table (18%) cream	250 mL
1/3 cup	freshly grated Parmesan cheese	75 mL
8 oz	bow tie pasta (farfalle)	250 g
1/3 cup	chopped fresh basil	75 mL
	Salt and freshly ground black pepper	

1. In a large saucepan, melt butter over medium heat. Add green onions, garlic and walnuts; cook, stirring, for 2 minutes or until onions are softened. Stir in cream and Parmesan. Keep warm over low heat; do not let mixture boil.

2. Cook pasta in a large pot of boiling salted water until tender but firm. Drain well; add to cream sauce along with basil and toss to coat. Season with salt and pepper to taste. Serve immediately.

SERVES 8

This impressive dish, which features plenty of vegetables, appeals to both vegetarians and meat eaters.

TIP
To make ahead, cover and refrigerate for up to one day.

Baked Polenta with Roasted Vegetables

Preheat oven to 425°F (220°C)
2 baking sheets
13-by 9-inch (3 L) baking dish, greased

2	zucchini	2
1	small eggplant (about 1 lb/500 g)	1
1	red bell pepper	1
1	yellow bell pepper	1
1	large red onion	1
2 tbsp	olive oil	25 mL
1 1/2 tsp	dried rosemary, crumbled	7 mL
1/2 tsp	salt	2 mL
1/2 tsp	freshly ground black pepper	2 mL
1/4 cup	chopped fresh parsley	50 mL
	Garlic Polenta (recipe follows)	
2 cups	tomato pasta sauce	500 mL
2 cups	shredded mozzarella cheese	500 mL
1/3 cup	freshly grated Parmesan cheese	75 mL

1. Halve zucchini lengthwise and thickly slice. Cut eggplant into 1/2-inch (1 cm) slices, then cut into 1 1/2 inch (4 cm) pieces. Cut peppers into 1-inch (2.5 cm) pieces. Cut onion into thin lengthwise wedges. Arrange vegetables on baking sheets. Drizzle with oil; sprinkle with rosemary, salt and pepper. Roast in preheated oven, stirring occasionally, for 25 to 30 minutes or until tender. Transfer to a bowl; stir in parsley.
2. Cut prepared polenta in half crosswise; using two lifters, gently transfer one half to baking dish. Spread with half the tomato sauce, then half the vegetables and half the mozzarella and Parmesan cheeses. Repeat layers. (Can be prepared up to this point, covered and refrigerated for up to two days.) Bake in 350°F (180°C) oven for 50 to 60 minutes or until piping hot in center and cheese is melted.

Garlic Polenta

Baking sheet, greased

3	cloves garlic, minced	3
2 tsp	salt	10 mL
2 cups	cornmeal	500 mL
⅓ cup	freshly grated Parmesan cheese	75 mL
2 tbsp	butter	25 mL

1. In a Dutch oven or large saucepan, bring 7 cups (1.75 L) water, garlic and salt to a boil; gradually whisk in cornmeal until thickened. Reduce heat to low; cook, stirring often with wooden spoon, for 15 to 20 minutes or until polenta is thick enough to mound on spoon. Stir in Parmesan cheese and butter.

2. Spread onto prepared baking sheet; cover with plastic wrap. Refrigerate for 30 minutes or until firm.

MAKES ABOUT
½ CUP (125 ML)

Pesto keeps well for up to a week in the refrigerator or pack into a small airtight container and freeze for up to one month.

TIP

Whenever you use a spoonful of the pesto, cover the surface of the pesto with a bit more oil to seal in flavors.

Basil Pesto

1½ cups	lightly packed fresh basil leaves	375 mL
2	cloves garlic, coarsely chopped	2
3 tbsp	pine nuts or lightly toasted walnuts	45 mL
¼ cup	olive oil (approx.)	50 mL
¼ cup	freshly grated Parmesan cheese	50 mL
	Salt and freshly ground black pepper	

1. In a food processor, combine basil, garlic and pine nuts. While machine is running, add oil in a stream and process until smooth. Add a bit more oil if pesto appears dry.
2. Stir in Parmesan cheese; season with salt and pepper to taste. Place in a small container; cover with a thin layer of oil and refrigerate.

MAKES ABOUT
¾ CUP (175 ML)

For a fast dinner suggestion, toss this pesto with 8 oz (250 g) pasta, cooked according to package directions, or swirl it into soup for a wonderful burst of flavor.

TIP

If fresh basil is unavailable, increase parsley to 1 cup (250 mL) and add 1 tbsp (15 mL) dried basil.

Sun-Dried Tomato Pesto

½ cup	sun-dried tomatoes	125 mL
½ cup	lightly packed fresh basil (see Tip, left)	125 mL
½ cup	lightly packed fresh parsley	125 mL
1	large clove garlic	1
⅓ cup	vegetable stock	75 mL
2 tbsp	olive oil	25 mL
⅓ cup	freshly grated Parmesan cheese	75 mL
½ tsp	freshly ground black pepper	2 mL

1. In a bowl, cover sun-dried tomatoes with boiling water; let stand for 10 minutes or until softened. Drain and pat dry; chop coarsely.
2. In a food processor, combine rehydrated tomatoes, basil, parsley and garlic. With motor running, add stock and oil in a stream. Stir in Parmesan cheese and pepper.

Best-Ever Macaroni and Cheese (page 199) ➢

SERVES 4 AS A MAIN COURSE OR 6 AS A SIDE DISH

Traditional paella is made in a wide shallow pan, but today's nonstick skillet makes a very good substitute and reduces the amount of oil needed for this dish.

TIP

Try a variety of different vegetables, including bite-size pieces of broccoli, cauliflower, asparagus, green beans, bell peppers and zucchini.

Spanish Vegetable Paella

Preheat oven to 375°F (190°C)

4 cups	assorted prepared vegetables (see Tip, left)	1 L
3½ cups	chicken or vegetable stock	875 mL
¼ tsp	saffron threads, crushed	1 mL
Pinch	hot pepper flakes	Pinch
	Salt	
2 tbsp	olive oil	25 mL
4	green onions, chopped	4
3	large cloves garlic, finely chopped	3
1½ cups	short-grain white rice, such as Arborio	375 mL

1. Cook vegetables (except peppers and zucchini) in a saucepan of boiling, lightly salted water, for 1 minute. Rinse under cold water to chill; drain well.

2. In the same saucepan, bring stock to a boil. Add saffron and hot pepper flakes; season with salt to taste. Keep warm.

3. In a large nonstick skillet, heat oil over medium-high heat. Add green onions and garlic; cook, stirring, for 1 minute. Add vegetables to skillet; cook, stirring often, for 4 minutes or until lightly colored. Stir in rice and hot stock mixture. Reduce heat so rice cooks at a gentle boil: cook, uncovered, without stirring, for 10 minutes or until most of the liquid is absorbed.

4. Cover skillet with lid or foil. (If skillet handle is not ovenproof, wrap in double layer of foil.) Bake for 15 minutes or until all liquid is absorbed and rice is tender. Remove; let stand, covered, for 5 minutes before serving.

◄ Spaghetti with Meatballs (page 203)

SERVES 4 TO 6

Nutritionists recommend adding more grain to our diets. Here's a dish to serve to your family that is not only great-tasting, but wholesome besides.

TIP

Other nuts, such as skinned hazelnuts or unblanched almonds, can be substituted for the walnuts.

Mushroom Barley Pilaf

1 tbsp	butter	15 mL
2 cups	sliced mushrooms	500 mL
1	small onion, chopped	1
1/2 tsp	dried thyme or marjoram leaves	2 mL
1 cup	pearl barley, rinsed	250 mL
2 1/2 cups	chicken or vegetable stock (approx.)	625 mL
1/3 cup	finely chopped walnuts or pecans	75 mL
1/4 cup	freshly grated Parmesan cheese	50 mL
2 tbsp	chopped fresh parsley	25 mL
	Salt and freshly ground black pepper	

1. In a medium saucepan, heat butter over medium heat. Add mushrooms, onion and thyme; cook, stirring, for 5 minutes or until softened.

2. Stir in barley and stock; bring to a boil. Reduce heat, cover and simmer, stirring occasionally and adding more stock if necessary, for 30 minutes or until barley is tender.

3. Stir in walnuts, Parmesan and parsley; season with salt and pepper to taste.

SERVES 6 TO 8

This herb-infused rice makes the perfect accompaniment to a wide range of dishes. Try it with fish, chicken, beef, lamb or pork.

TIP

To save time, make ahead and reheat in the microwave before serving.

VARIATION

Saffron Rice Pilaf

Substitute ¼ tsp (1 mL) crushed saffron threads for the thyme.

Herbed Rice Pilaf

2 tbsp	butter	25 mL
1	small onion, finely chopped	1
1	clove garlic, minced	1
½ tsp	dried thyme leaves	2 mL
	Freshly ground black pepper	
1½ cups	long-grain white rice	375 mL
3 cups	chicken or vegetable stock	750 mL
1	small red bell pepper, finely diced	1
¼ cup	chopped fresh parsley	50 mL

1. In a large saucepan, melt butter over medium heat. Add onion, garlic, thyme and pepper; cook, stirring often, for 3 minutes or until softened.
2. Add rice and stock; bring to a boil. Reduce heat to low; cover and simmer for 15 minutes or until most of stock is absorbed.
3. Stir in red pepper; cover and cook for 7 to 9 minutes more or until rice is tender. Stir in parsley; let stand, uncovered, for 5 minutes.

Vegetable Fried Rice

SERVES 4

Use this recipe as a guide to create your own versions of fried rice, depending on what type of veggies you have in the fridge. With rice cooked ahead, it takes no time to prepare this quick supper dish.

TIPS

Instead of peas, try substituting blanched diced carrots, snow peas cut into 1-inch (2.5 cm) pieces, 1 zucchini, halved lengthwise and sliced, and small broccoli florets.

VARIATION

Chicken or Pork Fried Rice

Cut 8 oz (250 g) chicken breasts or lean boneless pork loin into thin strips. In a skillet, heat 1 tbsp (15 mL) oil over medium-high heat; cook meat, stirring, for 5 minutes or until no longer pink. Remove; keep warm. Continue with recipe as directed. Return meat to skillet with bean sprouts.

1 tbsp	vegetable oil	15 mL
3	green onions, chopped	3
1½ tsp	minced fresh gingerroot	7 mL
1	clove garlic, minced	1
3 cups	cold cooked rice	750 mL
1 cup	frozen peas	250 mL
½	red bell pepper, cut into thin strips, 1½ inches (4 cm) long	½
2 cups	bean sprouts	500 mL
2 tbsp	soy sauce	25 mL
1 tsp	mild curry paste or powder (optional)	5 mL

1. In a large nonstick skillet, heat oil over high heat. Add green onions, ginger and garlic; cook, stirring, for 15 seconds or until fragrant. Add rice, peas and pepper; cook, stirring often, for 5 to 7 minutes or until rice is heated through and vegetables are tender.

2. In a small bowl, combine soy sauce and curry paste, if using; stir into rice mixture along with bean sprouts. Cook, stirring, for 1 to 2 minutes or until heated through. Serve immediately.

SERVES 8

Oven-baked risotto makes an elegant and colorful dish that's perfect for entertaining.

TIP

To make ahead, cover and refrigerate for up to one day. Increase baking time by 10 minutes.

Baked Risotto with Spinach

Preheat oven to 350°F (180°C)
13-by 9-inch (3 L) baking dish, greased

2	packages (each 10 oz/300 g) fresh spinach	1
2	leeks, cut in half lengthwise, then sliced crosswise, rinsed	2
2 tbsp	butter, divided	25 mL
1/2 tsp	salt	2 mL
1/4 tsp	freshly ground black pepper	1 mL
1/4 tsp	freshly grated nutmeg	1 mL
2 1/2 cups	short-grain rice, such as Arborio	625 mL
3	cloves garlic, finely chopped	3
7 cups	hot chicken or vegetable stock	1.75 L
4 oz	herb and garlic cream cheese or herb goat cheese	125 g
1/2 cup	freshly grated Parmesan cheese	125 mL

1. Rinse spinach; remove tough ends. Place in Dutch oven with just enough water clinging to leaves; cook, over medium-high heat, stirring, until just wilted. Drain well and squeeze dry; finely chop.
2. In a large nonstick skillet, melt 1 tbsp (15 mL) butter over medium heat; cook leeks, stirring, for 3 minutes or until softened. Add spinach, salt, pepper and nutmeg; cook, stirring, for 5 minutes or until vegetables are tender.
3. In a Dutch oven, heat remaining butter over medium heat; cook rice and garlic, stirring, for 2 minutes. Add 5 cups (1.25 L) hot stock; bring to a boil. Reduce heat to medium-low, cover and simmer for 15 minutes or until rice is almost tender and most of liquid is absorbed.
4. Stir in remaining stock and herbed cream cheese until blended; add spinach mixture. Spread in baking dish. Sprinkle with Parmesan. Bake in oven for 25 to 30 minutes or until center is piping hot and top is light golden.

SERVES 4 TO 6

Risotto is hugely popular these days. And no wonder — its creamy appeal makes it a modern comfort food. It may seem intimidating to make at home, but it's easy to do provided you don't wander away from the stove. What else is key about risotto? It waits for no one, so call everyone to the table as you add the last ladle of stock to the saucepan.

TIP

A proper risotto is made with Italian short-grain rice, which has a relatively high starch content. As it cooks, it gives off the starch and the constant stirring results in a creamy, moist texture similar to porridge. Arborio rice is the most widely available short-grain variety; look for the word superfino on the package to ensure you are buying a superior grade. Vialone nano and carnaroli are two other types of short-grain Italian rice that make wonderful risotto. They are not quite as starchy as Arborio and require slightly less stock in cooking.

Wild Mushroom Risotto

5 cups	lightly salted chicken or vegetable stock (approx.)	1.25 L
2 tbsp	butter	25 mL
2 tbsp	olive oil	25 mL
1 lb	assorted mushrooms, such as cremini, shiitake and oyster, coarsely chopped	500 g
2	cloves garlic, minced	2
1 tbsp	chopped fresh thyme or 1 tsp (5 mL) dried	15 mL
1/4 tsp	freshly ground black pepper	1 mL
1	small onion, finely chopped	1
1 1/2 cups	short-grain rice, such as Arborio	375 mL
1/2 cup	white wine or stock	125 mL
1/3 cup	freshly grated Parmesan cheese	75 mL
	Salt	
2 tbsp	chopped fresh parsley	25 mL

1. In a large saucepan, bring stock to a boil; reduce heat to low and keep hot.
2. In a heavy-bottomed medium saucepan, heat 1 tbsp (15 mL) each oil and butter over medium heat. Add mushrooms, garlic, thyme and pepper; cook, stirring often, for 5 to 7 minutes or until tender. Remove and set aside.
3. Add remaining butter and oil to saucepan; cook onion, stirring, for 2 minutes or until softened. Add rice; stir for 1 minute. Add wine; stir until absorbed.
4. Add 1 cup (250 mL) hot stock; adjust heat to a simmer so stock bubbles and is absorbed slowly.

5. When absorbed, continue adding 1 cup (250 mL) stock at a time, stirring almost constantly, for 15 minutes. Add mushroom mixture; cook, stirring often, adding more stock when absorbed, until rice is just tender but slightly firm in the center. Mixture should be creamy; add more stock or water, if necessary. (Total cooking time will be 20 to 25 minutes.)
6. Add Parmesan cheese; adjust seasoning with salt and pepper to taste. Spoon into warm shallow serving bowls or onto plates. Sprinkle with parsley; serve immediately.

SERVES 4

Attractive and colorful, this classic Southern specialty relies on the flavors of tomato, celery, thyme and bay leaf. It's a spicy one-dish meal that takes only 30 minutes to cook.

TIP

Today supermarkets stock frozen shrimp already peeled and deveined — a convenient option for this recipe.

VARIATION

Skillet Sausage and Rice Creole

Substitute 12 oz (375 g) mild or hot Italian sausages for the shrimp. Cut sausages in half lengthwise. Place cut side down in skillet; cook over medium heat, turning occasionally, for 10 minutes or until no longer pink. Cut into thick slices; add to recipe as you would the shrimp.

Skillet Shrimp and Rice Creole

1 tbsp	vegetable oil	15 mL
1	large onion, chopped	1
2	cloves garlic, finely chopped	2
2	stalks celery, chopped	2
1/2 tsp	dried thyme leaves	2 mL
1	bay leaf	1
1 cup	long-grain white rice	250 mL
1	red bell pepper, diced	1
1	can (14 oz/398 mL) tomatoes, including juice, chopped	1
1 cup	fish or chicken stock	250 mL
1/2 tsp	salt	2 mL
Pinch	cayenne pepper	Pinch
2	small zucchini, halved lengthwise and thinly sliced	2
1 lb	large shrimp, peeled and deveined, tails left on	500 g

1. In a large nonstick skillet, heat oil over medium heat. Add onion, garlic, celery, thyme and bay leaf; cook, stirring, for 5 minutes or until softened.
2. Stir in rice and red pepper; cook for 2 minutes. Add tomatoes with juice, stock, salt and a generous pinch cayenne pepper. Bring to a boil; reduce heat, cover and simmer for 15 minutes. Stir in zucchini; bury shrimp in rice. Cover and cook for 8 minutes or until zucchini are tender and shrimp are pink and firm.

SERVES 4 TO 6

If you have a vegetarian in the family, you can count on this Indian-inspired dish with its bold seasonings as a reliable main-course dish. A bowlful makes a quick and easy supper.

TIP

For a meat-lover's version of this dish, add chopped leftover roast lamb, roast beef or baked ham for the last 10 minutes of cooking.

Indian-Style Lentils

1 tbsp	vegetable oil	15 mL
1	medium onion, chopped	1
3	cloves garlic, finely chopped	3
1 tbsp	minced fresh gingerroot	15 mL
2 tsp	ground cumin	10 mL
1 tsp	ground coriander	5 mL
½ tsp	salt	2 mL
	Freshly ground black pepper	
1 cup	green lentils, rinsed and sorted	250 mL
1	can (19 oz/540 mL) tomatoes, including juice, chopped	1
1½ cups	vegetable or chicken stock	375 mL
⅓ cup	chopped fresh cilantro or parsley	75 mL

1. In a large saucepan, heat oil over medium heat. Add onion, garlic, ginger, cumin, coriander, salt and pepper; cook, stirring, for 3 minutes or until softened.
2. Add lentils, tomatoes with juice and stock. Bring to a boil; reduce heat, cover and simmer for 35 minutes or until lentils are tender. Stir in cilantro; adjust seasoning with salt and pepper to taste.

SERVES 6

It's Friday night. You've worked hard all week. Don't even bother setting the table. Here's a supper dish that's easy to balance on your lap while you relax in front of the TV. As an added bonus, this dish goes great with a cold beer.

TIP

Any kind of smoked sausage or ham works well. The smaller-sized green Laird lentils hold their shape in cooking and are the kind I prefer for this recipe.

Bistro Lentils with Smoked Sausage

3 1/2 cups	chicken or vegetable stock (approx.)	875 mL
1 1/2 cups	lentils, rinsed and sorted	375 mL
1/2 tsp	dried thyme leaves	2 mL
2 tbsp	olive oil	25 mL
1 cup	diced red onions	250 mL
3	cloves garlic, finely chopped	3
2	carrots, peeled and diced	2
1 cup	diced fennel or celery	250 mL
1	red bell pepper, diced	1
2 tbsp	balsamic vinegar	25 mL
8 oz	smoked sausage, such as kielbasa, cut into 1/2-inch (1 cm) chunks	250 g
	Freshly ground black pepper	
1/4 cup	chopped fresh parsley	50 mL

1. In a large saucepan, bring stock to a boil over high heat. Add lentils and thyme; reduce heat to medium-low, cover and simmer for 25 to 30 minutes or until lentils are just tender but still hold their shape.

2. Meanwhile, heat oil in a large nonstick skillet over medium heat. Add onions, garlic, carrots and fennel; cook, stirring often, for 8 minutes. Add red pepper; cook, stirring, for 2 minutes more or until vegetables are just tender. Stir in vinegar; remove from heat.

3. Add vegetables and smoked sausage to lentils in saucepan; season with pepper to taste. Cover and cook for 5 to 8 minutes more or until sausage is heated through. (Add more stock or water, if necessary, to prevent lentils from sticking.) Stir in parsley. Serve warm or at room temperature.

SERVES 8

Here's an old-time favorite that stirs memories of the pioneer spirit. This rustic dish is a winter standby and wonderful when served with home-baked bread.

VARIATION

For a vegetarian version, omit bacon and cook onions and garlic in 2 tbsp (25 mL) vegetable oil.

Molasses Baked Beans

Preheat oven to 300°F (150°C)
12-cup (3 L) casserole dish or bean pot

1 lb	dried Great Northern or white pea beans, rinsed and picked over (about 2¼ cups/550 mL)	500 g
6	slices lean smoky bacon, chopped	6
1	large onion, chopped	1
3	cloves garlic, finely chopped	3
1	can (7½ oz/213 mL) tomato sauce	1
⅓ cup	fancy molasses	75 mL
¼ cup	packed brown sugar	50 mL
2 tbsp	balsamic vinegar	25 mL
2 tsp	dry mustard	10 mL
1 tsp	salt	5 mL
¼ tsp	freshly ground black pepper	1 mL

1. In a Dutch oven or large saucepan, combine beans with 6 cups (1.5 L) cold water. Bring to a boil over high heat; boil for 2 minutes. Remove from heat, cover and let stand for 1 hour.
2. Drain beans and cover with 8 cups (2 L) cold water. Bring to a boil; reduce heat, cover and simmer for 30 to 40 minutes or until beans are just tender but still hold their shape. Drain, reserving 2 cups (500 mL) cooking liquid. Place beans in casserole dish or bean pot.
3. Meanwhile, in a saucepan, cook bacon over medium heat, stirring often, for 5 minutes or until crisp. Drain all but 2 tbsp (25 mL) fat from pan. Add onion and garlic; cook, stirring, for 3 minutes or until softened.
4. Add 2 cups (500 mL) reserved bean-cooking liquid, tomato sauce, molasses, brown sugar, balsamic vinegar, mustard, salt and pepper. Stir into beans.
5. Cover and bake in preheated oven for 2½ to 3 hours or until most of liquid has been absorbed.

SERVES 8

A simple combo of beans and vegetables is a terrific side dish or main course that will delight not only the vegetarians in the crowd but everyone else as well. As a prelude to dinner, your home will be filled with the heavenly aroma of garlic from the crunchy crumb topping.

TIP

To make fresh bread crumbs, process 2 thick slices crusty bread in a food processor until fine.

Baked White Beans with Garlic Crumb Crust

Preheat oven to 350°F (180°C)
10-cup (2.5 L) shallow baking dish, greased

3 tbsp	olive oil	45 mL
2 cups	chopped Spanish onion	500 mL
3	cloves garlic, finely chopped	3
2 tbsp	balsamic vinegar	25 mL
5	tomatoes, seeded and diced	5
1 tbsp	chopped fresh thyme or 1 tsp (5 mL) dried thyme leaves	15 mL
1	large bay leaf	1
	Salt and freshly ground black pepper	
2	zucchini, halved lengthwise, thickly sliced	2
1	red bell pepper, diced	1
1	yellow bell pepper, diced	1
2	cans (each 19 oz/ 540 mL) white kidney beans, drained and rinsed	2

GARLIC CRUMB CRUST

1 ½ cups	soft fresh bread crumbs (see Tip, left)	375 mL
¼ cup	chopped fresh parsley	50 mL
2	cloves garlic, minced	2
2 tbsp	olive oil	25 mL

1. In a Dutch oven or large saucepan, heat oil over medium heat. Cook onions and garlic, stirring often, for 5 minutes or until softened. Add balsamic vinegar and cook until evaporated. Add tomatoes, thyme and bay leaf; season with salt and pepper. Bring to boil. Reduce heat, cover and simmer for 20 minutes.

2. Add zucchini and peppers; cook for 5 to 7 minutes or until vegetables are tender-crisp. Gently stir in beans.

3. Spoon mixture into prepared baking dish. (Can be prepared up to this point, covered and refrigerated for up to one day.)

4. Garlic Crumb Crust: In a bowl, combine bread crumbs, parsley and garlic. Drizzle with olive oil and toss to coat. Sprinkle crumb topping over beans; bake for 35 to 45 minutes or until bubbly and top is golden.

SERVES 8

Looking for a meal-in-one dish for a casual get-together? Count on this layered rendition of enchiladas to deliver raves when a gang descends to watch the big game on television.

TIP

To make ahead, cover and refrigerate for up to one day or overwrap in heavy-duty foil and freeze for up to one month. Let thaw completely in refrigerator for up to 24 hours. Increase baking time by 15 minutes.

Southwest Tortilla Vegetable Bake

Preheat oven to 350°F (180°C)
13-by 9-inch (3 L) baking dish, greased

1 tbsp	vegetable oil	15 mL
1	large onion, chopped	1
3	cloves garlic, minced	3
2	large green bell peppers, diced	2
2 tsp	dried oregano leaves	10 mL
2 tsp	ground cumin	10 mL
1	can (12 oz/341 mL) corn kernels, drained	1
1	jar (26 oz/700 mL) medium salsa	1
2	cans (each 19 oz/ 540 mL) black beans, drained and rinsed	2
2 tsp	chili powder	10 mL
8 oz	cream cheese, softened	250 g
3/4 cup	sour cream or yogurt	175 mL
1/2 cup	chopped fresh cilantro or parsley	125 mL
7	large 9-inch (23 cm) flour tortillas	7
2 cups	shredded mozzarella cheese	500 mL

1. In a large nonstick skillet, heat oil over medium heat; cook onion, garlic, peppers, oregano and cumin, stirring often, for 10 minutes or until vegetables are tender. Remove from heat; stir in corn and 1 1/2 cups (375 mL) salsa.
2. In a bowl, using a fork, mash beans with chili powder. In a separate bowl, blend cream cheese with sour cream; stir in cilantro.
3. Arrange three flour tortillas in prepared baking dish, covering bottom and sides. Spread with half the bean mixture; layer with half the vegetable and cream cheese mixtures. Top with two tortillas, tucking in sides. Repeat layers. Top with remaining two tortillas; spread with remaining salsa.
4. Sprinkle with cheese; cover loosely with foil. Bake in oven for 30 minutes. Uncover and bake for 25 minutes longer or until filling is bubbly. Let stand 5 minutes before cutting.

Vegetables

Fluffy Garlic Mashed Potatoes

SERVES 6

The secret to these creamy mashed potatoes is buttermilk. It adds a tangy flavor and keeps the potatoes moist so they reheat beautifully the next day.

6	large Russet or Yukon Gold potatoes (about 3 lbs/1.5 kg)	6
2 tbsp	butter or olive oil	25 mL
2	cloves garlic, finely chopped or more to taste	2
1/2 cup	milk	125 mL
3/4 cup	buttermilk or sour cream (approx.)	175 mL
	Salt and freshly ground black pepper or nutmeg	

1. Peel potatoes and cut into 3-inch (8 cm) chunks. In a large saucepan, cook potatoes in boiling salted water until tender, about 20 minutes or until fork-tender. (Yukon Gold potatoes take a few minutes longer.) Drain well and return to saucepan. Place over low heat and dry 1 to 2 minutes.
2. Press potatoes through a food mill or ricer or mash with potato masher or use an electric mixer at low speed until very smooth. (Do not use a food processor or the potatoes will turn into glue.)
3. In a small saucepan, heat butter and garlic over medium-low heat for 1 to 2 minutes; do not let garlic brown. Add milk and heat until piping hot. Beat garlic mixture into potatoes along with enough buttermilk or sour cream to make a smooth purée. Adjust seasoning with salt and pepper or nutmeg to taste.
4. Place over medium heat, stirring occasionally, until potatoes are piping hot. Can be made a few hours ahead and reheated. Beat in additional milk or buttermilk to make potatoes creamy, if necessary.

VARIATION

Roasted Garlic Mashed Potatoes

Beat in a whole bulb of roasted garlic (instead of fresh garlic) in the above recipe. It may seem like a lot, but once roasted, garlic loses its harsh taste and becomes very mild and buttery.

To roast garlic: Trim 1/4 inch (0.5 cm) off the larger stem end of a whole bulb of garlic. Place cut-side down on a sheet of foil. Drizzle with 2 tsp (10 mL) olive oil. Wrap and place in small casserole dish. Roast in 350°F (180°C) oven for about 45 minutes or until soft. Squeeze the whole garlic bulb so pulp slips out of skins; add to potatoes when mashing. I often roast several heads at a time and refrigerate the roasted garlic to use during the week.

Creamy Mashed Potato Casserole

SERVES 6

Everyone's favorite do-ahead mashed potato casserole — perfect for a roast turkey or roast beef family dinner. For lump-free mashed potatoes, use a food mill or ricer instead of a potato masher.

Preheat oven to 350°F (180°C)
8-cup (2 L) casserole dish, greased

6	large Russet potatoes, peeled and quartered (about 3 lbs/1.5 kg)	6
4 oz	cream cheese, softened, cubed	125 g
3/4 cup	hot milk (approx.)	175 mL
	Salt and freshly grated nutmeg	
1/2 cup	shredded Cheddar cheese	125 mL
1/4 cup	fine dry bread crumbs	50 mL
1/2 tsp	paprika	2 mL

1. Peel potatoes and cut into 3-inch (8 cm) chunks. In a large saucepan, cook potatoes in boiling salted water until tender, about 20 minutes or until fork-tender. (Yukon Gold potatoes take a few minutes longer.) Drain well and return to saucepan. Place over low heat and dry 1 to 2 minutes.
2. Press potatoes through a food mill or ricer or mash with potato masher or use an electric mixer at low speed until very smooth. (Do not use a food processor or the potatoes will turn into glue.)
3. In a small bowl, combine cheddar cheese, bread crumbs and paprika. Sprinkle evenly over potatoes.
4. Bake, uncovered, in oven for 40 to 50 minutes or until top is golden and a knife inserted in center is hot to the touch.

TIPS

Casserole can be prepared ahead, covered and refrigerated for up to two days. Increase baking time by 10 minutes.

The type of potatoes used determines how fluffy your mashed potatoes will be. The starchy Russet or baking variety produces fluffy mashed potatoes. Yellow-fleshed potatoes, such as Yukon Gold, have a slightly buttery taste and make delicious mashed potatoes with a creamier texture. Regular white potatoes also make a creamy purée, although not as flavorful. New potatoes are not suitable for mashing as they don't have the starch content of storage potatoes.

SERVES 4

I wouldn't dream of serving a baked ham without this favorite side dish. Use your food processor to quickly slice the potatoes.

TIP

To make ahead, layer potatoes in cream sauce in dish, cover and refrigerate for up to one day.

VARIATION

Scalloped Potatoes with Ham and Swiss Cheese

Add 8 oz (250 g) smoked ham, cut into 1-inch (2.5 cm) strips, along with potatoes in the sauce. Substitute Swiss Gruyère cheese for the Cheddar cheese.

Classic Scalloped Potatoes

Preheat oven to 350°F (180°C)
11-by 9-inch (2.5 L) baking dish, greased

2 tbsp	butter	25 mL
1	large onion, halved lengthwise, thinly sliced	1
2 tbsp	all-purpose flour	25 mL
1 1/2 cups	milk	375 mL
2 tsp	Dijon mustard	10 mL
1/2 tsp	salt	2 mL
Pinch	freshly grated nutmeg	Pinch
6	medium potatoes (about 2 lbs/1 kg)	6
1 cup	shredded aged Cheddar cheese	250 mL

1. In a saucepan, melt butter over medium heat. Cook onion, stirring often, for 3 minutes or until softened. Sprinkle with flour; stir in milk, mustard, salt and nutmeg. Bring to a boil, stirring, until sauce thickens.
2. Peel and thinly slice potatoes; rinse under cold water. Drain; wrap in dry clean towel to dry. Stir into sauce; bring to a boil over medium heat. Spoon into baking dish; sprinkle with cheese. Bake for 45 to 50 minutes or until potatoes are tender and top is golden.

SERVES 4 TO 6

Some people think there can never be enough potato recipes in a cookbook — and I agree. Potatoes are soothing, earthy and one of the best comfort foods around. No matter how you prepare them they always taste wonderful. Here's an update of a French classic with half the calorie-rich cream replaced by flavorful stock. It's a perfect accompaniment to a Sunday roast or as a main course dish served with a crisp tossed salad.

TIP

Recipe can easily be doubled and baked in a 13-by 9-inch (3 L) baking dish.

Gruyère Scalloped Potatoes

Preheat oven to 375°F (190°C)
11-by 9-inch (2.5 L) baking dish, greased

6	medium Russet or Yukon Gold potatoes (about 2 lbs/1 kg)	6
	Salt, freshly ground black pepper and grated nutmeg	
½ cup	chicken stock	125 mL
½ cup	whipping (35%) cream	125 mL
1	clove garlic, minced	1
1 cup	shredded Gruyère or Cheddar cheese	250 mL

1. Peel and thinly slice potatoes; rinse under cold water. Drain; wrap in dry clean towel to dry. Arrange slices in prepared baking dish. Season with salt, pepper and nutmeg.
2. In a small saucepan, bring stock, cream and garlic to a boil. (Or place in a large glass measure; microwave at High for 2½ minutes or until almost boiling.) Pour over potatoes. Cover with lid or foil.
3. Bake in preheated oven for 40 minutes. Sprinkle with cheese; bake, uncovered, for 20 to 25 minutes more or until cheese is bubbly and golden.

SERVES 6

These traditional Irish mashed potatoes are made with butter and green onions and are the perfect companion to a rich dark stew.

VARIATION

Instead of green onions, use ⅓ cup (75 mL) snipped fresh chives or parsley.

Champ

6	medium Russet or Yukon Gold potatoes, peeled and quartered (about 2 lbs/1 kg)	6
¾ cup	milk (approx.)	175 mL
¾ cup	chopped green onions	175 mL
2 tbsp	butter	25 mL
	Salt and freshly ground black pepper	
	Chopped green onion tops	

1. Peel potatoes and cut into 3-inch (8 cm) chunks. In a large saucepan, cook potatoes in boiling salted water until tender, about 20 minutes or until fork-tender. (Yukon Gold potatoes take a few minutes longer.) Drain well and return to saucepan. Place over low heat and dry 1 to 2 minutes.

2. Press potatoes through a food mill or ricer or mash with potato masher or use an electric mixer at low speed until very smooth. (Do not use a food processor or the potatoes will turn into glue.)

3. Meanwhile, in a small saucepan, combine milk, green onions and butter. Place over medium-low heat for 5 minutes, or until piping hot. Using an electric mixer, beat in milk mixture, adding more milk if necessary, until potatoes are creamy. Season with salt and pepper to taste.

4. Place pan over medium-low heat, if necessary, to reheat until piping hot. Spoon into serving bowl and sprinkle with green onion tops.

SERVES 6

With the shortcut microwave method, you'll also find this versatile dish a breeze to make for quick family suppers.

Easy Parmesan Potato Bake

Preheat oven to 375°F (190°C)
11-by 9-inch (2.5 L) baking dish, greased

6	medium potatoes, peeled and thinly sliced (about 2 lbs/1 kg)	6
1 cup	chicken or vegetable stock	250 mL
1 tbsp	melted butter or olive oil	15 mL
1	large clove garlic, minced	1
1/4 tsp	salt	1 mL
1/4 tsp	freshly ground black pepper	1 mL
1/3 cup	freshly grated Parmesan cheese	75 mL
1 tbsp	chopped fresh parsley	15 mL

1. Layer potatoes in prepared baking dish. In a large glass measuring cup, combine stock, butter, garlic, salt and pepper; pour over potatoes. Sprinkle with Parmesan and parsley.
2. Bake in oven for 50 to 60 minutes or until potatoes are tender and top is golden brown.

Quick Microwave-Broiler Method

1. Preheat broiler. Layer potatoes in baking dish; pour stock mixture over. Cover with lid or microwave-safe plastic wrap; turn back one corner to vent. Microwave at High for 8 minutes. Rearrange potatoes slices. Cover and microwave at High for another 6 to 8 minutes or until potatoes are tender when pierced with a fork. Sprinkle with Parmesan and parsley. Place under broiler, about 5 inches (12 cm) from heat; cook for 2 to 3 minutes or until nicely browned.

SERVES 4

You won't believe how fantastic these homemade French fries taste. This two-step frying method results in wonderfully crisp potatoes that are not greasy. Fry potato strips in a large saucepan on your stovetop or use an electric deep fryer, a nifty new kitchen appliance that takes the worry out of cooking with hot oil.

TIP

Place the fried potatoes on a heavy brown paper bag covered with paper towels to absorb the excess oil.

Perfect French Fries

Deep-fry thermometer

4	large or 6 medium Russet potatoes (about 2 lbs/1 kg)	4
8 cups	vegetable oil (approx.)	2 L
	Salt	

1. Peel potatoes and cut into long strips ½-inch by ½-inch (1 cm) in diameter. Rinse in several changes cold water to remove starch. Cover with cold water until ready to cook. Drain well; wrap in clean dry kitchen towel to dry potatoes thoroughly.

2. Place enough oil in a large saucepan to come 3-inches (8 cm) up sides of pan. Insert a deep-fry thermometer into oil; place over medium-high heat. Heat oil to 325°F (160°C).

3. Add potato strips in batches; fry for 8 to 10 minutes or until potatoes start to brown. Remove with slotted spoon and drain on paper towels. (Can be prepared up to this point 1 hour before serving; remove pan from heat.)

4. Place pan over high heat and reheat oil to 375°F (190°C). Add potatoes in batches; fry briefly for 1 to 2 minutes or until crisp and golden brown. Remove with slotted spoon; drain on paper towels. Season with salt; serve immediately.

SERVES 4

If you love French fries (and who doesn't?), but you're concerned about calories, here's the next best thing to deep frying.

TIP

Dark rimmed baking sheets attract the oven heat and will roast the potatoes faster and give them a more intense color than shiny aluminum ones.

Oven French Fries

Preheat oven to 450°F (230°C)
2 baking sheets, greased

4	large or 6 medium Russet potatoes (about 2 lbs/1kg)	4
2 tbsp	olive or vegetable oil	25 mL
	Salt	

1. Peel potatoes and cut into long strips ½-inch by ½-inch (1 cm) in diameter. Rinse in several changes cold water to remove starch. Cover with cold water until ready to cook. Drain well; wrap in clean dry kitchen towel to dry potatoes thoroughly.
2. Place potatoes on baking sheets; drizzle with oil and toss to coat evenly. Arrange in a single layer. Roast in oven for 25 to 30 minutes, stirring occasionally, until tender and golden brown.

SERVES 4

If you're like me, you'll come to rely on this breezy side dish as the perfect complement to a Sunday roast. I also like it with Quick Bistro-Style Steak (see recipe, page 98) and other grilled meats.

TIP

Peel the potatoes if you like, but I find the potatoes are tastier with the skin left on.

Roasted Garlic Potatoes

Preheat oven to 400°F (200°C)
13-by 9-inch (3 L) baking dish, greased

4	large Russet potatoes, scrubbed and cut into 1-inch (2.5 cm) chunks (about 2 lbs/1 kg)	4
2 tbsp	olive oil	25 mL
4	cloves garlic, slivered	4
	Salt and freshly ground black pepper	
1 tbsp	chopped fresh parsley	15 mL

1. Cook potato chunks in a large saucepan of boiling salted water for 5 minutes; drain well. Spread in baking dish. Drizzle with oil and garlic; season with salt and pepper to taste.
2. Roast for 40 minutes, stirring occasionally, until potatoes are tender and golden. Sprinkle with parsley.

SERVES 4

This classic comfort food, called kugel, is a staple in Jewish cooking. It's a delicious accompaniment to roasted meats and chicken.

TIP

Wrapping the grated potatoes in a clean dry towel gets rid of excess starch. Make sure to grate potatoes just before using since they discolor quickly.

Potato Pudding

Preheat oven to 350°F (180°C)
8-inch (2 L) square baking dish, well-greased

2	eggs	2
2 tbsp	all-purpose flour	25 mL
1 tbsp	chopped fresh parsley	15 mL
1	large clove garlic, minced	1
3/4 tsp	salt	4 mL
1/4 tsp	freshly ground black pepper	1 mL
1	medium onion	1
6	medium potatoes (about 2 lbs/1 kg)	6
1 tbsp	vegetable oil	15 mL

1. In a bowl, beat eggs; stir in flour, parsley, garlic, salt and pepper. Using a food processor, grate onion; fold into egg mixture.
2. Peel potatoes; wash and cut into quarters. Grate using a food processor. Wrap in a large clean kitchen towel; squeeze out excess moisture. Stir into onion mixture until combined. (Do this quickly before potatoes discolor.)
3. Spread in baking dish. Drizzle with oil and spread evenly. Bake in oven for about 1 hour or until top is nicely browned. Cut into squares and serve.

SERVES 4 AS MAIN COURSE OR 6 AS SIDE DISH

Don't even bother with meat. This melt-in-the-mouth veggie dish is a scrumptious meal in itself. Hearty potatoes, sweet tomatoes and delicate zucchini are heavenly when sprinkled with a golden cheese and crumb topping.

TIP

Just add warm crusty bread to this vegetable medley for an easy supper.

Tomato, Zucchini and Potato Bake

Preheat oven to 350°F (180°C)
13-by 9-inch (3 L) baking dish, lightly greased

4	medium ripe tomatoes	4
	Salt	
2 tbsp	olive oil	25 mL
4	medium potatoes, peeled and thinly sliced (about 1 1/2 lbs/750 g)	4
1	medium onion, thinly sliced	1
3	cloves garlic, finely chopped	3
1 1/2 tsp	dried Italian herbs or dried oregano leaves	7 mL
	Freshly ground black pepper	
3	small zucchini, thinly sliced (about 1 lb/500 g)	3
1 cup	shredded Gruyère, Provolone or mozzarella cheese	250 mL
1/4 cup	freshly grated Parmesan cheese	50 mL
1/2 cup	soft fresh bread crumbs	125 mL
1/4 cup	finely chopped fresh parsley	50 mL

1. Halve tomatoes crosswise and squeeze out seeds. Thinly slice and place on paper towels to drain. Season lightly with salt.
2. In a large nonstick skillet, heat oil over medium heat. Add potatoes, onion, garlic and Italian herbs; cook, stirring often, for 8 to 10 minutes or until potatoes are softened. Season with salt and pepper.
3. Layer half the sliced tomatoes, half the zucchini and half the potato mixture in prepared baking dish. Repeat layers again in same order. (The recipe can be prepared to this point up to one day ahead, then covered and refrigerated.)
4. In a bowl, combine cheeses, bread crumbs and parsley; sprinkle over top.
5. Bake in preheated oven for 40 to 45 minutes or until top is golden and vegetables are tender.

SERVES 4

Baked potatoes stuffed with a variety of fillings is a popular meal in my house. I make them ahead for those nights when everyone is on a different schedule. The potatoes need only a quick reheat in the microwave as each person walks through the door for an instant supper.

TIPS

To oven bake potatoes: Place in 400°F (200°C) oven for 1 hour or until potatoes give slightly when squeezed.

To microwave: Arrange potatoes in a circle 1-inch (2.5 cm) apart on a paper towel. Microwave at High, turning halfway through cooking, until potatoes are just tender when pierced with a skewer. Microwave cooking times at High: 1 potato, 4 to 5 minutes; 2 potatoes, 6 to 8 minutes; 4 potatoes, 10 to 12 minutes.

For moist potatoes wrap cooked potatoes individually in foil. For drier potatoes, wrap in a dry towel. Let stand 5 minutes.

Beef-Stuffed Spuds

Preheat oven to 400°F (200°C)
13-by 9-inch (3 L) baking dish

4	large baking potatoes (each 10 oz/300 g)	4
8 oz	lean ground beef or veal	250 g
1/3 cup	finely chopped onions	75 mL
1	clove garlic, minced	1
1 tsp	Worcestershire sauce	5 mL
	Salt and freshly ground black pepper	
1/2 cup	sour cream, plain yogurt or buttermilk (approx.)	125 mL
1 cup	shredded Cheddar cheese	250 mL
2 tbsp	chopped fresh parsley	25 mL

1. Scrub potatoes well and pierce skins with a fork in several places to allow steam to escape. Bake or microwave potatoes (see Tips, left).
2. In a large nonstick skillet over medium-high heat, cook beef, breaking up with a wooden spoon, for 4 minutes or until no longer pink.
3. Reduce heat to medium. Add onions, garlic and Worcestershire sauce; season with salt and pepper. Cook, stirring often, for 4 minutes or until onions are softened.
4. Cut warm potatoes in half lengthwise. Carefully scoop out each potato, leaving a 1/4-inch (0.5 cm) shell; set shells aside.
5. In a bowl, mash potatoes with potato masher or fork; beat in enough sour cream until smooth. Stir in beef mixture, half the cheese and all the parsley; season with salt and pepper to taste. Spoon into potato shells; top with remaining cheese.
6. Arrange in baking dish; bake in preheated oven for 15 minutes or until cheese is melted. Or place on microwave-safe rack or large serving plate; microwave at Medium-High for 5 to 7 minutes or until heated through and cheese melts.

SERVES 4

These delicious baked potatoes are great to pack along to work if you have the use of a microwave for reheating.

TIP

Cheddar and broccoli are a classic combo, but get adventurous with whatever cheese and vegetables are in the fridge. Another favorite is mozzarella cheese and lightly sautéed mushrooms and diced red peppers seasoned with basil.

Broccoli and Cheese-Stuffed Potatoes

Preheat oven to 400°F (200°C)
13-by 9-inch (3 L) baking dish

4	large baking potatoes (each 10 oz/300 g)	4
3 cups	small broccoli florets and peeled, chopped stems	750 mL
½ cup	sour cream, plain yogurt or buttermilk (approx.)	125 mL
2	green onions, chopped	2
1 ⅓ cups	shredded Cheddar or Gruyère cheese	325 mL
	Salt and cayenne pepper	

1. Scrub potatoes well and pierce skins with a fork in several places to allow steam to escape. Bake or microwave potatoes (see Tips, page 251).
2. In a saucepan, cook or steam broccoli until just tender-crisp. (Or place in covered casserole and microwave at High for 3 minutes.) Drain well.
3. Cut a thin slice from tops of warm potatoes. Scoop out potato leaving a ¼-inch (0.5 cm) shell, being careful not to tear the skins.
4. In a bowl, mash potato with potato masher or fork; beat in enough sour cream until smooth. Add broccoli, green onions and 1 cup (250 mL) cheese. Season with salt and a dash of cayenne pepper to taste.
5. Spoon filling into potato shells, mounding the tops. Arrange in shallow baking dish; sprinkle with remaining cheese. Bake in preheated oven for 20 minutes or until cheese melts. Or place on a microwave-safe rack and microwave at Medium-High for 5 to 7 minutes or until heated through and cheese melts.

SERVES 6

I love the way oven-roasting sweetens and concentrates the flavors of these sturdy root vegetables. This dish is a natural with stew and mashed potatoes.

TIP

We're used to roasting potatoes, so moving onto other vegetables isn't that much of a shift in our cooking style. Try this treatment with other vegetables such as peppers, winter squash, beets, cauliflower and even asparagus. You'll be amazed with the results. Use oil instead of butter and add a sprinkling of dried herbs, if you like. Reduce cooking time according to the size and type of vegetables.

Oven-Roasted Root Vegetables

Preheat oven to 400°F (200°C)
13-by 9-inch (3 L) baking dish, lightly greased

3	medium carrots	3
2	medium parsnips	2
½	small rutabaga (about 8 oz/250 g)	½
1	medium red onion, cut into wedges	1
2	cloves garlic, cut into slivers	2
¼ cup	dry sherry or chicken stock	50 mL
2 tbsp	melted butter	25 mL
½ tsp	salt	2 mL
¼ tsp	freshly ground black pepper	1 mL
2 tbsp	finely chopped fresh parsley	25 mL

1. Peel carrots, parsnips and rutabaga; cut into 2-by ½-inch (5 by 1 cm) strips. Place in prepared baking dish along with onion and garlic.
2. In a small bowl, combine sherry and butter; drizzle over vegetables. Sprinkle with salt and pepper.
3. Cover dish with foil; bake for 30 minutes. Remove foil; bake for 25 to 30 minutes more, stirring occasionally, until vegetables are tender and light golden. Sprinkle with parsley before serving.

SERVES 6

Snowy cauliflower topped with cheese and nuts makes the perfect side dish for a Sunday roast. For vegetarians, it becomes a main course dish when served along with grains or a bowl of pasta.

TIP

Sprinkle the garlic-crumb mixture over other vegetables such as broccoli, Brussels sprouts or spinach. Unblanched almonds, pecans or walnuts can replace the hazelnuts.

Cauliflower with Hazelnut Crumb Topping

Preheat broiler
12-by 8-inch (2.5 L) shallow baking dish, lightly greased

2 tbsp	butter	25 mL
1/4 cup	hazelnuts, finely chopped	50 mL
1/2 cup	soft fresh bread crumbs	125 mL
1	large clove garlic, minced	1
1/2 cup	finely shredded Gruyère or aged Cheddar cheese	125 mL
2 tbsp	chopped fresh parsley	25 mL
1	medium cauliflower, broken into florets	1

1. In a medium skillet, melt butter over medium heat. Add hazelnuts and cook, stirring, for 1 minute or until lightly toasted. Add bread crumbs and garlic; cook, stirring, for 1 minute more or until crumbs are lightly colored. Remove from heat; let cool.
2. In a bowl, combine crumb mixture, cheese and parsley.
3. In a large saucepan of boiling salted water, cook cauliflower for 3 to 5 minutes or until tender-crisp. Drain well. Place in baking dish; sprinkle with crumb mixture. Place under preheated broiler for 1 to 2 minutes or until topping is lightly browned.

SERVES 6

This hearty vegetable dish is reminiscent of Swiss cheese fondue. It can even stand in for a light, satisfying supper when paired with crusty bread and a tossed salad.

TIP

Nutmeg is a key flavoring in this dish. Whole nutmeg is preferable to the pre-ground variety. Find it in the spice section of supermarkets and use a special grater available in kitchenware shops.

Cauliflower Fondue Bake

Preheat oven to 375°F (190°C)
8-inch (2 L) square baking dish, greased

1	medium cauliflower, broken into florets	1
2 tbsp	butter	25 mL
2 tbsp	all-purpose flour	25 mL
1/2 cup	milk	125 mL
1/2 cup	dry white wine	125 mL
1 1/2 cups	shredded Gruyère cheese	375 mL
	Salt and freshly grated nutmeg (see Tip, left)	

1. In a large saucepan of boiling salted water, cook cauliflower for 3 to 5 minutes or until tender-crisp. Drain well; place in baking dish.
2. In the same saucepan, melt butter over medium heat; blend in flour and cook, stirring, for 15 seconds or until bubbly. Whisk in milk in a stream; cook until smooth and very thick. Whisk in wine in a stream; cook, stirring, until thickened and bubbly. Reduce heat to low; gradually add cheese, a handful at a time, stirring, until cheese melts and sauce is smooth. Season with salt and generous pinch of nutmeg to taste. Sauce will be thick.
3. Pour evenly over cauliflower. (The dish can be prepared to this point up to a day ahead; cover and refrigerate.) Bake for 20 to 25 minutes (up to 10 minutes longer, if refrigerated) or until cauliflower is just tender and top is lightly browned.

SERVES 6

This simple vegetable side dish appears at all our family gatherings including Christmas and Thanksgiving. It's a hit with everybody. Serve the cheese sauce with other vegetables including cauliflower and Brussels sprouts.

TIP

Hot milk is the secret to lump-free sauce; microwave milk at High for 2 minutes.

Steamed Broccoli with Cheddar Cheese Sauce

8-cup (2 L) casserole dish

8 cups	broccoli stems and florets (1 large bunch)	2 L
2 tbsp	butter	25 mL
2 tbsp	all-purpose flour	25 mL
1 cup	hot milk	250 mL
1 cup	shredded aged Cheddar cheese	250 mL
	Salt and cayenne pepper	

1. Steam broccoli for 5 minutes or until just tender. Drain well and place in casserole dish.
2. Meanwhile, in a small saucepan, melt butter over medium heat. Whisk in flour, stirring, for 15 seconds or until foamy. Whisk in milk in a stream.
3. Bring to boil; cook, stirring, for 1 minute or until thickened. Reduce heat to low and whisk in cheese, until melted. Season with salt and pinch of cayenne pepper to taste. Pour over broccoli and serve immediately.

Broccoli and Cheese-Stuffed Potatoes (page 252) ➢

SERVES 6

When locally grown asparagus appears at the market, it's one of my rites of spring. I prepare them tossed with crunchy almonds and melting Parmesan — and it's every bit as pleasing as a buttery Hollandaise.

TIP

Try making this dish with green beans. Trim and cut into 1½-inch (4 cm) lengths and cook in boiling water for about 5 minutes or until tender-crisp.

Asparagus with Parmesan and Toasted Almonds

1½ lbs	asparagus	750 g
¼ cup	sliced blanched almonds	50 mL
2 tbsp	butter	25 mL
2	cloves garlic, finely chopped	2
¼ cup	freshly grated Parmesan cheese	50 mL
	Salt and freshly ground black pepper	

1. Snap off asparagus ends; cut spears on the diagonal into 2-inch (5 cm) lengths. In a large nonstick skillet, bring ½ cup (125 mL) water to a boil; cook asparagus for 2 minutes (start timing when water returns to a boil) or until just tender-crisp. Run under cold water to chill; drain and reserve.
2. Dry the skillet and place over medium heat. Add almonds and toast, stirring often, for 2 to 3 minutes or until golden. Remove and reserve.
3. Increase heat to medium-high. Add butter to skillet; cook asparagus and garlic, stirring, for 4 minutes or until asparagus is just tender.
4. Sprinkle with Parmesan; season with salt and pepper. Transfer to serving bowl; top with almonds.

◄ Asparagus with Parmesan and Toasted Almonds (see recipe above)

SERVES 4

Roasting brings out the best in many vegetables including asparagus. The oven-roasting method is much simpler and more flavorful than the traditional way of cooking asparagus in a steamer.

Oven-Roasted Asparagus

Preheat oven to 425°F (220°C)
Baking sheet, greased

1 lb	asparagus	500 g
1 tbsp	olive oil	15 mL
	Salt and freshly ground black pepper	
1 tbsp	balsamic vinegar	15 mL

1. Snap off tough asparagus ends. If large, peel stalks. Arrange in single layer on prepared baking sheet. Drizzle with oil; season with salt and pepper.
2. Roast in oven, stirring occasionally, for 12 to 15 minutes or until almost tender.
3. Drizzle balsamic vinegar over asparagus and toss to coat. Roast for 3 to 5 minutes more or until tender-crisp. Serve immediately.

SERVES 4

This is a favorite dish to make in late summer when young beans and ripe tomatoes are at their best. But even in winter, with vine-ripened greenhouse tomatoes and imported fresh beans, this recipe is still good. If bits of tomato skin in the sauce bother you, peel the tomatoes before dicing.

TIP

For a quick supper, toss vegetable sauce with 8 oz (250 g) cooked pasta, such as penne, and sprinkle generously with Parmesan cheese. Also substitute other vegetables, such as fennel, asparagus or broccoli, for the beans.

Green Beans Stewed with Tomatoes

1 lb	green beans	500 g
1 tbsp	olive oil	15 mL
1	small red onion, halved lengthwise, thinly sliced	1
2	cloves garlic, thinly sliced	2
1 tsp	dried basil leaves	5 mL
2	ripe tomatoes, diced	2
1 tbsp	balsamic vinegar	15 mL
2 tbsp	water (approx.)	25 mL
1/4 tsp	salt	1 mL
1/4 tsp	freshly ground black pepper	1 mL

1. Trim ends of beans; cut into 1 1/2-inch (4 cm) lengths. In a saucepan, cook beans in lightly salted boiling water, for 3 minutes (start timing when water returns to a boil) or until still crisp. Drain well; reserve.
2. Meanwhile, in a large nonstick skillet, heat oil over medium heat. Add onion, garlic and basil; cook, stirring, for 2 minutes or until softened.
3. Stir in tomatoes, vinegar, water, salt and pepper; cook, stirring often, for 3 minutes or until sauce-like.
4. Add beans; cover and simmer for 8 to 10 minutes, stirring occasionally, until tender. Add more water, if necessary, to keep mixture moist. Serve warm or at room temperature.

SERVES 4 TO 6

Fresh corn is a real summer treat. Serve this tasty summer side dish with grilled meats.

TIP

Fresh corn works best, but frozen kernels can be substituted. To cut corn kernels from cobs, stand ears on end and cut straight down using a small sharp knife.

Easy Skillet Corn with Tomatoes and Basil

2 tsp	vegetable or olive oil	10 mL
3	green onions, sliced	3
1	small green bell pepper, diced	1
3 cups	uncooked corn kernels (about 5 ears of corn)	750 mL
2	tomatoes, seeded and diced	2
2 tbsp	chopped fresh basil leaves or 1 tsp (5 mL) dried	25 mL
Pinch	granulated sugar	Pinch
	Salt and freshly ground black pepper	

1. In a large nonstick skillet, heat oil over medium-high heat. Add green onions, green pepper, corn, tomatoes and basil (if using dried); cook, stirring often, for 5 to 7 minutes (8 to 10 minutes, if using frozen corn) or until corn is tender.
2. Add sugar; season with salt and pepper to taste. Sprinkle with chopped basil (if using fresh).

SERVES 4

This is one of my favorite choices to accompany a holiday roast or turkey. Packages of ready-to-cook, peeled whole baby carrots are widely available in supermarkets. They certainly make a cook's life easier — especially when you're preparing a mammoth family dinner and plan to serve several dishes.

TIPS

If doubling the recipe, glaze vegetables in a large nonstick skillet to evaporate the stock quickly.

Try this tasty treatment with a combination of blanched carrots, rutabaga and parsnip strips, too.

Lemon-Glazed Baby Carrots

1 lb	peeled baby carrots	500 g
1/4 cup	chicken or vegetable stock	50 mL
1 tbsp	butter	15 mL
1 tbsp	packed brown sugar	15 mL
1/2 tsp	grated lemon zest	2 mL
1 tbsp	fresh lemon juice	15 mL
1/4 tsp	salt	1 mL
	Freshly ground black pepper	
1 tbsp	finely chopped fresh parsley or chives	15 mL

1. In a medium saucepan, cook carrots in boiling salted water for 5 to 7 minutes (start timing when water returns to a boil) or until just tender-crisp; drain and return to saucepan.
2. Add stock, butter, brown sugar, lemon zest and juice, salt and pepper to taste. Cook, stirring often, for 3 to 5 minutes or until liquid has evaporated and carrots are nicely glazed.
3. Sprinkle with parsley or chives and serve.

SERVES 4

Use this recipe as a guideline and then get creative with whatever vegetables you have in the fridge. You'll need about 5 cups (1.25 L) in total.

TIPS

Vegetables that take longer to cook, such as carrots, broccoli and cauliflower, should be added to the skillet first before adding quick-cooking ones like peppers and zucchini.

You can also toss the cooked vegetables with 4 oz (125 g) cooked spaghettini for an easy pasta supper.

Teriyaki Vegetable Stir-Fry

2 tbsp	teriyaki or soy sauce	25 mL
2 tbsp	water	25 mL
1 tbsp	rice vinegar	15 mL
2 tsp	packed brown sugar	10 mL
1 tsp	cornstarch	5 mL
1	large clove garlic, minced	1
1 tbsp	vegetable oil	15 mL
2 cups	small cauliflower or broccoli florets	500 mL
1	red bell pepper, cut into 2-inch (5 cm) strips	1
2	small zucchini, halved lengthwise and thinly sliced	2

1. In a glass measuring cup, combine teriyaki sauce, water, vinegar, brown sugar, cornstarch and garlic; set aside.
2. In a wok or large nonstick skillet, heat oil over high heat. Add cauliflower and cook, stirring, for 1 minute. Add red pepper and zucchini; cook, stirring, for 2 minutes.
3. Reduce heat to medium. Stir teriyaki sauce and add to skillet. Cook, stirring, until sauce is slightly thickened. Cover and cook for 1 minute or until vegetables are tender-crisp.

SERVES 4 TO 6

I love the combination of sweet potatoes and apples accented with maple syrup. It's great served with pork or chicken.

TIP

You can make this vegetable dish a day ahead; cover and refrigerate. To reheat, cover and microwave at High until piping hot.

VARIATION

Instead of sweet potatoes, use 2 lbs (1 kg) butternut squash, peeled and seeds removed.

Microwave Sweet Potato Purée with Apples

8-cup (2 L) casserole dish, greased

1 tbsp	butter	15 mL
1	small onion, chopped	1
3	sweet potatoes, peeled and cut into 1½-inch (4 cm) chunks (about 2 lbs/1 kg)	3
2	apples, peeled, cored and chopped	2
¼ cup	maple syrup	50 mL
	Salt, freshly ground black pepper and grated nutmeg	

1. In casserole dish, combine butter and onion; microwave at High for 2 minutes or until onion is softened. Add sweet potatoes and apples; drizzle with maple syrup. Cover and microwave at High for 20 to 25 minutes, stirring once, until sweet potatoes are very tender.
2. In a food processor, purée in batches until smooth. Place in a serving dish; season with salt, pepper and nutmeg to taste.

SERVES 6

Team this creamy vegetable dish with a simple roast of pork or chicken with crispy potato wedges.

Creamed Spinach and Mushroom Bake

Preheat oven to 375°F (190°C)
Shallow 8-cup (2 L) baking dish, greased

2	packages (each 10 oz/300 g) fresh spinach	2
2 tbsp	butter	25 mL
1	leek, white and light green part only, chopped	1
8 oz	shiitake or portobello mushrooms, sliced and chopped	250 g
1 cup	whipping (35%) cream	250 mL
1 tsp	grated orange zest	5 mL
	Salt, freshly ground black pepper and grated nutmeg	

CRUMB TOPPING

1/2 cup	fresh baguette bread crumbs	125 mL
1/3 cup	shredded Gruyère or Parmesan cheese	75 mL
1/4 cup	finely chopped walnuts	50 mL

1. Rinse spinach in cold water; remove large stems. Place in Dutch oven or large saucepan with just enough water clinging to leaves; cook, over medium-high heat, stirring, until just wilted. Drain well and squeeze dry; finely chop.
2. In a large nonstick skillet, heat butter over medium-high heat. Cook leeks and mushrooms, stirring, for 5 minutes or until tender. Stir in spinach, cream and orange zest. Cook until piping hot. Season with salt, pepper and nutmeg to taste. Transfer to baking dish. (Can be prepared up to this point, covered and refrigerated for two days.)
3. Crumb Topping: In a bowl, combine bread crumbs, cheese and walnuts. Sprinkle over spinach. Bake in oven for about 30 minutes or until top is golden and center is piping hot.

SERVES 4

If the soft texture of a squash purée doesn't appeal to you, try this easy stir-fry instead.

TIP

To prepare squash, peel using a vegetable peeler or paring knife. Cut into lengthwise quarters and seed. Cut into thin ¼-inch (0.5 cm) by 1½-inch (4 cm) pieces.

Butternut Squash with Snow Peas and Red Pepper

1 tbsp	vegetable oil	15 mL
5 cups	prepared butternut squash (see Tip, left)	1.25 L
4 oz	snow peas, ends trimmed	125 g
1	red bell pepper, cut into thin strips	1
1 tbsp	packed brown sugar	15 mL
1½ tsp	grated fresh gingerroot	7 mL
	Salt and freshly ground black pepper	

1. In a large nonstick skillet, heat oil over medium-high heat. Cook squash, stirring, for 3 to 4 minutes or until almost tender.
2. Add snow peas, pepper, brown sugar and ginger. Cook, stirring often, for 2 minutes or until vegetables are tender-crisp. Season with salt and pepper to taste.

SERVES 4

For a modern spin of an Oktoberfest dinner, spoon cabbage in center of serving plates and top with grilled sausages or smoked pork chops.

Sweet-and-Spicy Cabbage

1	large pear or apple	1
2 tbsp	vegetable oil	25 mL
1/2	red onion, cut into thin wedge strips	1/2
1/2 tsp	hot pepper flakes or to taste	2 mL
1/2	small Savoy cabbage, finely shredded	1/2
2 tbsp	rice vinegar	25 mL
1 tbsp	liquid honey	15 mL
	Salt	

1. Cut pear into quarters and core (not necessary to peel). Thinly slice, then cut slices in half.

2. In a large nonstick skillet, heat oil over high heat until almost smoking. Add pear, onion and hot pepper flakes; stir-fry for 1 minute. Add cabbage and stir-fry for 1 minute more or until wilted.

3. Stir in rice vinegar and honey; cook, stirring, for 30 seconds. Season with salt to taste; serve immediately.

SERVES 8

I consider this recipe a convenience food. I keep containers of sweet-and-sour red cabbage in my freezer, ready to microwave at a moment's notice to serve along with pork chops or roasts.

TIPS

Depending on how sweet-and-sour you like your red cabbage, add more brown sugar and vinegar to taste. Most cooked red cabbage recipes, this one included, call for vinegar or wine. This adds not only flavor, but acidity, which preserves the cabbage's bright red color.

To freeze, pack cabbage into containers; it freezes well for up to three months.

Sweet-and-Sour Red Cabbage with Apples

2 tbsp	butter	25 mL
1	large onion, finely chopped	1
2	apples, peeled, cored and diced	2
1 cup	chicken or vegetable stock	250 mL
1/2 cup	red wine or additional stock	125 mL
1/3 cup	red wine vinegar	75 mL
1/3 cup	packed brown sugar	75 mL
1	bay leaf	1
1/2 tsp	salt	2 mL
1/4 tsp	ground cinnamon	1 mL
1/4 tsp	freshly ground black pepper	1 mL
Pinch	ground cloves	Pinch
1	medium red cabbage, finely shredded (about 10 cups/2.5 L)	1
1 1/2 tsp	cornstarch	7 mL
1 tbsp	cold water	15 mL

1. In a Dutch oven or large saucepan, heat butter over medium heat. Add onion and apples; cook, stirring often, for 5 minutes or until softened.
2. Add stock, wine, vinegar, brown sugar, bay leaf, salt, cinnamon, pepper and ground cloves. Bring to a boil; stir in cabbage.
3. Cover and simmer over medium-low heat, stirring occasionally, for 45 minutes or until cabbage is tender.
4. Blend cornstarch with water; stir into cabbage. Cook 3 minutes more or until sauce is slightly thickened. Remove bay leaf before serving.

SERVES 4

This colorful vegetable medley is a great summer side dish.

TIP

To toast the pine nuts, place in dry skillet over medium heat, stirring, for 3 to 4 minutes.

Cherry Tomato and Zucchini Sauté with Basil

1 tbsp	olive oil	15 mL
3	small zucchini, halved lengthwise and thinly sliced	3
2 cups	cherry tomatoes, halved	500 mL
1/2 tsp	ground cumin (optional)	2 mL
2	green onions, sliced	2
2 tsp	balsamic vinegar	10 mL
	Salt and freshly ground black pepper	
2 tbsp	chopped fresh basil or mint	25 mL
2 tbsp	lightly toasted pine nuts (optional)	25 mL

1. In a large nonstick skillet, heat oil over high heat. Add zucchini and cook, stirring, for 1 minute. Add cherry tomatoes, cumin, if using, green onions and balsamic vinegar. Cook, stirring, for 1 to 2 minutes or until zucchini is tender-crisp and tomatoes are heated through. Season with salt and pepper to taste.
2. Sprinkle with basil and pine nuts, if using, and serve immediately.

Salads

ALL ABOUT OLIVE OIL

Olive oil is the pressed juice from olives, a fruit, and there are dozens of varieties, each with its own distinct flavor and characteristics.

Olive oils add not only great flavor to foods, they have certain health advantages. Rich in monounsaturated fats, olive oils reduce the level of harmful cholesterol in our blood and at the same time leave the good cholesterol intact.

There are two grades of oil available in our market. *Extra virgin olive oil* is the best quality, retaining the fresh, natural flavor of the olives with a maximum acidity level of 1% oleic acid. It's ideal for cooking, salads and flavoring dishes before serving. *Regular olive oil* comes from olives that have been refined to produce a colorless and flavorless oil. Virgin olive oil is added to give it some added character. It is used primarily in cooking. "Light" olive oil is not lighter in calories, only in flavor. It's a refined oil and overpriced when compared to other quality oils in the same price bracket. If you want a mild-flavored oil, mix vegetable oil with some good-quality extra virgin instead.

What to look for in an oil

Olives oils are a lot like wines — there are many to choose from and they vary greatly in price and quality. Sample a variety to decide what appeals most to your taste buds, as well as budget.

- Read the bottle label to help you make an informed choice. Lower-priced brands of oils, although bottled in a particular country, are often a blend from several different countries in the Mediterranean. The more expensive olive oils, however, often include the name of the producer and region, along with a vintage date on their labels.

- Don't judge an oil by its color. Oils range from buttery yellow to vivid green depending on the olive variety and stage of ripeness at harvest time. Color does, however, give a clue to flavor. Generally, light-colored oils are more subtle than the robust darker oils.

- Olive oil loses it flavor and color over time, so use soon after purchase. Store oils in a cool, dark place, away from direct light. Do not store in the refrigerator. When properly capped, oil will keep for one year.

SERVES 6

The king of tossed salads was named after a Tijuana restaurateur by the name of Caesar Cardini. Here, mayonnaise gives this classic salad an even creamier texture than the original.

TIPS

Raw or coddled eggs are considered taboo in salads because they may contain salmonella bacteria. Mayonnaise is used instead.

Make sure salad greens are washed and dried thoroughly, preferably in a salad spinner, for best results. Homemade croutons make a definite flavor difference but 3 cups (750 mL) store-bought croutons work in a pinch.

Caesar Salad

1/3 cup	olive oil	75 mL
2 tbsp	light mayonnaise	25 mL
2 tbsp	fresh lemon juice	25 mL
2 tbsp	water	25 mL
1 tsp	Dijon mustard	5 mL
2	cloves garlic, minced	2
3	anchovy fillets, chopped or 1 tbsp (15 mL) anchovy paste	3
1/4 tsp	freshly ground black pepper	1 mL
1	large head Romaine lettuce, torn into bite-size pieces (about 12 cups/3 L)	1
6	slices bacon, cooked crisp and crumbled (optional)	6
	Garlic croutons (see recipe below)	
1/3 cup	freshly grated Parmesan cheese	75 mL
	Salt	

1. In a food processor, combine oil, mayonnaise, lemon juice, water, mustard, garlic, anchovy fillets and pepper; process until smooth and creamy.
2. Arrange lettuce in salad bowl; pour dressing over and toss lightly. Add croutons; sprinkle with crumbled bacon, is using, and Parmesan cheese. Toss again. Taste and season with salt and pepper, if needed. Serve immediately.

Garlic Croutons

Preheat oven to 375°F (190°C)

4 cups	cubed crusty bread, cut into 1/2-inch (1 cm) pieces	1 L
2 tbsp	olive oil	25 mL
1	clove garlic, minced	1
2 tbsp	freshly grated Parmesan cheese	25 mL

1. Place bread cubes in a bowl. Combine oil and garlic; drizzle over bread cubes and toss. Sprinkle with Parmesan and toss again. Arrange on baking sheet in single layer. Toast in preheated oven, stirring once, for about 10 minutes or until golden.

SERVES 8 TO 10

Remember the layered salads of the 1950s — the ones made with shredded iceberg lettuce, sliced cooked eggs and frozen peas crowned with heavy mayonnaise? This updated version layers colorful vegetables that accent the flavors of Greece with a garlic-yogurt dressing and feta cheese topping.

TIP

To serve, spoon down through the vegetable layers so each serving has a little bit of everything.

To ripen tomatoes, see Tip, page 50.

Layered Greek Salad

4 cups	plain yogurt	1 L
2	cloves garlic, minced	2
2 tbsp	olive oil	25 mL
2 tbsp	red wine vinegar	25 mL
1 tsp	salt	5 mL
1 tsp	granulated sugar	5 mL
1 tsp	dried oregano leaves	5 mL
1/4 tsp	freshly ground black pepper	1 mL
1	small head Romaine lettuce, shredded (about 8 cups/2 L, packed)	1
1	small Spanish onion, diced	1
1	red bell pepper, diced	1
1	green bell pepper, diced	1
1/2	seedless cucumber, cubed	1/2
1/4 cup	chopped fresh parsley	50 mL
1 1/2 cups	crumbled feta cheese (about 6 oz/175 g)	375 mL
2	ripe tomatoes, cut into wedges	2
12	Kalamata olives	12

1. Place yogurt in cheesecloth-lined sieve set over a bowl. Cover and refrigerate for 4 hours or until reduced to about 2 1/2 cups (625 mL). Transfer to bowl; discard whey. Stir in garlic, oil, vinegar, salt, sugar, oregano and pepper.
2. Line bottom of 8- or 9-inch (20 or 23 cm) round glass salad bowl with lettuce. Next, layer separately the onion, red pepper, green pepper and cucumber.
3. Spread top with yogurt mixture. Refrigerate, loosely covered, for 8 hours or overnight. Sprinkle with parsley and feta. Garnish with tomato wedges and olives.

SERVES 6 TO 8

The vegetables can be prepared earlier in the day and refrigerated. Toss them with the vinaigrette just before serving to prevent them from getting waterlogged.

Summer Garden Salad

2 pints	cherry tomatoes, halved or quartered, if large	1 L
1	red bell pepper, diced	1
1	yellow bell pepper, diced	1
1	green bell pepper, diced	1
1	sweet onion, such as Vidalia, coarsely chopped	1
½	seedless cucumber, quartered lengthwise, thickly sliced	½
⅓ cup	olive oil	75 mL
¼ cup	sherry or red wine vinegar	50 mL
½ tsp	salt	2 mL
¼ tsp	freshly ground black pepper	1 mL
⅓ cup	coarsely chopped fresh parsley	75 mL

1. In a large serving bowl, combine tomatoes, peppers, onion and cucumber.

2. In another bowl, whisk together oil, vinegar, salt and pepper.

3. Just before serving, pour vinaigrette over vegetables; sprinkle with parsley. Serve immediately.

yes

Spinach, Mushroom and Carrot Salad

SERVES 6 TO 8

This party salad is not complicated to make, neither is it expensive to prepare. But the flavors make it special enough to serve for company — with tangy lime juice, mustard and cumin balancing the sweetness of raisins and carrots.

TIP

This colorful salad can be made up to 4 hours ahead and refrigerated. Add the dressing and toss just before serving.

VARIATION

Use ¾ tsp (4 mL) dried fines herbes instead of cumin.

1	package (10 oz/300 g) fresh spinach, stemmed and coarsely chopped (about 8 cups/2 L)	1
1½ cups	sliced mushrooms	375 mL
2 cups	peeled shredded carrots	500 mL
1½ cups	seedless cucumber, halved lengthwise and sliced	375 mL
1	small red onion, thinly sliced	1
⅓ cup	dark raisins	75 mL

DRESSING

¼ cup	olive oil	50 mL
2 tbsp	fresh lime juice	25 mL
1 tbsp	liquid honey	15 mL
2 tsp	Dijon mustard	10 mL
¾ tsp	ground cumin	4 mL
1	clove garlic, minced	1
½ tsp	salt	2 mL
¼ tsp	freshly ground black pepper	1 mL

1. In a serving bowl, layer one-third of the shredded spinach, all the sliced mushrooms, another one-third of the spinach, all the shredded carrots, then remaining spinach. Layer cucumbers, onion and raisins over top. Cover and refrigerate up to 4 hours.
2. Dressing: In a bowl, whisk together oil, lime juice, honey, mustard, cumin, garlic, salt and pepper. Just before serving, drizzle over salad and toss gently.

SERVES 4

There are so many wonderful mushroom varieties in supermarkets these days. Feel free to use any mushroom combination, depending on what's available, when you make this earthy starter or luncheon salad. Select apple varieties, such as Cortland or Granny Smith, which resist browning when sliced.

TIPS

Most produce stores sell mixes of exotic greens, but you can make your own mixture using radicchio, arugula and oak leaf lettuces.

Toast walnuts in a 350°F (180°C) oven for 7 to 9 minutes.

VARIATION

Instead of goat cheese, use brie or a creamy blue cheese.

Warm Mushroom and Goat Cheese Salad

6 cups	Mesclun or mixed salad greens	1.5 L
1	large apple, quartered and cored	1
1	goat cheese log (5 oz/150 g) cut into 8 slices	1
2 tbsp	olive oil	25 mL
8 oz	cremini mushrooms, thickly sliced	250 g
4 oz	assorted mushrooms, such as oyster, shiitake and porcini, thickly sliced	125 g
½ cup	sliced green onions	125 mL
¼ cup	liquid honey	50 mL
¼ cup	cider vinegar	50 mL
¼ tsp	salt	1 mL
¼ tsp	freshly ground black pepper	1 mL
½ cup	coarsely chopped toasted walnuts	125 mL

1. Divide salad greens among four plates. Cut apple quarters into 8 thin slices; arrange in a circle in middle of each plate. Place 2 slices goat cheese in center of each circle. (Can be done shortly before serving, covered and refrigerated.)

2. In a large nonstick skillet, heat oil over medium-high heat. Cook mushrooms, stirring, for 3 to 5 minutes or until tender.

3. Add green onions, honey, vinegar, salt and pepper; cook, stirring, for 15 seconds or until hot. Remove from heat. Spoon warm mushroom mixture over salad greens. Sprinkle with walnuts. Serve immediately.

SERVES 4

You'll find that kids love this stir-fry version of a cabbage salad — and so will you. It's a great way to appreciate this nutritious and economical vegetable.

TIP

Buy a convenient bag of shredded cabbage at your supermarket and this salad is made in no time.

Warm Bacon Cabbage Slaw

1/4 cup	sour cream or plain yogurt	50 mL
2 tbsp	light mayonnaise	25 mL
2 tbsp	cider vinegar	25 mL
1 tbsp	Dijon mustard	15 mL
1 tbsp	packed brown sugar	15 mL
4	slices bacon, chopped	4
4 cups	shredded green cabbage	1 L
2	stalks celery, sliced	2
3	green onions, sliced	3
	Salt and freshly ground black pepper	

1. In a small bowl, whisk together sour cream, mayonnaise, vinegar, mustard and brown sugar.
2. In large nonstick skillet over medium-high heat, cook bacon, stirring, for 3 minutes or until crisp. Transfer to paper towels to drain. Drain all but 2 tsp (10 mL) fat from skillet. Add cabbage, celery and green onions; cook, stirring, for 2 to 3 minutes or until cabbage is wilted.
3. Remove from heat; stir in sour cream mixture. Sprinkle with bacon; season with salt and pepper to taste. Serve immediately.

SERVES 6

A family barbecue and picnic calls for a generous bowl of old-fashioned cabbage slaw with a creamy mayonnaise-mustard dressing.

VARIATION

Waldorf Coleslaw

Substitute 2 chopped large stalks celery for the carrots, add 2 diced apples and 3/4 cup (175 mL) walnuts.

Creamy Coleslaw

8 cups	finely shredded green cabbage	2 L
5	green onions, sliced	5
2	carrots, peeled and shredded	2
2 tbsp	chopped fresh parsley	25 mL
1/2 cup	light mayonnaise	125 mL
2 tbsp	liquid honey	25 mL
2 tbsp	cider vinegar	25 mL
1 tbsp	Dijon mustard	15 mL
1/2 tsp	celery seeds (optional)	2 mL
1/2 tsp	salt	2 mL
1/4 tsp	freshly ground black pepper	1 mL

1. In a serving bowl, combine cabbage, green onions, carrots and parsley.
2. In another bowl, stir together mayonnaise, honey, vinegar, mustard, celery seeds, if using, salt and pepper. Pour over cabbage mixture; toss to coat well. Refrigerate until ready to serve.

SERVES 4

This delectable grilled salad can be made with whatever vegetables you have on hand. Other vegetables suggestions include sliced baby eggplant, thickly sliced fennel or thick asparagus spears.

TIP

Soak bamboo skewers in cold water for 15 minutes to prevent them from burning when grilling the vegetables.

Grilled Vegetable Salad

Preheat barbecue
Bamboo skewers

1	Vidalia onion	1
1	red bell pepper	1
1	yellow bell pepper	1
3	small zucchini	3

DRESSING

2 tbsp	olive oil	25 mL
1 tbsp	balsamic vinegar	15 mL
1 tbsp	red wine vinegar	15 mL
1 tsp	Dijon mustard	5 mL
1	large clove garlic, minced	1
1 tbsp	finely chopped fresh parsley	15 mL
2 tsp	finely chopped fresh rosemary or thyme leaves	10 mL
1/2 tsp	salt	2 mL
1/2 tsp	freshly ground black pepper	2 mL

1. Slice onion into four rounds; insert small bamboo skewers through slices to prevent them from falling apart when grilling. Cut peppers into quarters; remove ribs and seeds. Cut zucchini crosswise into halves and then cut each piece in half lengthwise. Arrange vegetables on a baking sheet.
2. Dressing: In a bowl, combine oil, vinegars, mustard, garlic, parsley, rosemary, salt and pepper. Brush vegetables with vinaigrette and let marinate at room temperature for 30 minutes or for up to 4 hours.
3. Place on greased grill over medium-high heat; grill for 12 to 15 minutes, turning occasionally; remove vegetables as they become tender-crisp. Transfer to a serving platter; serve warm or at room temperature.

SERVES 6

Bean salad is another staple we've grown up with over the years. Originally this salad used canned string beans, but fresh beans give it a new lease on taste, as does the addition of fiber-packed chickpeas.

VARIATION

Instead of chickpeas, you can try canned mixed beans. This includes a combination of chickpeas, red and white kidney beans and black-eyed peas. It's available in supermarkets.

Bean Salad with Mustard-Dill Dressing

1 lb	green beans	500 g
1	can (19 oz/540 mL) chickpeas, drained and rinsed	1
1/3 cup	chopped red onions	75 mL

DRESSING

2 tbsp	olive oil	25 mL
2 tbsp	red wine vinegar	25 mL
1 tbsp	Dijon mustard	15 mL
1 tbsp	granulated sugar	15 mL
1/4 tsp	salt	1 mL
1/4 tsp	freshly ground black pepper	1 mL
2 tbsp	finely chopped fresh dill	25 mL

1. Trim ends of beans; cut into 1-inch (2.5 cm) lengths. In a large pot of boiling salted water, cook beans for 3 to 5 minutes (start timing when water returns to a boil) or until tender-crisp. Drain; rinse under cold water to chill. Drain well.
2. In a serving bowl, combine green beans, chickpeas and onions.
3. Dressing: In a small bowl, whisk together oil, vinegar, mustard, sugar, salt and pepper until smooth. Stir in dill.
4. Pour over beans and toss well. Refrigerate until serving time.

MAKES ½ CUP (125 ML)

Why buy expensive bottled salad dressings when it's so convenient to have this great-tasting salad dressing on hand? Make a double batch and store in a covered container in the refrigerator to use at a moment's notice.

French Salad Dressing

⅓ cup	olive or vegetable oil	75 mL
2 tbsp	red wine vinegar	25 mL
1½ tsp	Dijon mustard	7 mL
1	clove garlic, minced	1
1 tsp	dried fines herbes	5 mL
Pinch	granulated sugar	Pinch
	Salt and freshly ground black pepper	

1. In a bowl, stir together oil, vinegar, mustard, garlic and fines herbes. Season with sugar, salt and pepper to taste. Store in covered jar in the refrigerator.

SERVES 6

When preparing this dish ahead, I like to keep the blanched green beans, tomatoes and dressing separate and toss them just before serving to prevent the salad from getting soggy.

TIP

Use the terrific mustardy dressing with other favorite vegetable salad mixtures and crisp greens.

Green Bean and Plum Tomato Salad

1 lb	young green beans, trimmed	500 g
8	small plum tomatoes (about 1 lb/500 g)	8
2	green onions, sliced	2

DRESSING

1/4 cup	olive oil	50 mL
4 tsp	red wine vinegar	20 mL
1 tbsp	grainy mustard	15 mL
1	clove garlic, minced	1
1/2 tsp	granulated sugar	2 mL
1/4 tsp	salt	1 mL
1/4 tsp	freshly ground black pepper	1 mL
1/4 cup	chopped fresh parsley	50 mL

1. In a medium saucepan of boiling salted water, cook beans for 3 to 5 minutes or until just tender-crisp. Drain and rinse under cold water to chill; drain well. Pat dry with paper towels or wrap in a clean, dry towel.
2. Cut plum tomatoes in half lengthwise; using a small spoon, scoop out centers. Cut each piece again in half lengthwise; place in a bowl. Just before serving, combine beans, tomatoes and green onions in a serving bowl.
3. Dressing: In a small bowl, whisk together oil, vinegar, mustard, garlic, sugar, salt and pepper. Stir in parsley. Pour dressing over salad and toss well.

SERVES 6

If anything signals the arrival of summer days and backyard barbecues, it's a trusty potato salad. My version goes beyond tossing potatoes with mayonnaise. In this recipe, warm potatoes are steeped in a tasty marinade before mayonnaise is introduced. The result? A summertime family favorite.

TIP

You can also add 3 chopped hard-cooked eggs and ¾ cup (175 mL) frozen peas, rinsed under hot water and drained well.

Best-Ever Potato Salad

6	new medium potatoes (about 2 lbs/1 kg)	6
2 tbsp	red wine vinegar	25 mL
1 tbsp	Dijon mustard	15 mL
1	clove garlic, minced	1
4	green onions, sliced	4
2	stalks celery, diced	2
¼ cup	chopped fresh parsley or dill	50 mL
½ cup	light mayonnaise	125 mL
¼ cup	sour cream or plain yogurt	50 mL
½ tsp	salt	2 mL
	Freshly ground black pepper	

1. In a medium saucepan of boiling salted water, cook whole potatoes for 20 to 25 minutes until just tender. Drain; when cool enough to handle, peel and cut into ½-inch (1 cm) cubes. Place in a serving bowl.
2. In a small bowl, stir together vinegar, mustard and garlic; pour over warm potatoes and toss gently. Let cool to room temperature. Stir in onions, celery and parsley.
3. In a bowl, combine mayonnaise, sour cream, salt and pepper to taste. Fold into potato mixture until evenly coated. Refrigerate until serving time.

SERVES 6

Here, I've borrowed ingredients from the popular Caesar salad dressing to give new potatoes a tasty twist. If you like, cook or microwave 4 bacon strips until crisp, then crumble and sprinkle over salad along with the parsley.

TIPS

Refrigerate the salad if making ahead, but let it come to room temperature before serving.

Use potatoes the same size so they cook evenly.

Caesar Potato Salad

2 lbs	small new potatoes, scrubbed	1 kg
1/4 cup	light mayonnaise	50 mL
2 tbsp	olive oil	25 mL
2 tbsp	fresh lemon juice	25 mL
2 tsp	Dijon mustard	10 mL
1 1/2 tsp	anchovy paste or 2 minced anchovy fillets	7 mL
1 tsp	Worcestershire sauce	5 mL
1	large clove garlic, minced	1
	Salt and freshly ground black pepper	
	Romaine lettuce	
2 tbsp	chopped fresh parsley	25 mL

1. In a large saucepan of boiling salted water, cook potatoes for 15 minutes or until just tender when pierced. Drain; let cool slightly. Cut into halves or quarters. Place in a bowl.
2. In a small bowl, whisk together mayonnaise, oil, lemon juice, mustard, anchovy paste, Worcestershire sauce and garlic; season with salt and pepper to taste. Pour over warm potatoes; gently toss to coat. Cover and refrigerate up to 4 hours.
3. Arrange in a lettuce-lined serving bowl; sprinkle with parsley.

SERVES 4 TO 6

Why settle for take-out at your supermarket deli when you can make this chunky potato and egg salad flecked with dill pickles? Add crusty rolls and sliced cold cuts for a ready-to-go picnic lunch.

TIP

Can be prepared ahead, covered and refrigerated, for up to two days.

Deli Egg and Potato Salad

1 1/2 lbs	small new potatoes	750 g
1/3 cup	light mayonnaise	75 mL
1/3 cup	sour cream	75 mL
1 tbsp	grainy mustard	15 mL
1/2 tsp	salt	2 mL
1/4 tsp	freshly ground black pepper	1 mL
4	hard-cooked eggs, chopped (see Tip, page 72)	4
1/2 cup	diced celery	125 mL
1/2 cup	diced dill pickle	125 mL
3	green onions, sliced	3
2 tbsp	chopped fresh dill or parsley	25 mL

1. In a saucepan of lightly salted boiling water, cook potatoes for 15 minutes or until tender. Drain; when cool enough to handle, cut into 1/2-inch (1 cm) cubes.
2. In a bowl, combine mayonnaise, sour cream, mustard, salt and pepper. Fold in potatoes, eggs, celery, pickles, onions and dill; stir gently until coated.

Italian Pasta Salad

SERVES 6

Pasta salads are always a hit. They brighten up a buffet, backyard barbecue or your dinner table. Served with Herbed Garlic Bread (see recipe, page 92), this salad is a meal in itself.

8 oz	pasta such as fusilli or penne	250 g
4 oz	Provolone cheese, cut into small cubes	125 g
1 cup	cherry tomatoes, halved or quartered, if large	250 mL
1/3 cup	diced red onions	75 mL
1/2	large red bell pepper, cut into thin 1 1/2-inch (4 cm) strips	1/2
1/2	large green bell pepper, cut into thin 1 1/2-inch (4 cm) strips	1/2
1/3 cup	Kalamata olives (optional)	75 mL
1/3 cup	finely chopped fresh parsley	75 mL
DRESSING		
1/4 cup	olive oil	50 mL
2 tbsp	red wine vinegar	25 mL
1 tbsp	Dijon mustard	15 mL
1	large clove garlic, minced	1
1 tsp	dried basil leaves	5 mL
1 tsp	dried oregano leaves	5 mL
1/2 tsp	salt	2 mL
1/4 tsp	freshly ground black pepper	1 mL

1. Cook pasta in a large pot of boiling salted water until tender but still firm. Drain; rinse under cold water and drain well.
2. In a large serving bowl, combine pasta, cheese cubes, tomatoes, onions, peppers, olives and parsley.
3. Dressing: In a bowl, combine oil, vinegar, mustard, garlic, basil, oregano, salt and pepper.
4. Pour dressing over pasta mixture; toss until well-coated. Let stand at room temperature for up to 30 minutes, allowing flavors to blend. Refrigerate if making ahead.

TIP

Dried basil and oregano can be replaced with 1 tbsp (15 mL) each chopped fresh. (As a general rule, when substituting fresh for dried herbs use three times the amount of fresh for the dried.)

VARIATION

You can also add 8 oz (125 g) pepperoni, salami or ham, cut into thin 1-inch (2.5 cm) strips.

SERVES 6

Cut preparation time way down by using store-bought tzatziki in this salad. The garlicky Greek sauce made with yogurt and cucumber is not only great for souvlaki, but also makes a delicious salad dressing to use instead of mayonnaise.

TIPS

To seed tomatoes, cut in half crosswise and gently squeeze out seeds.

Tzatziki sauce can be stored in a covered container in refrigerator for up to five days. This recipe makes about 2 cups (500 mL).

Great Greek Pasta Salad

8 oz	penne or spiral pasta	250 g
1	small red onion, chopped	1
2	red bell peppers, diced	2
3/4 cup	crumbled feta cheese	175 mL
1/2 cup	Kalamata olives	125 mL
1/4 cup	chopped fresh parsley	50 mL

DRESSING

3/4 cup	Tzatziki Sauce (see recipe below)	175 mL
2 tbsp	olive oil	25 mL
1 tbsp	red wine vinegar	15 mL
1 tsp	dried oregano leaves	5 mL
1/4 tsp	freshly ground black pepper	1 mL

1. Cook pasta in a large pot of boiling salted water until tender but firm. Drain; rinse under cold water to chill. Drain well. In a serving bowl, combine pasta, onion, peppers, feta, olives and parsley.
2. Dressing: In a bowl combine Tzatziki Sauce, oil, vinegar, oregano and pepper; toss with pasta mixture to coat. Cover and refrigerate. Remove from fridge 30 minutes before serving.

Tzatziki Sauce

3 cups	plain yogurt	750 mL
1 cup	finely chopped cucumber	250 mL
1 tsp	salt	5 mL
2	cloves garlic, minced	2
2 tsp	fresh lemon juice or red wine vinegar	10 mL

1. Place yogurt in a coffee-filter or double paper towel-lined sieve set over a bowl; cover and let drain in the refrigerator for 4 hours or until reduced to 1 1/2 cups (375 mL).
2. In a bowl, sprinkle cucumber with salt. Let stand 20 minutes. Drain in a sieve; squeeze out excess moisture and pat dry with paper towels. In a bowl, combine yogurt, cucumber, garlic and lemon juice.

SERVES 8

Your turn to bring the salad to the next reunion or neighborhood get-together? Here's a sure-fire winner that can be easily doubled to feed as many folks as the occasion demands. Even better, it can be made a day ahead.

TIP

To cook the rice, rinse ¾ cup (175 mL) basmati rice under cold water; drain. In a medium saucepan, bring 1½ cups (375 mL) water to a boil. Add rice and ½ tsp (2 mL) salt; cover and simmer for 15 minutes or until tender. Spread hot rice on baking sheet to cool.

Speedy Mexicali Rice and Black Bean Salad

2 cups	cooked basmati rice (see Tip, left)	500 mL
1	can (19 oz/540 mL) black beans, drained and rinsed	1
1 cup	cooked corn kernels	250 mL
1	red bell pepper, diced	1
4	green onions, sliced	4

DRESSING

½ cup	sour cream	125 mL
2 tbsp	olive oil	25 mL
4 tsp	fresh lime or lemon juice	20 mL
1 tsp	dried oregano leaves	5 mL
1 tsp	ground cumin	5 mL
½ tsp	hot pepper sauce	2 mL
½ cup	chopped fresh cilantro or parsley	125 mL

1. In a large serving bowl, combine rice, black beans, corn, red pepper and green onions.

2. Dressing: In a bowl, combine sour cream, olive oil, lime juice, oregano, cumin and hot pepper sauce. Pour over rice mixture; toss well. Cover and refrigerate for up to 8 hours. Stir in cilantro just before serving.

SERVES 8

The Lebanese salad, tabbouleh, made with nutty-tasting bulgur, is a good example of the vibrant comfort foods from the Mediterranean that have become so popular in recent years. This refreshing green salad is often displayed next to traditional favorites, such as potato salad and coleslaw, in the deli section of supermarkets. But you'll find it very inexpensive and easy to make in your home kitchen.

TIPS

Bulgur is precooked cracked wheat that has been dried; it needs only to be soaked in water before using.

This salad keeps well for several days. It's better to add the tomatoes as a garnish just before serving to prevent the salad from becoming soggy.

Tabbouleh

3/4 cup	fine bulgur	175 mL
2 cups	finely chopped fresh parsley, preferably flat leaf	500 mL
4	green onions, finely chopped	4
1/4 cup	finely chopped fresh mint or 2 tbsp (25 mL) dried crumbled (optional)	50 mL
1/4 cup	olive oil	50 mL
1/4 cup	fresh lemon juice	50 mL
1 tsp	salt	5 mL
1/2 tsp	paprika	2 mL
1/4 tsp	freshly ground black pepper	1 mL
2	tomatoes, seeded and diced	2

1. Place bulgur in a bowl; add cold water to cover. Let stand for 30 minutes. Drain in a fine sieve. Using the back of a spoon, or with your hands, squeeze out as much water as possible.

2. In a serving bowl, combine softened bulgur, parsley, onions and mint, if using.

3. In a small bowl, stir together oil, lemon juice, salt, paprika and pepper. Pour over bulgur mixture; toss well. Cover and refrigerate until serving time. Just before serving, sprinkle with tomatoes.

Green Bean and Plum Tomato Salad (page 281) ➢
Overleaf: Caesar Salad (page 271)

Cookies, Muffins and Breads

Classic Chocolate Chip Cookies (page 291)

BAKING TIPS

Perfectly Baked Cookies

- Place baking sheet on middle rack of oven. Bake only one sheet at a time.
- Wipe sheets with paper towels or a damp cloth to remove grease.
- Let sheets cool completely before using again to prevent dough from melting and spreading out too much during baking.
- Double the recipe, bake half and freeze dough to bake later.
- To grease pans and baking sheets, solid vegetable shortening or unsalted or lightly salted butter is recommended.

Cutting Bars or Squares

- Line sides and bottom of baking pan with foil.
- Bake as directed and let bars cool completely in pan.
- Place in freezer for up to 30 minutes or until partially frozen.
- Lift out entire batch. Cut into bars or squares with a sharp knife.
- Arrange in cookie tin with waxed paper separating the layers and freeze. Most bars, like cookies, freeze well.

About Nuts

- Toasting Nuts: Place on baking sheet in 350°F (180°C) oven for about 6 to 8 minutes or until lightly fragrant. You'll find the nuts easier to chop when warm, too.
- Nothing ruins baked goods more than rancid nuts, in particular walnuts. Taste before purchasing, if possible, to make sure nuts are fresh. Store them in a covered container in the fridge or freezer.

Bread Baking Know-How

- For yeast to work properly, liquids must be at the correct temperature to activate the yeast. Liquids that are too hot will kill the action of yeast and dough will not rise. Cold temperatures will shock the yeast and it will not have its full leavening strength. Use a thermometer for accuracy.
- Do not work in too much flour when mixing and kneading, or dough will be heavy. Depending on the humidity of the flour used, you may need less or more than the amount called for.
- To measure flour correctly for all baking, give flour a quick stir, spoon into dry measure and use a knife to level the top.

MAKES 40 COOKIES

I'm never short of taste testers when the first warm batch of these cookies come out of the oven. My family loves them flecked with chocolate chips and walnuts. Served with a cold glass of milk, they're pure heaven.

VARIATION

Double Chocolate Chunk Cookies

Decrease all-purpose flour to 1½ cups (375 mL). Sift flour with ½ cup (125 mL) cocoa powder and baking soda. Replace chocolate chips with white chocolate chunks instead.

Classic Chocolate Chip Cookies

Preheat oven to 350°F (180°C)
Cookie sheets, lightly greased

¾ cup	butter, softened	175 mL
¾ cup	granulated sugar	175 mL
½ cup	packed brown sugar	125 mL
2	eggs	2
2 tsp	vanilla	10 mL
1¾ cups	all-purpose flour	425 mL
½ tsp	baking soda	2 mL
½ tsp	salt	2 mL
1½ cups	semi-sweet chocolate chips	375 mL
1 cup	chopped walnuts or pecans (optional)	250 mL

1. In a large bowl, using an electric mixer, cream butter with granulated and brown sugars until fluffy; beat in eggs and vanilla until smooth.
2. In another bowl, stir together flour, baking soda and salt. Beat into creamed mixture until combined; stir in chocolate chips and walnuts, if using.
3. Drop by tablespoonfuls (15 mL) about 2 inches (5 cm) apart onto cookie sheets.
4. Bake one sheet at time on middle rack in preheated oven for 10 to 12 minutes or until edges are firm. (Bake for the shorter time if you prefer cookies with a soft chewy center.) Cool for 2 minutes on baking sheets; remove to wire rack and cool completely.

MAKES 36 COOKIES

Kids love home-baked cookies especially moist and chewy ones like these made with wholesome oatmeal.

TIP

Use whatever combination of dried fruits and nuts appeals to your family or whatever you happen to have on hand. Just add 1½ cups (375 mL) in total to the batter.

Scrumptious Oatmeal Cookies

Preheat oven to 350°F (180°C)
Cookie sheets, greased

¾ cup	butter, softened	175 mL
1¼ cups	packed brown sugar	300 mL
1	egg	1
1 tsp	vanilla	5 mL
1½ cups	all-purpose flour	375 mL
½ tsp	baking soda	2 mL
¼ tsp	salt	1 mL
1½ cups	old-fashioned rolled oats	375 mL
¾ cup	sliced almonds or chopped pecans	175 mL
¾ cup	dried cherries, dried cranberries, raisins or chocolate chips	175 mL

1. In a bowl, cream butter and sugar until fluffy. Beat in egg and vanilla.
2. In another bowl, stir together flour, baking soda and salt. Stir into butter mixture, mixing well. Stir in rolled oats, almonds and dried cherries.
3. Drop by heaping tablespoonfuls (15 mL) about 2 inches (5 cm) apart onto prepared cookie sheets and flatten with a fork.
4. Bake one sheet at a time on middle rack in preheated oven for 12 to 14 minutes or until edges are golden. Let stand for 5 minutes; remove cookies with a spatula to a rack and let cool.

MAKES 40 COOKIES

These crisp cookies are sure to satisfy a craving for something sweet and indulgent.

Peanut Butter Cookies

Preheat oven to 375°F (190°C)
Cookie sheets, lightly greased

1/2 cup	butter, softened, or shortening	125 mL
2/3 cup	smooth peanut butter	150 mL
1 cup	packed brown sugar	250 mL
1	egg	1
1 tsp	vanilla	5 mL
1 3/4 cups	all purpose flour	425 mL
1/2 tsp	baking soda	2 mL
1/4 tsp	salt	1 mL

1. In a bowl, cream butter, peanut butter and brown sugar until fluffy. Beat in egg and vanilla.
2. In another bowl, stir together flour, baking soda and salt. Stir into creamed mixture.
3. Form into 1-inch (2.5 cm) balls and place 2 inches (5 cm) apart on prepared cookie sheets. Using the tines of a fork, flatten by making criss-cross patterns on tops.
4. Bake one sheet at a time on middle rack in preheated oven for 11 to 13 minutes or until light golden. Transfer to a rack to cool.

MAKES 60 COOKIES

A favorite since my university days, these spice cookies would provide fuel for cram sessions before exams. Now, continuing the tradition, my kids bake a batch when they have to hit the books.

TIP

Be sure to use fresh baking soda as it makes these cookies crisp and light. Like baking powder, an open box of baking soda has a shelf life of only six months, so make sure to replenish both regularly. As a reminder, write the date when they need to be replaced on the container.

Gingersnaps

Preheat oven to 350°F (180°C)
Cookie sheets, lightly greased

1/2 cup	shortening	125 mL
1/2 cup	butter, softened	125 mL
3/4 cup	packed brown sugar	175 mL
1/4 cup	fancy molasses	50 mL
1	egg	1
2 1/4 cups	all-purpose flour	550 mL
1 1/2 tsp	baking soda	7 mL
1 1/2 tsp	ground ginger	7 mL
1 tsp	ground cinnamon	5 mL
1 tsp	ground cloves	5 mL
1/4 tsp	salt	1 mL
	Granulated sugar	

1. In a large bowl, cream shortening and butter with sugar until light and fluffy; beat in molasses and egg until creamy.

2. In another bowl, sift together flour, baking soda, ginger, cinnamon, ground cloves and salt. Stir into creamed mixture to make a soft dough. Refrigerate for 1 hour or until firm.

3. Shape dough into 1-inch (2.5 cm) balls; roll in bowl of granulated sugar. Arrange 2 inches (5 cm) apart on prepared cookie sheets. Flatten to 1/4 inch (0.5 cm) thickness using bottom of large glass dipped in sugar.

4. Bake in preheated oven for 12 to 14 minutes or until golden. Cool 2 minutes on baking sheets; transfer to rack and let cool.

MAKES 48 COOKIES

The secret to this tender, easy-to-make shortbread is to have a light touch and not to over handle the dough.

Scottish Shortbread

Preheat oven to 300°F (150°C)
Cookie sheets

1 cup	unsalted butter, softened	250 mL
1/2 cup	superfine sugar	125 mL
2 cups	all-purpose flour	500 mL
1/2 tsp	salt	2 mL

1. In a bowl, cream butter with wooden spoon until fluffy. Beat in sugar, a spoonful at time, until well blended. Stir in flour and salt; gather into a ball.
2. On a lightly floured work surface, gently knead four or five times until smooth. Roll out a portion of the dough on a lightly floured surface to 1/3-inch (0.8 cm) thickness. Cut out shapes using cooking cutters and place on cookie sheets.
3. Bake one sheet at a time on middle rack in preheated oven for 25 to 30 minutes or until edges are light golden. Transfer cookies to rack to cool.

MAKES 32 BROWNIES

So moist and chewy, these brownies will disappear in no time. Luckily, this recipe makes a big batch, so you can stash half in the freezer — which is certainly recommended, if you want them to last more than a day!

Fudgy Chocolate Brownies

Preheat oven to 350°F (180°C)
13-by 9-inch (3.5 L) baking pan, greased

1 cup	butter, softened	250 mL
1 1/2 cups	granulated sugar	375 mL
4	eggs	4
2 tsp	vanilla	10 mL
1 cup	all-purpose flour	250 mL
1 cup	cocoa powder	250 mL
3/4 tsp	baking powder	4 mL
1/2 tsp	salt	2 mL
1 cup	walnuts, chopped	250 mL
FROSTING		
1 cup	confectioner's (icing) sugar	250 mL
1/3 cup	cocoa powder	75 mL
2 tbsp	butter, softened	25 mL
2 tbsp	milk	25 mL

1. In a bowl, using an electric mixer, cream butter with sugar until light and fluffy. Beat in eggs, one at a time, until incorporated; add vanilla.
2. In a separate bowl, sift together flour, cocoa powder, baking powder and salt. Beat into butter mixture to make a smooth batter. Fold in walnuts.
3. Spread in prepared baking pan. Bake on middle rack in preheated oven for 25 to 30 minutes or until cake tester inserted in center comes out clean. Place pan on rack to cool completely.
4. Frosting: In a bowl, using an electric mixer, cream confectioner's sugar, cocoa powder, butter and milk until smooth. Spread over slightly warm brownies. When set, cut into bars.

MAKES 32 BROWNIES

These brownies are the perfect chocolate indulgence — rich, dense and chocolatey with a crunchy layer of toffee. Baking is a breeze with this streamlined recipe that requires only a saucepan and a baking pan lined with foil for easy clean up.

TIP

Look for Skor toffee bits in the baking section of supermarkets. If unavailable, use 5 finely chopped Skor bars instead. Reduce chocolate chips to ¾ cup (175 mL).

Skor Fudge Brownies

Preheat oven to 350°F (180°C)
13-by 9-inch (3.5 L) baking pan, bottom and sides lined with heavy foil with edges overhanging the sides

1 cup	butter, cut into pieces	250 mL
6 oz	unsweetened chocolate, coarsely chopped (6 squares)	175 g
2 cups	granulated sugar	500 mL
4	eggs	4
2 tsp	vanilla	10 mL
1¼ cups	all-purpose flour	300 mL
¼ tsp	salt	1 mL
1	package (8 oz/227 g) Skor toffee bits	1
1 cup	semi-sweet chocolate chips	250 mL

1. In a medium saucepan, melt butter and chocolate over medium heat, stirring often, until melted and smooth.
2. Remove from heat; stir in sugar. Beat in eggs and vanilla. Stir in flour and salt to make a smooth batter.
3. Spread evenly in prepared baking pan. Bake on middle rack in preheated oven for 18 minutes or until top is almost set. Sprinkle Skor toffee bits over top and return pan to oven.
4. Bake for 8 to 10 minutes more or until a toothpick inserted in center comes out with a few moist crumbs clinging to it.
5. Place pan on a rack; sprinkle with chocolate chips. Let stand for 5 minutes or until chocolate is melted. Spread evenly. Let cool until chocolate is set.
6. Lift brownies out of pan; carefully remove foil and cut into bars using a sharp knife.

MAKES 36 SQUARES

These classy lemon treats with a shortbread crust are always appreciated when friends are invited for a fresh-brewed cup of tea or coffee.

Luscious Lemon Squares

Preheat oven to 350°F (180°C)
8-inch (2 L) square baking pan

1 cup	all-purpose flour	250 mL
1/4 cup	granulated sugar	50 mL
1/2 cup	butter, cut into pieces	125 mL
FILLING		
2	eggs	2
1 cup	granulated sugar	250 mL
2 tbsp	all-purpose flour	25 mL
1/2 tsp	baking powder	2 mL
Pinch	salt	Pinch
1 tbsp	grated lemon zest	15 mL
1/4 cup	fresh lemon juice	50 mL
	Confectioner's (icing) sugar	

1. In a bowl, combine flour and sugar; cut in butter with a pastry blender to make coarse crumbs. Press into bottom of baking pan. Bake in preheated oven for 18 to 20 minutes or until light golden. Let cool on rack.

2. Filling: In a bowl, beat eggs with sugar, flour, baking powder, salt, lemon zest and juice. Pour over base.

3. Bake for 25 to 30 minutes or until filling is set and light golden. Place pan on rack to cool. Dust with confectioner's sugar; cut into small squares.

MAKES 16 SQUARES

Here's a heritage recipe that never grows old. My version of date squares has a burst of lemon in the filling, which only enhances its traditional appeal.

TIP

Rather than using a knife to cut sticky dried fruits like dates and apricots, you'll find that kitchen scissors do a better job.

Fabulous Date Squares

Preheat oven to 350°F (180°C)
8-inch (2 L) square baking pan

FILLING

3 cups	chopped pitted dates (about 12 oz/375 g)	750 mL
1 cup	water	250 mL
1/4 cup	packed brown sugar	50 mL
1 tsp	grated lemon zest	5 mL

CRUMB LAYER

1 1/2 cups	quick-cooking rolled oats	375 mL
1 cup	all-purpose flour	250 mL
3/4 cup	packed brown sugar	175 mL
1/2 tsp	baking powder	2 mL
1/4 tsp	salt	1 mL
3/4 cup	cold butter, cut into pieces	175 mL

1. Filling: In a saucepan, combine dates, water, brown sugar and lemon zest. Place over medium heat; cook, stirring, for 8 to 10 minutes or until dates form a smooth paste. Let cool.
2. Crumb Layer: In a bowl, combine rolled oats, flour, brown sugar, baking powder and salt. Cut in butter with a pastry cutter or fork to make coarse crumbs.
3. Press two-thirds of crumb mixture in bottom of baking pan. Spread evenly with date filling. Sprinkle with remaining crumb mixture, pressing down lightly.
4. Bake in preheated oven for 30 minutes or until golden. Let cool on a rack; cut into squares.

MAKES 24 BARS

Ideal for school lunches, these chewy bars travel well. I like to package bars individually in plastic wrap, place in a covered container and freeze. It's so easy to pop a bar from the freezer into lunch bags or take them along for snacks.

Lunch Box Oatmeal-Raisin Bars

Preheat oven to 350°F (180°C)
13-by 9-inch (3.5 L) baking pan, lined with foil, greased

2⁄3 cup	packed brown sugar	150 mL
1⁄3 cup	butter	75 mL
1⁄3 cup	golden corn syrup	75 mL
2 1⁄2 cups	quick-cooking rolled oats	625 mL
1⁄4 cup	all-purpose flour	50 mL
1⁄2 cup	raisins or chopped dried apricots	125 mL
1	egg	1
1 tsp	vanilla	5 mL

1. In a glass bowl, combine brown sugar, butter and corn syrup. Microwave at High for 2 minutes; stir until smooth. Microwave 1 minute more or until sugar dissolves and mixture comes to a full boil.
2. Stir in rolled oats, flour and raisins. In a small bowl, beat egg with vanilla. Stir into rolled-oats mixture.
3. Spread evenly in prepared pan. Bake in preheated oven for 20 to 25 minutes or until golden around edges. Let cool 10 minutes in pan. Lift out foil; cut into 3-by 1 1⁄2-inch (8 by 4 cm) bars. Transfer to a rack to complete cooling.

MAKES 24 BARS

Peanut butter fans will love these no-bake bars. They're a breeze to make and taste so much better than the expensive packaged snack bars sold in supermarkets.

TIP

Wrap bars individually in plastic wrap and freeze. Then, when making school lunches, just pop a pre-wrapped bar into each lunch bag.

Peanutty Cereal Snacking Bars

13-by 9-inch (3.5 L) baking pan, greased

1 cup	smooth or chunky peanut butter (regular or light)	250 mL
2⁄3 cup	liquid honey or golden corn syrup	150 mL
4 cups	toasted rice cereal	1 L
2 cups	muesli-type cereal with fruit and nuts	500 mL

1. In a large saucepan, combine peanut butter and honey; cook over medium heat, stirring constantly, until smooth. (Or place in large glass bowl and microwave at High for 2 minutes, or until smooth, stirring once.)

2. Fold in cereals until evenly coated. Press firmly into prepared baking pan. Let cool; cut into 3-by 1½-inch (8 by 4 cm) bars.

MAKES 24 BARS

Making these bars is a lot less work than making a batch of cookies. Save even more time by using a food processor to make the shortbread base.

Easy Apricot Pecan Bars

Preheat oven to 350°F (180°C)
8-inch (2 L) square baking pan, lined with greased foil

1 cup	all-purpose flour	250 mL
6 tbsp	butter, cut into pieces	90 mL
1/4 cup	packed brown sugar	50 mL

TOPPING

1 cup	dried apricots	250 mL
1	egg	1
1 tsp	vanilla	5 mL
3/4 cup	packed light brown sugar	175 mL
2 tbsp	all-purpose flour	25 mL
1/2 tsp	baking powder	2 mL
1/2 cup	chopped pecans or walnuts	125 mL

1. In a food processor, combine flour, butter and brown sugar; process to make fine crumbs. Press mixture evenly in bottom of prepared baking pan. Bake for 15 minutes or until light golden. Let cool; leave oven on.
2. Topping: Place apricots in a small saucepan; cover with water. Bring to a boil; cook for 3 to 5 minutes or until softened. Drain well; let cool slightly. Using scissors, cut into slivers.
3. In a bowl, beat egg with vanilla; stir in brown sugar, flour and baking powder. Add apricots. Spread mixture evenly over baked crust; sprinkle with pecans. Bake in preheated oven for 22 to 25 minutes or until top is golden brown. Place on rack; let cool.
4. Lift bars out of pan; remove foil. Cut into bars.

MAKES 18 TARTS

Scrumptious is the best way to describe these old-time favorite tarts with a moist, not too sweet, filling.

Butter Tarts

Preheat oven to 425°F (220°C)
2 large muffin pans, lightly greased

	Pastry for double crust 9-inch (23 cm) pie (see recipe, page 171)	
½ cup	raisins, currants, chopped walnuts or pecans	125 mL
FILLING		
2	eggs	2
¾ cup	corn syrup	175 mL
¾ cup	packed brown sugar	175 mL
¼ cup	butter, melted	50 mL
2 tsp	vanilla	10 mL
2 tsp	fresh lemon juice	10 mL
¼ tsp	salt	1 mL

1. On a lightly floured surface, roll out pastry to ⅛-inch (0.25 cm) thickness. Cut out 4-inch (10 cm) rounds and fit into muffin cups. Sprinkle raisins in bottom.

2. Filling: In a bowl, beat eggs. Stir in corn syrup, brown sugar, butter, vanilla, lemon juice and salt. Spoon 2 tbsp (25 mL) filling into each tart shell.

3. Bake on rack in lower third of preheated oven for 14 to 16 minutes or until pastry is golden and filling is bubbly. Remove from oven; let stand for 1 minute. Run a knife around pastry edge to loosen tarts; using a pastry spatula, carefully remove to a rack to cool.

MAKES 12 LARGE MUFFINS

I discovered that these wholesome muffins have great appeal. As a food columnist for The Gazette *newspaper in Montreal, this recipe was featured in one of my weekly columns. The maple syrup amount was omitted due to a technical problem when going to press and the paper received more than 500 telephone calls from readers requesting how much maple syrup to add to the recipe. Here it is — with the right amount of maple syrup!*

Maple Walnut Apple Muffins

Preheat oven to 400°F (200°C)
Muffin pan, greased or with paper liners

1 1/4 cups	all-purpose flour	300 mL
2 1/2 tsp	baking powder	12 mL
1/2 tsp	baking soda	2 mL
1/4 tsp	salt	1 mL
1/3 cup	finely chopped walnuts	75 mL
1	egg	1
1 cup	rolled oats	250 mL
1 cup	coarsely grated apple	250 mL
2/3 cup	maple syrup	150 mL
1/2 cup	plain yogurt	125 mL
1/4 cup	vegetable oil	50 mL

1. In a bowl, combine flour, baking powder, baking soda, salt and walnuts.
2. In another bowl, beat egg. Stir in oats, grated apple, maple syrup, yogurt and oil. Stir into flour mixture just until combined; do not over mix.
3. Spoon batter into prepared muffin cups. Bake in preheated oven for 20 minutes or until tops are springy to the touch. Let muffins cool slightly; transfer to rack to cool.

MAKES 16 LARGE MUFFINS

Packed with nuts, fruits and carrots, these scrumptious muffins are perfect for breakfast. But they are just as tasty for afternoon snacks or stowed away in a lunch box.

TIP

Have only one muffin pan? Place muffin paper liners in 6-oz (175 mL) glass custard cups or small ramekins and fill with extra batter. Place in oven and bake alongside muffin pan.

Carrot-Raisin Muffins

Preheat oven to 375°F (190°C)
2 muffin pans, well-greased or with paper liners

2 cups	all-purpose flour	500 mL
3/4 cup	granulated sugar	175 mL
1 1/2 tsp	ground cinnamon	7 mL
1 tsp	baking powder	5 mL
1 tsp	baking soda	5 mL
1/2 tsp	freshly grated nutmeg	2 mL
1/2 tsp	salt	2 mL
1 1/2 cups	grated carrots (about 3 medium)	375 mL
1 cup	grated peeled apples	250 mL
1/2 cup	raisins	125 mL
1/2 cup	sweetened shredded coconut	125 mL
1/2 cup	chopped walnuts (optional)	125 mL
2	eggs	2
2/3 cup	plain yogurt	150 mL
1/3 cup	vegetable oil	75 mL

1. In a large bowl, stir together flour, sugar, cinnamon, baking powder, baking soda, nutmeg and salt. Stir in carrots, apples, raisins, coconut and walnuts, if using.
2. In another bowl, beat eggs; add yogurt and oil. Stir into flour mixture just until combined. (Batter will be very thick.)
3. Spoon batter into prepared muffins cups filling almost to the top.
4. Bake in preheated oven for 25 to 30 minutes or until tops spring back when lightly touched. Let cool in pans for 5 minutes; transfer muffins to a rack and cool.

MAKES 12 MUFFINS

When it comes to celebrating the pleasures of summer fruits, nothing beats juicy blueberries. They are especially welcome when teamed with lemon in these deliciously moist muffins.

TIP

To minimize the problem of frozen blueberries tinting the batter blue, place berries in a sieve and quickly rinse under cold water to get rid of any ice crystals. Blot dry with paper towels. Place berries in a bowl and toss with 2 tbsp (25 mL) of the muffin flour mixture. Use immediately; fold into batter with a few quick strokes.

Blueberry Cornmeal Muffins

Preheat oven to 400°F (200°C)
Muffin pan, well-greased or with paper liners

1 1/2 cups	all-purpose flour	375 mL
1/3 cup	cornmeal	75 mL
1/2 cup	granulated sugar	125 mL
2 1/2 tsp	baking powder	12 mL
1/4 tsp	salt	1 mL
1	egg	1
3/4 cup	milk	175 mL
1/4 cup	butter, melted	50 mL
1 tsp	grated lemon zest	5 mL
1 cup	fresh or frozen blueberries	250 mL

1. In a bowl, stir together flour, cornmeal, sugar, baking powder and salt.
2. In another bowl, beat egg. Stir in milk, melted butter and lemon zest. Combine with dry ingredients until just mixed. Gently fold in blueberries.
3. Spoon into prepared muffin cups so they are three-quarters full.
4. Bake in preheated oven for 20 to 24 minutes or until top is firm to the touch and lightly browned. Remove from pans and let muffins cool on rack.

MAKES 12 MUFFINS

Bran muffins are never out of style. Nicely moistened with molasses, these muffins will become a morning favorite.

TIP

Always measure the oil before measuring sticky sweeteners such as molasses or honey. (For recipes that don't call for oil, spray measure with nonstick vegetable spray or lightly coat with oil. You'll find every last drop of sweetener will easily pour out.)

Bran Muffins

Preheat oven to 400°F (200°C)
Muffin pan, well-greased or with paper liners

2	eggs	2
1 cup	buttermilk	250 mL
1⁄3 cup	packed brown sugar	75 mL
1⁄4 cup	vegetable oil	50 mL
1⁄4 cup	fancy molasses	50 mL
1 1⁄4 cups	whole wheat flour	300 mL
1 cup	natural bran	250 mL
1 tsp	baking soda	5 mL
1⁄2 tsp	baking powder	2 mL
1⁄4 tsp	salt	1 mL
1⁄2 cup	raisins or chopped apricots	125 mL

1. In a bowl, beat eggs. Add buttermilk, brown sugar, oil and molasses.
2. In another bowl, combine flour, bran, baking soda, baking powder and salt. Stir into liquid ingredients to make a smooth batter; fold in raisins.
3. Spoon into prepared muffin cups so they are three-quarters full.
4. Bake in preheated oven for 20 to 24 minutes or until tops spring back when lightly touched. Let cool 10 minutes; remove from pan and cool on racks.

MAKES 12 MUFFINS

Whip up this batch of muffins and they'll be gone in no time. They are especially child-friendly, but they'll also be enjoyed by the adults in the house.

TIP

Don't overmix the batter. Use quick gentle strokes to combine the dry and liquid ingredients together. It's normal to have a few lumps remaining in the batter.

Banana Spice Muffins

Preheat oven to 400°F (200°C)
Muffin pan, well-greased or with paper liners

1	egg	1
1 cup	mashed ripe bananas (about 3)	250 mL
3/4 cup	packed brown sugar	175 mL
1/2 cup	plain yogurt	125 mL
1/4 cup	vegetable oil	50 mL
2 cups	all-purpose flour	500 mL
1 1/2 tsp	baking powder	7 mL
1 1/2 tsp	ground cinnamon	7 mL
1/2 tsp	baking soda	2 mL
1/2 tsp	freshly grated nutmeg	2 mL
1/4 tsp	ground cloves	1 mL
1/4 tsp	salt	1 mL
1/2 cup	raisins	125 mL

1. In a bowl, beat egg. Stir in bananas, brown sugar, yogurt and oil until smooth.
2. In another bowl, combine flour, baking powder, cinnamon, baking soda, nutmeg, cloves and salt; stir into banana mixture until just combined. Fold in raisins.
3. Spoon batter into prepared muffin cups until level with top of pan. Bake in preheated oven for 20 to 25 minutes or until top springs back when lightly touched. Transfer muffins to a rack and let cool.

MAKES 1 LOAF

Everyone has a recipe for banana bread in their files. I've included my best. It's a simple bread that just relies on the flavor of banana and walnuts. Honey gives extra moistness that keeps it fresh for days — if it lasts that long.

TIPS

Lining the bottom of baking pan with waxed or parchment paper ensures you'll never have trouble removing the bread from the pan.

Left with ripe bananas on your counter but have no time to bake a bread? Simply freeze whole bananas with the peel, then leave at room temperature to defrost. Or, peel and mash bananas; pack into containers and freeze for up to two months. Defrost at room temperature. Frozen banana purée may darken slightly but will not affect the delicious baked results.

Banana Nut Bread

Preheat oven to 325°F (160°C)
9-by 5-inch (2 L) loaf pan, greased

1¾ cups	all-purpose flour	425 mL
1 tsp	baking soda	5 mL
½ tsp	salt	2 mL
2	eggs	2
1 cup	mashed ripe bananas (about 3 ripe)	250 mL
⅓ cup	vegetable oil	75 mL
½ cup	liquid honey	125 mL
⅓ cup	packed brown sugar	75 mL
½ cup	chopped walnuts	125 mL

1. In a bowl, sift together flour, baking soda and salt.
2. In another bowl, beat eggs. Stir in bananas, oil, honey and brown sugar.
3. Stir dry ingredients into banana mixture until combined. Fold in walnuts.
4. Pour batter in prepared loaf pan. Bake in preheated oven for 1¼ hours or until cake tester inserted in center comes out clean. Let pan cool on rack for 15 minutes. Run knife around edge; turn out loaf and let cool on rack.

Lemon Yogurt Loaf

MAKES 1 LOAF

Here's a lemony-flavored loaf that stays moist for days — if it lasts that long.

TIP

I like to double this recipe so that I have an extra loaf handy in the freezer. Wrap in plastic wrap, then in foil and freeze for up to one month.

VARIATION

Lemon Poppy Seed Loaf

Stir 2 tbsp (25 mL) poppy seeds into flour mixture before combining with yogurt mixture.

Preheat oven to 350°F (180°C)
9-by 5-inch (2 L) loaf pan, greased

1¾ cups	all-purpose flour	425 mL
1 tsp	baking powder	5 mL
½ tsp	baking soda	2 mL
¼ tsp	salt	1 mL
2	eggs	2
¾ cup	granulated sugar	175 mL
¾ cup	plain yogurt	175 mL
⅓ cup	vegetable oil	75 mL
1 tbsp	grated lemon zest	15 mL
TOPPING		
⅓ cup	fresh lemon juice	75 mL
⅓ cup	granulated sugar	75 mL

1. In a bowl, combine flour, baking powder, baking soda and salt. In another large bowl, beat eggs. Stir in sugar, yogurt, oil and lemon zest. Fold in flour mixture to make a smooth batter.
2. Spoon into prepared pan; bake in preheated oven for 50 to 60 minutes or until cake tester inserted in center comes out clean. Place pan on rack.
3. Topping: In a small saucepan, heat lemon juice and sugar; bring to a boil. Cook, stirring, until sugar is dissolved. (Or place in a glass bowl and microwave at High for 1 minute, stirring once.) Pour over hot loaf in pan; let cool completely before turning out of pan.

MAKES 1 LOAF

This bread is so much easier to bake than pumpkin pie, but still loaded with all the spice-scented flavors we love.

Orange Pumpkin Loaf

Preheat oven to 350°F (180°C)
9-by 5-inch (2 L) loaf pan, greased

1 cup	all-purpose flour	250 mL
3/4 cup	whole wheat or all-purpose flour	175 mL
2 tsp	baking powder	10 mL
1/2 tsp	baking soda	2 mL
1/2 tsp	salt	2 mL
1 1/2 tsp	ground cinnamon	7 mL
1/2 tsp	freshly grated nutmeg	2 mL
1/4 tsp	ground cloves or allspice	1 mL
1 1/4 cups	packed brown sugar	300 mL
2	eggs	2
1 cup	canned pumpkin purée (not pie filling)	250 mL
1/3 cup	vegetable oil	75 mL
2 tsp	grated orange zest	10 mL
1/4 cup	orange juice	50 mL

1. In a bowl, combine flours, baking powder, baking soda and salt; stir well.
2. In a small bowl, combine cinnamon, nutmeg and cloves. Transfer 1 tsp (5 mL) of the spice mixture to another bowl; add 2 tbsp (25 mL) brown sugar. Set aside for topping.
3. Place remaining spices and brown sugar in a bowl; add eggs and beat well. Stir in pumpkin, oil, orange zest and juice. Stir dry ingredients into pumpkin mixture until combined.
4. Spoon batter into prepared loaf pan. Sprinkle top with reserved spiced-sugar mixture. Bake on middle rack in preheated oven for 50 to 55 minutes or until toothpick inserted in center comes out clean. Let pan cool on rack for 15 minutes; turn loaf out and let cool completely.

MAKES 12 BUNS

Mashed potatoes are the secret ingredient that keep these sticky buns extra moist. A word of warning to the calorie-conscious: It is next to impossible to eat just one of these buns!

TIP

To make buns for morning coffee or brunch, prepare dough the day before (no need to let it rise) and place in a covered bowl in the fridge overnight. Next morning, punch down the dough and let it warm up to room temperature. A quick way to warm it is in the microwave at Low; check every few minutes and turn often. Roll out dough, spread with filling and continue with recipe as directed.

Sticky Cinnamon Buns

Preheat oven to 375°F (190°C)
13-by 9-inch (3.5 L) baking pan, well-greased

1 cup	peeled potatoes, cut into ½-inch (1 cm) cubes	250 mL
¼ cup	butter, cubed	50 mL
1 cup	milk	250 mL
3¼ cups	all-purpose flour (approx.)	800 mL
¼ cup	granulated sugar	50 mL
1	package (2¼ tsp/11 mL) quick-rise instant yeast	1
1 tsp	salt	5 mL
½ tsp	ground cinnamon	2 mL
FILLING		
⅓ cup	maple syrup	75 mL
⅓ cup	butter, melted	75 mL
¾ cup	packed brown sugar	175 mL
½ cup	raisins	125 mL
½ cup	chopped pecans	125 mL
1½ tsp	ground cinnamon	7 mL

1. In a small saucepan, combine potatoes and water; simmer, covered, for 13 to 15 minutes or until very tender. Add butter; stir until melted.

2. Pour into a large bowl. Using an electric mixer, beat potatoes until smooth. Add milk, 1½ cups (375 mL) flour, sugar, yeast, salt and cinnamon. Beat for 2 minutes at medium speed until smooth. Using a wooden spoon, stir in 1½ cups (375 mL) more flour to make a soft, slightly sticky dough.

3. Turn out onto floured board; knead, adding just enough flour to prevent dough from sticking, for 5 minutes or until smooth and elastic. Shape into a ball, cover with an inverted bowl and let rise for 20 minutes.

4. Filling: Combine maple syrup and 2 tbsp (25 mL) melted butter; pour into prepared baking pan. In a bowl, combine brown sugar, raisins, pecans and cinnamon; sprinkle ¾ cup (175 mL) over maple mixture in pan.
5. Punch down dough; roll out to 18- by 10-inch (45 by 25 cm) rectangle.
6. Brush with 2 tbsp (25 mL) melted butter; sprinkle with remaining raisin mixture leaving a ½-inch (1 cm) border along long sides. Roll up from one long side, pinching edges to seal. Cut dough into 12 slices; place, cut-side down, in pan. Brush with remaining melted butter. Cover and let rise in warm place for 45 to 60 minutes or until doubled in bulk.
7. Bake in preheated oven for 30 to 35 minutes or until golden. Let cool on rack for 5 minutes; invert onto a large serving platter.

MAKES 2 LOAVES

There's nothing more welcoming than the aroma of home-baked bread when you walk in the door. Who can wait to cut into a warm loaf so tasty, you don't need butter?

Honey Oatmeal Bread

Preheat oven to 375°F (190°C)
Two 9-by 5-inch (2 L) loaf pans, greased

1	package (2¼ tsp/11 mL) active dry yeast	1
1 tsp	granulated sugar	5 mL
1 cup	milk	250 mL
¼ cup	dark honey, such as buckwheat, or fancy molasses	50 mL
2 tbsp	butter	25 mL
2½ tsp	salt	12 mL
1 cup	old-fashioned rolled oats	250 mL
2 cups	whole wheat flour	500 mL
3 cups	all-purpose flour (approx.)	750 mL
2 tsp	melted butter	10 mL
1	egg white	1
	Additional rolled oats	

1. Place ½ cup (125 mL) lukewarm water in a glass measuring cup; sprinkle with yeast and sugar. Let stand until foamy.
2. In a saucepan, combine 1 cup (250 mL) lukewarm water, milk, honey, 2 tbsp (25 mL) butter and salt. Heat over medium heat, stirring, until bubbles appear around edge.
3. Place rolled oats in a large mixing bowl; pour in hot mixture. Let cool until lukewarm; if using a thermometer, temperature should read 105° to 115°F (40° to 45°C).
4. Stir in whole wheat flour and dissolved yeast; beat vigorously with a wooden spoon for 1 minute or until smooth. Stir in enough all-purpose flour to make a stiff dough that leaves sides of bowl.
5. Turn out onto a floured board and knead, adding just enough flour to prevent dough from sticking, for 7 to 9 minutes or until smooth and elastic.

6. Shape into a ball; place in well-buttered bowl. Turn dough to coat in butter. Cover with plastic wrap, then with clean dry towel; let rise in warm place until doubled in bulk, about 1½ to 2 hours.
7. Punch down dough; knead for 1 minute to get rid of air bubbles. Divide in two. Shape into loaves and place in prepared loaf pans. Brush tops with 2 tsp (10 mL) melted butter. Cover with clean towel; let rise in a warm place for 1¼ hours or until almost doubled in bulk.
8. Lightly beat egg white with 1 tsp (5 mL) water; brush tops of loaves. Sprinkle each loaf with 1 tbsp (15 mL) rolled oats.
9. Bake in preheated oven for 45 minutes or until bottom of loaves when removed from pans sound hollow when tapped. Remove loaves from oven, turn out of pans and let cool on racks.

MAKES ABOUT 12 SCONES

Bring out the clotted cream or the sweet butter. Set out the thick jam or fruit preserves. Brew a steaming pot of tea, invite some good friends over, then spoil them with these tender, light scones.

VARIATION

Apricot and Candied Ginger Scones

Substitute slivered dried apricots for the currants and add 2 tbsp (25 mL) finely chopped candied ginger to flour mixture.

Tea Time Scones

Preheat oven to 400°F (200°C)
Large baking sheet, greased

2 cups	all-purpose flour	500 mL
1/4 cup	granulated sugar	50 mL
1 tbsp	baking powder	15 mL
1/2 tsp	baking soda	2 mL
1/2 tsp	salt	2 mL
1/2 cup	cold butter, cut into pieces	125 mL
1/2 cup	dried currants or raisins	125 mL
1	egg	1
1/2 cup	buttermilk	125 mL
TOPPING		
1 tbsp	buttermilk	15 mL
2 tsp	granulated sugar	10 mL

1. In a large bowl, stir together flour, sugar, baking powder, baking soda and salt. Cut in butter using a pastry blender or fork to make coarse crumbs. Stir in currants or raisins.
2. In another bowl, beat egg with buttermilk; stir into dry ingredients to make a soft dough.
3. Turn out onto floured board and knead dough gently three to four times; pat or roll out using a floured rolling pin into a circular shape about 3/4 inch (2 cm) thick. Cut out rounds using a 2 1/2-inch (6 cm) floured cutter; arrange on prepared baking sheet.
4. Brush with buttermilk and sprinkle with sugar. Bake in preheated oven for 16 to 20 minutes or until golden. Transfer to rack.

MAKES 12 BISCUITS

Serve these wonderful biscuits straight from the oven. Consider baking a double batch if expecting a hungry crowd.

TIP

To assemble recipe ahead, place dry ingredients in a bowl. Cut in butter, add cheese, cover and refrigerate. While oven is preheating, stir in the milk and continue with recipe.

Cheddar Drop Biscuits

Preheat oven to 400°F (200°C)
Baking sheet, greased

2 cups	all-purpose flour	500 mL
1 tbsp	baking powder	15 mL
1/2 tsp	salt	2 mL
1/3 cup	butter, at room temperature, cut into pieces	75 mL
1 cup	coarsely shredded aged Cheddar cheese	250 mL
2 tbsp	chopped fresh chives (optional)	25 mL
1 cup	milk	250 mL
	Additional chopped chives	

1. In a large bowl, combine flour, baking powder and salt. Cut in butter using a pastry blender or two knives to make coarse crumbs. Add cheddar cheese and chives, if using.
2. Stir in milk to make a soft, sticky dough. Drop twelve heaping tablespoonfuls (15 mL) onto prepared baking sheet. Sprinkle tops with chopped chives.
3. Bake on middle rack in preheated oven for 18 to 20 minutes or until edges are golden. Transfer biscuits to a rack to cool.

MAKES 1 LOAF

Old-fashioned soda bread is a wonderful accompaniment to a hearty soup or stew. Any leftovers are delicious toasted and spread with butter and homemade preserves.

Whole-Grain Irish Soda Bread

Preheat oven to 375°F (190°C)
Cookie sheet, greased

2 cups	whole wheat flour	500 mL
1 2/3 cups	all-purpose flour	400 mL
2/3 cup	old-fashioned rolled oats	150 mL
1 tbsp	granulated sugar	15 mL
1 1/2 tsp	baking soda	7 mL
1/2 tsp	salt	2 mL
2 cups	buttermilk	500 mL
TOPPING		
1 tbsp	buttermilk	15 mL
1 tbsp	old-fashioned rolled oats	15 mL

1. In a large bowl, combine flours, rolled oats, sugar, baking soda and salt. Stir well. Make a well in center; add buttermilk. Stir until a soft dough forms.

2. Turn out onto lightly floured board; knead five or six times until smooth. Shape dough into a ball; pat into an 8-inch (20 cm) round. Place on prepared cookie sheet. With a sharp knife dipped in flour, cut a large 1/2-inch (1 cm) deep cross on top of loaf.

3. Topping: Brush loaf with buttermilk and sprinkle with oats. Bake in preheated oven for 50 to 60 minutes until well risen and golden; loaf sounds hollow when tapped on base. Immediately wrap in clean, dry tea towel; set aside to cool. This prevents crust from becoming too hard.

SERVES 4

Expecting company and want to get a head start on the cooking? Here's a great breakfast dish that can be assembled a day ahead or frozen. When ready to serve, arrange the toasts on greased baking sheets and pop in the oven while you make the coffee.

TIPS

Freeze unbaked slices in a single layer on a baking sheet lined with plastic wrap; when frozen, transfer to plastic storage bags and freeze. No need to defrost before baking; bake as directed in recipe, increasing baking time by about 5 minutes.

Buy bread that is 4 inches (10 cm) in diameter or increase slices to 10 if slightly smaller.

VARIATION

Fruit Kabobs

Add colorful fruit kabobs to dress up the breakfast plate. Thread assorted fresh fruit chunks, such as apple, banana, strawberries, kiwi, pear and pineapple, onto 4-inch (10 cm) small bamboo skewers. (Trim or cut skewers in half, if necessary, to get the right length.)

Oven French Toast

Preheat oven to 425°F (220°C)
13-by 9-inch (3 L) baking dish
Baking sheet, well-greased

4	eggs	4
1 cup	milk	250 mL
1 tbsp	granulated sugar	15 mL
1 tsp	vanilla	5 mL
8	slices day-old French bread, cut ¾ inch (2 cm) thick	8
¼ cup	melted butter	50 mL
2 tbsp	granulated sugar	25 mL
¾ tsp	ground cinnamon	4 mL

1. In a bowl, whisk together eggs, milk, 1 tbsp (15 mL) granulated sugar and vanilla. Arrange bread slices in a single layer in baking dish. Pour egg mixture over. Turn slices over and let stand until egg mixture is absorbed. Cover and refrigerate until ready to bake. (Recipe can be prepared up to this point the night before.)
2. Arrange toasts in a single layer on prepared sheet and brush tops with half of melted butter.
3. Bake in preheated oven for 10 minutes. Turn slices over; brush tops with remaining melted butter. Bake for 8 minutes longer or until puffed and golden.
4. In a shallow bowl, combine 2 tbsp (25 mL) granulated sugar and cinnamon. Dip baked slices in sugar mixture and lightly coat on both sides. Serve with maple syrup and, if desired, accompany with fruit kabobs (see Variation, left).

MAKES ABOUT 18 PANCAKES

If I had to name one dish that would bring my kids out from under their down comforters on a lazy weekend morning, this would be it. For a different twist, try these irresistible pancakes topped with spiced pear slices, too.

TIPS

To keep pancakes warm, place on rack in warm oven.

Extra pancakes can be wrapped and frozen, then popped in the toaster for a quick breakfast.

To get a head start on a weekend breakfast, I measure out the dry ingredients for several batches of pancakes in advance, place in plastic bags and store in the cupboard. Beat in the liquid ingredients and the batter is ready for the griddle.

Buttermilk Pancakes with Spiced Maple Apples

SPICED MAPLE APPLES

2 tbsp	butter	25 mL
4	apples or pears, peeled, cored and sliced	4
1/3 cup	maple syrup	75 mL
1/2 tsp	ground cinnamon	2 mL
1/2 tsp	ground ginger	2 mL
1/4 tsp	freshly grated nutmeg	1 mL

PANCAKES

1 3/4 cups	all-purpose flour	425 mL
1 tbsp	granulated sugar	15 mL
2 tsp	baking powder	10 mL
1/2 tsp	baking soda	2 mL
1/2 tsp	salt	2 mL
2	eggs	2
2 cups	buttermilk	500 mL
2 tbsp	melted butter	25 mL

1. Spiced Maple Apples: In a large nonstick skillet, melt butter over medium-high heat. Add apples, maple syrup, cinnamon, ginger and nutmeg; cook, stirring often, for 5 minutes or until apples are just tender. Keep warm.

2. Pancakes: In a bowl, combine flour, sugar, baking powder, baking soda and salt. In another bowl, beat eggs; add buttermilk and melted butter. Whisk into flour mixture to make a smooth thick batter.

3. On an oiled griddle or in a large nonstick skillet over medium heat, drop 1/4 cupfuls (50 mL) of batter and spread to a 4-inch (10 cm) circle. Cook for about 1 1/2 minutes or until bubbles appear on top; turn over and cook until browned on other side. Serve with spiced maple apples over top.

Carrot-Raisin Muffins (page 305) ➢
Overleaf: Farmhouse Apple Pie (page 349)

Cakes, Pies and Desserts

continued on next page

< Strawberry Cream Cake (page 326)

BAKING TIPS

- Incorrect measurement is a major cause of baking failures. Use a liquid cup measure for fluids and a dry measure for dry ingredients such as flour. Spoon ingredient into dry measure and level off using a knife. Do not pack the dry measure down by tapping on the counter top; this increases the amount.
- In baking, always use large eggs, not medium or extra large, either of which can affect the baking result.
- Ingredients, such as eggs and butter, should be used at room temperature. Leave eggs on the counter for 30 minutes or place in a bowl of warm (not hot) water for 10 minutes.
- To soften butter, microwave on Defrost and check at 15-second intervals.
- Replace your supplies of baking powder and baking soda every six months; once opened, they oxidize and lose their leavening power.
- Replenish your spices regularly; buy the freshest dried fruits and nuts.
- For walnuts, the light-colored Californian walnuts are preferred.
- Always store nuts in a container in the refrigerator or freezer to keep them fresh
- For perfect cakes, loaves, bars and squares, it's essential to use the correct size of baking pan specified in each recipe.
- When a recipe calls for a baking pan, it refers to a metal pan, while a baking dish refers to glass.
- Light baking sheets, particularly the nonstick variety, are generally better than dark sheets, which attract heat and cause cookies to bake faster and/or cause the undersides to darken too quickly.
- To grease pans or baking sheets, solid vegetable shortening or unsalted or lightly salted butter is recommended.

SERVES 10 TO 12

More commonly known as fruit platz, this delectable recipe was given to me by a Mennonite family in Niagara whose ancestors settled the region over two centuries ago. It makes use of seasonal fruits from sweet-and-sour pitted cherries, raspberries, sliced peaches, nectarines, apricots to blue plums.

TIP

For a smaller-size cake, halve the ingredients and bake in a buttered 8-inch (2 L) square pan for 35 to 40 minutes.

Mennonite Streusel Cake

Preheat oven to 350°F (180°C)
13-by 9-inch (3.5 L) baking pan, generously greased

2 cups	all-purpose flour	500 mL
½ cup	granulated sugar	125 mL
1 tbsp	baking powder	15 mL
¼ tsp	salt	1 mL
⅓ cup	butter, softened	75 mL
1	egg	1
1 cup	half-and-half (10%) cream	250 mL
1½ tsp	vanilla or grated lemon zest	7 mL
4 cups	fresh or frozen blueberries or other seasonal sliced fruits	1 L

CRUMB TOPPING

1 cup	all-purpose flour	250 mL
¾ cup	packed brown sugar	175 mL
½ cup	butter, softened	125 mL

1. In a large bowl, combine flour, sugar, baking powder and salt. Cut in butter using a pastry blender or two knives to make coarse crumbs. In another bowl, beat egg with cream and vanilla. Stir into flour mixture to make a thick batter.
2. Drop tablespoonfuls of batter into prepared baking dish and spread evenly. Top with blueberries in a single layer.
3. Crumb Topping: In a bowl, combine flour and brown sugar. Cut in butter using a pastry blender or two knives to make coarse crumbs. Sprinkle evenly over fruit. Bake on middle rack in preheated oven for 45 to 50 minutes or until crumb topping is golden. Place on a rack and let cool. Cut into squares and serve.

SERVES 10 TO 12

Here's a cake that is so moist with just a hint of spice. Topped with a luscious orange frosting, it's sure to please the most discerning carrot cake fan.

TIP

To soften cream cheese, place in glass bowl and microwave at Medium for 45 to 60 seconds.

Carrot Cake with Orange Cream Cheese Frosting

Preheat oven to 350°F (180°C)
13-by 9-inch (3.5 L) baking pan, greased

2 cups	all-purpose flour	500 mL
2 tsp	baking powder	10 mL
1 ½ tsp	ground cinnamon	7 mL
½ tsp	salt	2 mL
3	eggs	3
1 ⅓ cups	granulated sugar	325 mL
¾ cup	vegetable oil	175 mL
⅓ cup	orange juice	75 mL
2 cups	finely shredded carrots	500 mL
1 cup	chopped walnuts or pecans	250 mL
ORANGE CREAM CHEESE FROSTING		
4 oz	cream cheese, softened	125 g
2 cups	confectioner's (icing) sugar	500 mL
1 tsp	finely grated orange zest	5 mL

1. In a bowl, combine flour, baking powder, cinnamon and salt. In another bowl, beat eggs with sugar, oil and orange juice; stir in carrots and walnuts. Stir in flour mixture until combined; spread batter in prepared baking pan.
2. Bake in preheated oven for 35 to 40 minutes or until cake tester inserted in center comes out clean. Place on rack to cool.
3. Orange Cream Cheese Frosting: In a bowl, using an electric mixer, beat cream cheese, confectioner's sugar and orange zest until smooth. Spread evenly over cake.

SERVES 8 TO 10

Nothing is more seductive than crimson strawberries, cold whipped cream and buttery-lemon cake. For me, this perfect summer dessert beats out shortcake hands down as the ultimate strawberry creation.

TIPS

Strawberries can be replaced with other small fruits such as raspberries, blueberries or blackberries. Or use a combination of several berries.

To make your own superfine sugar, place granulated sugar in a food processor; process until very fine.

For fluffy whipped cream, make sure whipping cream is very cold before beating. As well, place the beaters and bowl in the freezer for 10 minutes before you start.

Strawberry Cream Cake

Preheat oven to 350°F (180°C)
9-inch (23 cm) springform pan, greased and floured

SPONGE CAKE		
3	eggs	3
1 cup	granulated sugar	250 mL
1 ½ cups	all-purpose flour	375 mL
2 tsp	baking powder	10 mL
¼ tsp	salt	1 mL
¾ cup	milk	175 mL
⅓ cup	butter, melted	75 mL
1 tsp	grated lemon zest	5 mL
FILLING		
1 ½ cups	whipping (35%) cream	375 mL
1 tsp	vanilla	5 mL
¼ cup	superfine sugar	50 mL
3 cups	sliced strawberries	750 mL
1 cup	whole small strawberries	250 mL
	Mint sprigs	

1. Sponge Cake: In a bowl, using an electric mixer at high speed, beat eggs and sugar for 3 minutes or until thick and creamy.
2. In a separate bowl, combine flour, baking powder and salt. In a glass measuring cup, combine milk, melted butter and lemon zest.
3. Beat dry ingredients into egg mixture alternately with milk mixture until batter is just smooth.
4. Pour into prepared pan. Bake in preheated oven for 35 minutes or until cake tester inserted in center comes out clean.
5. Let cake cool for 5 minutes; run knife around edge and remove sides. Place on rack to cool completely. Using a long serrated knife, slice cake horizontally to make three layers each about ½ inch (1 cm) thick.

VARIATION

Raspberry Cream Cake

When fresh berries are unavailable, substitute 1 package (10 oz/300 g) individually frozen raspberries. Do not defrost. Set aside 12 frozen berries; place in freezer and use to garnish top shortly before serving. Spread cake layers with whipped cream and reserved frozen berries; refrigerate. Dessert can be assembled up to 4 hours ahead of serving time.

6. Filling: In a bowl, using an electric mixer, whip cream until soft peaks form. Beat in vanilla and sugar, a spoonful at a time, until stiff peaks form.
7. Arrange one cake layer, cut side up on a large serving plate. Spread with one-third of the whipped cream; top with half the sliced berries including some juice. Arrange second cake layer on top. Spread with one-third of the whipped cream and remaining sliced berries with juice. Arrange third layer on top; spread top with remaining whipped cream. Garnish with small whole berries and mint sprigs.

SERVES 8

I keep individual quick-frozen berries stocked in my freezer to make this delectable cake year-round.

TIP

If using frozen berries, individual quick-frozen berries do not need to be defrosted before adding to batter.

Sour Cream Raspberry Coffee Cake

Preheat oven to 350°F (180°C)
9-inch (23 cm) springform pan, greased

1 1/2 cups	all-purpose flour	375 mL
3/4 cup	granulated sugar	175 mL
1/2 cup	sweetened shredded coconut	125 mL
2 tsp	baking powder	10 mL
1/2 tsp	baking soda	2 mL
Pinch	salt	Pinch
2	eggs	2
1 cup	sour cream	250 mL
1 tsp	vanilla	5 mL
1 cup	fresh or frozen raspberries or blueberries	250 mL

CRUMB TOPPING

1/3 cup	packed brown sugar	75 mL
1/4 cup	quick-cooking rolled oats	50 mL
1/4 cup	all-purpose flour	50 mL
1/4 cup	sweetened shredded coconut	50 mL
1/2 tsp	ground cinnamon	2 mL
1/4 cup	butter, cut into pieces	50 mL

1. In a bowl, combine flour, sugar, coconut, baking powder, baking soda and salt. In another bowl, beat eggs with sour cream and vanilla. Stir in flour mixture; mix well. Gently fold in raspberries; spread batter in prepared pan.

2. Crumb Topping: In a bowl, combine brown sugar, oats, flour, coconut and cinnamon. Cut in butter using a pastry blender or two knives to make coarse crumbs. Sprinkle evenly over top.

3. Bake on middle rack in preheated oven for 40 to 45 minutes or until tester inserted in center comes out clean. Set cake on rack to cool. Serve warm or at room temperature.

SERVES 8

This coffee cake is welcome at brunch, afternoon tea or dessert time. Make it year-round with other seasonal fruits such as pears, apples, pitted cherries or plums.

TIP

To peel peaches, plunge in boiling water for 15 to 30 seconds to loosen skins.

Peach Almond Cake

Preheat oven to 350°F (180°C)
9-inch (23 cm) springform pan or cake pan, greased

1 ½ cups	all-purpose flour	375 mL
¾ cup	granulated sugar	175 mL
1 ½ tsp	baking powder	7 mL
½ tsp	baking soda	2 mL
¼ tsp	salt	1 mL
2	eggs	2
½ cup	plain yogurt	125 mL
¼ cup	butter, melted	50 mL
½ tsp	almond extract	2 mL
3	peaches, peeled and sliced	3
3 tbsp	sliced blanched almonds	45 mL
2 tbsp	granulated sugar	25 mL
½ tsp	ground cinnamon	2 mL

1. In a mixing bowl, stir together flour, ¾ cup (175 mL) sugar, baking powder, baking soda and salt.
2. In another bowl, beat eggs, yogurt, melted butter and almond extract until smooth. Stir into dry ingredients to make a smooth thick batter. Spread in prepared pan. Arrange peaches on top in a circular fashion.
3. In a small bowl, combine almonds, 2 tbsp (25 mL) sugar and cinnamon. Sprinkle over peaches. Bake in preheated oven for 45 to 50 minutes or until cake tester inserted in center comes out clean.

SERVES 12

This crowd-pleasing cake is as easy to make as a batch of muffins. Serve it as a dessert or enjoy it with a fresh-brewed cup of coffee or tea.

TIP

To freeze, wrap in plastic wrap, then in foil. Cake freezes well for up to one month.

Blueberry Crumb Cake

Preheat oven to 350°F (180°C)
9-inch (23 cm) springform pan, greased

CRUMB TOPPING

1/2 cup	all-purpose flour	125 mL
1/3 cup	packed brown sugar	75 mL
1 tsp	ground cinnamon	5 mL
1/4 cup	butter, cut into pieces	50 mL

CAKE

2 cups	all-purpose flour	500 mL
1 cup	granulated sugar	250 mL
2 1/2 tsp	baking powder	12 mL
1/2 tsp	baking soda	2 mL
1/2 tsp	salt	2 mL
2 cups	fresh or frozen blueberries	500 mL
2	eggs	2
3/4 cup	plain yogurt	175 mL
1/3 cup	butter, melted	75 mL
1 1/2 tsp	grated lemon zest	7 mL

1. Crumb Topping: In a bowl, combine flour, brown sugar and cinnamon. Cut in butter with a pastry blender or two knives until crumbly.
2. Cake: In a large mixing bowl, stir together flour, sugar, baking powder, baking soda and salt. Toss blueberries with 2 tbsp (25 mL) of the flour mixture; set aside.
3. In another bowl, beat eggs, yogurt, melted butter and lemon zest. Stir in flour mixture to make a smooth batter. Gently fold in floured blueberries. (Batter will be thick.)
4. Spoon into prepared pan. Sprinkle top with crumb mixture. Bake in preheated oven for 50 to 60 minutes or until cake tester inserted in center comes out clean. Let cool on rack. Run a knife around edge; remove side of pan, remove base and transfer cake to serving plate.

Double Chocolate Snacking Cake

SERVES 12

Zucchini gives this cake a rich, moist texture. There's no visible trace of it when the cake is baked, so it's perfect to serve to reluctant zucchini eaters. I don't bother to peel the zucchini, but you can if you prefer. Shredding the zucchini in a food processor saves time.

TIPS

If you don't have a flour sifter, sift the dry ingredients through a fine-meshed sieve to remove any lumps.

The chocolate glaze is optional; instead, you can sift confectioner's sugar over cake just before serving.

Preheat oven to 350°F (180°C)
13-by 9-inch (3.5 L) cake pan, greased

2	eggs	2
1 cup	sour cream or plain yogurt	250 mL
1/2 cup	vegetable oil	125 mL
2 tsp	vanilla	10 mL
2 cups	finely shredded zucchini	500 mL
2 1/4 cups	all-purpose flour	550 mL
1 1/3 cups	granulated sugar	325 mL
1/2 cup	cocoa powder	125 mL
1 tsp	baking powder	5 mL
1 tsp	baking soda	5 mL
1/2 tsp	salt	2 mL
3/4 cup	semi-sweet chocolate chips	175 mL
3/4 cup	chopped walnuts	175 mL

CHOCOLATE GLAZE (OPTIONAL)

1 cup	confectioner's (icing) sugar	250 mL
2 tbsp	cocoa powder	25 mL
2 tbsp	milk	25 mL

1. In a large bowl, beat eggs, sour cream, oil and vanilla. Stir in shredded zucchini.
2. In another bowl, sift together flour, sugar, cocoa, baking powder, baking soda and salt. Stir into creamed mixture until just combined. Fold in chocolate chips and walnuts.
3. Spread batter evenly in pan. Bake for 45 to 50 minutes or until a cake tester inserted in center comes out clean. Let stand on rack for 15 minutes to cool.
4. Chocolate Glaze: In a bowl combine confectioner's sugar, cocoa powder and milk; stir to make a smooth, spreadable glaze. Spread glaze, if using, over warm cake; let cool completely.

SERVES 8

Moist, rich and chocolatey — everything that you would expect in an old-fashioned layer cake. Serve as is or top with a scoop of vanilla ice cream for added indulgence.

Sour Cream Fudge Layer Cake with Chocolate Frosting

Preheat oven to 350°F (180°C)
Two 9-inch (2.5 L) round baking pans, bottoms lined with parchment paper

1 cup	strong coffee	250 mL
4 oz	unsweetened chocolate, chopped (4 squares)	125 g
1 cup	sour cream	250 mL
1½ tsp	baking soda	7 mL
¼ tsp	salt	1 mL
¾ cup	butter, softened	175 mL
1¾ cups	granulated sugar	425 mL
2	eggs	2
2 tsp	vanilla	10 mL
2¼ cups	all-purpose flour	550 mL

CHOCOLATE FROSTING

2½ cups	confectioner's (icing) sugar	625 mL
½ cup	cocoa powder	125 mL
½ cup	butter, softened	125 mL
3 tbsp	dark rum, coffee-flavored liqueur or milk	45 mL
3 tbsp	sour cream or milk (approx.)	45 mL

1. Brush parchment and sides of baking pan with melted butter and dust with cocoa powder, shaking out excess.
2. In a large glass bowl, microwave coffee and chocolate at High for 1 to 2 minutes, stirring once, until piping hot and chocolate is melted. Let cool to room temperature.
3. In a bowl, whisk together sour cream, baking soda and salt.

4. In large bowl, using an electric mixer, cream butter and sugar until fluffy. Beat in eggs, one at a time, until incorporated. Beat in chocolate-coffee mixture and vanilla. Beat in half of the flour with half of the sour cream mixture; beat in remaining flour and sour cream mixture to make a smooth batter. Spread evenly in prepared pans.
5. Bake in preheated oven for 35 to 40 minutes or until cake feels firm in the center and edges begin to pull away from sides. Leave in pans for 5 minutes; turn out onto wire racks to cool. (Cake layers can be wrapped in plastic wrap then in foil; freeze for up to one month.)
6. Chocolate Frosting: In a bowl, sift confectioner's sugar with cocoa powder. Using an electric mixer on low speed, beat in butter and rum until smooth. Beat in enough sour cream to make a spreadable frosting.
7. Arrange one cake layer on a large plate. Spread with some of the frosting. Top with second layer and spread frosting over tops and sides of cake.

SERVES 8

The combination of chocolate swirling through thick cream cheese on top of a chocolate nut crust makes this a decadent splurge. It's hard to resist having seconds.

TIPS

To prevent the top of the cheesecake from cracking, don't overbake it; it should still appear slightly underbaked in the center.

Chocolate baking crumbs are available in the baking or cookie section of supermarkets.

To melt chocolate, place in bowl and microwave at Medium for 2½ to 3 minutes.

Chocolate Swirl Cheesecake

Preheat oven to 325°F (160°C)
9-inch (23 cm) springform pan, ungreased

CRUST		
1 cup	chocolate baking crumbs	250 mL
⅓ cup	chopped walnuts or pecans	75 mL
2 tbsp	butter, melted	25 mL
2 tbsp	granulated sugar	25 mL
FILLING		
1 lb	cream cheese, softened (two 8 oz/250 g packages)	500 g
⅔ cup	granulated sugar	150 mL
3	eggs	3
½ cup	sour cream	125 mL
1½ tsp	vanilla	7 mL
3 oz	semi-sweet chocolate, melted (3 squares)	90 g

1. Crust: In a food processor, combine crumbs, walnuts, butter and sugar. Process using on-off turns until nuts are finely chopped. Press in bottom and 1 inch (2.5 cm) up sides of springform pan. Bake in preheated oven for 10 minutes or until just set. Let cool.
2. Filling: In a large bowl, using electric mixer, beat cream cheese and sugar until smooth. Beat in eggs, one at a time, until incorporated. Beat in sour cream and vanilla.
3. Transfer 1 cup (250 mL) of the batter to a bowl; stir in melted chocolate until smooth.
4. Spoon white batter into prepared pan. Top with six distinct spoonfuls of chocolate batter. Using a knife, cut through batter in a zigzag pattern being careful not to cut through to crust.
5. Bake in preheated oven for 30 minutes or until firm around outside and slightly moist in center. Turn off oven, leave door ajar and let cake cool in oven for 1 hour. Remove and carefully run a knife around outside edge; refrigerate.

SERVES 8

Can't decide to have a slice of cheesecake or wedge of pie? This delicious dessert satisfies both cravings in one slice.

Blueberry Cheesecake Tart

Preheat oven to 350°F (180°C)
10-inch (25 cm) tart pan with removable bottom, lightly greased

1 ½ cups	all-purpose flour	375 mL
¼ cup	granulated sugar	50 mL
¼ tsp	baking powder	1 mL
Pinch	salt	Pinch
½ cup	cold butter, cut into pieces	125 mL
1	egg yolk	1

FILLING

12 oz	cream cheese	375 g
½ cup	granulated sugar	125 mL
2	eggs	2
1 ½ tsp	finely grated lemon zest	7 mL
2 tbsp	fresh lemon juice	25 mL
1 ½ cups	fresh or frozen blueberries	375 mL

1. In a food processor, combine flour, sugar, baking powder and salt. Add butter; process to make fine crumbs. In a small bowl, beat egg yolk with 2 tbsp (25 mL) water. Pour over flour mixture; process, using on-off turns, until dough begins to come together. Gather into a ball; flatten into a flat round. Wrap in plastic wrap and refrigerate for one hour.

2. Place dough between two sheets of parchment paper or plastic wrap. Roll out into a 12-inch (30 cm) round. Remove top parchment paper and flip dough into tart pan. Remove parchment paper and press dough into pan; turn edges over and press into sides of pan. (If dough tears, pinch to seal.) Prick pastry with a fork; bake in preheated oven for 20 minutes or until light golden. Place on rack to cool.

3. In a bowl, using an electric mixer, beat cream cheese and sugar. Beat in eggs, lemon zest and juice.

4. Arrange blueberries in single layer in partially baked tart shell; pour filling over berries to cover. Bake in preheated oven for 35 minutes or until center is set. Place on rack to cool; refrigerate.

SERVES 8 TO 10

Making a cheesecake may seem like a half-day production, but not with this no-bake method that is guaranteed to win raves for the cook.

TIP

Can be made the day ahead, cover and refrigerate.

Luscious Tropical Cheesecake

Preheat oven to 350°F (180°C)
9-inch (23 cm) springform pan, ungreased

CRUST

1 cup	digestive cookie or graham wafer crumbs	250 mL
2 tbsp	granulated sugar	25 mL
2 tbsp	butter, melted	25 mL

FILLING

1	can (14 oz/398 mL) crushed pineapple	1
1	package (1/4 oz/7 g) unflavored gelatin	1
8 oz	cream cheese, softened and cubed	250 g
1 cup	ricotta cheese	250 mL
1/2 cup	granulated sugar	125 mL
1 1/2 tsp	grated orange zest	7 mL
1 cup	whipping (35%) cream	250 mL
1/2 cup	sweetened shredded coconut, toasted	125 mL

1. Crust: In a bowl, combine cookie crumbs, sugar and butter. Press in bottom of springform pan. Bake for 8 minutes or until set. Chill until firm. Fit a 3-inch (8 cm) wide strip of waxed or parchment paper around inside of pan.
2. Filling: Drain pineapple in sieve set over bowl; press with rubber spatula to extract juice. Pour 1/2 cup (125 mL) of the juice into a small saucepan; sprinkle gelatin over. Let stand for 5 minutes to soften. Cook over low heat, stirring, until gelatin is dissolved. (Or put juice and gelatin in a measuring cup; let stand 5 minutes to soften, then microwave at Medium for 1 minute.) Let cool slightly.

TIP

To toast coconut, place on baking sheet in a 350°F (180°C) oven, stirring once, for 5 to 6 minutes.

3. In a food processor, combine cream cheese, ricotta, sugar and warm gelatin mixture; process until smooth. Transfer to a large bowl; stir in drained pineapple and orange zest.
4. In a bowl, using an electric mixer, whip cream until stiff peaks form. Fold into pineapple mixture until smooth. Pour into prepared pan; smooth top and sprinkle with toasted coconut. Chill until set, about 4 hours. Remove side of pan and waxed or parchment paper; arrange on a serving plate.

SERVES 8 TO 10

No longer are tart, crimson cranberries merely an accompaniment to turkey. They star in a number of dessert recipes including this crumb-topped torte.

TIPS

Buy extra bags of cranberries on special and tuck into your freezer for year-round use.

Cranberries freeze well for up to one year and can be used in any recipe calling for fresh berries. This delicious cake can be made ahead and frozen.

Cranberry Cheese Torte

9-inch (23 cm) springform pan, greased and floured

CHEESE FILLING

8 oz	cream cheese, softened	250 g
1/3 cup	granulated sugar	75 mL
1	egg	1
1 tbsp	all-purpose flour	15 mL
1 tbsp	fresh lemon juice	15 mL
1 tsp	grated lemon zest	5 mL

CRUMB TOPPING

3/4 cup	all-purpose flour	175 mL
1/3 cup	packed brown sugar	75 mL
1/2 tsp	ground cinnamon	2 mL
1/3 cup	cold butter, cut into pieces	75 mL
1/3 cup	chopped pecans	75 mL

CAKE BATTER

2 cups	fresh or frozen cranberries, chopped	500 mL
3/4 cup	granulated sugar	175 mL
1/3 cup	butter, softened	75 mL
2	eggs	2
1 tsp	vanilla	5 mL
1 1/4 cups	all-purpose flour	300 mL
1 1/4 tsp	baking powder	6 mL
1/4 tsp	salt	1 mL
1/3 cup	milk	75 mL

1. Cheese Filling: In a bowl, beat cream cheese and sugar until creamy. Beat in egg, flour, lemon juice and zest until smooth.
2. Crumb Topping: In a bowl, combine flour, brown sugar and cinnamon. Cut in butter with a pastry blender or two knives to make coarse crumbs. Stir in pecans.

3. Cake Batter: In a bowl, combine cranberries with ¼ cup (50 mL) sugar; reserve. In a large bowl, cream butter and remaining sugar until light and fluffy. Beat in eggs and vanilla until smooth. Combine flour, baking powder and salt. Add to creamed mixture alternately with milk to make a smooth batter.
4. Spread in prepared springform pan. Sprinkle with 1 cup (250 mL) of the cranberry mixture; spoon cheese filling over. Top with remaining cranberry mixture. Sprinkle with crumb topping.
5. Bake in preheated oven for 50 to 55 minutes or until top is golden and cheese filling is set. Cool in pan on wire rack for 30 minutes before removing sides. Refrigerate until serving time.

MAKES 1 LOAF

Microplane zester/graters have become today's handy new kitchen gadget to shred citrus peel. They come in a variety of grate sizes from fine to coarse and also work magic when grating fresh ginger and hard cheeses such as Parmesan.

Golden Citrus Fruitcake

Preheat oven to 300°F (150°C)
9-by 5-inch (2 L) loaf pan, greased, bottom and sides lined with parchment paper and greased
Shallow pan of water placed on bottom rack in oven

1½ cups	chopped dried apricots	375 mL
1 cup	chopped dried figs	250 mL
1 cup	golden raisins	250 mL
1 cup	dark raisins or pecans	250 mL
½ cup	orange-flavored liqueur or orange juice	125 mL
¾ cup	butter, softened	175 mL
¾ cup	granulated sugar	175 mL
3	eggs	3
1 tbsp	finely grated orange zest	15 mL
1 tbsp	finely grated lemon zest	15 mL
1¾ cups	all-purpose flour	425 mL
1½ tsp	baking powder	7 mL
¼ tsp	salt	1 mL
	Additional orange-flavored liqueur (optional)	

1. In a large glass bowl, combine apricots, figs, golden and dark raisins and orange-flavored liqueur. Microwave at High for 2 minutes, stirring once. Let cool, stirring occasionally.

2. In a large bowl, using an electric mixer, cream butter and sugar until fluffy. Beat in eggs, one at a time, until incorporated. Stir in orange and lemon zests.

3. In another bowl, stir together flour, baking powder and salt. Using electric mixer, beat into creamed mixture until combined. Using a spatula, fold in fruit mixture including any remaining liqueur that hasn't been absorbed by the fruit.

4. Spoon batter into prepared pan. Bake in preheated oven for 2 hours or until cake tester inserted in center comes out clean. Transfer to a rack. Let stand for 15 minutes. Lift cake out of pan and place on rack until cool.
5. Remove parchment paper. If desired, wrap cake in cheesecloth and drizzle with about 2 tbsp (25 mL) orange-flavored liqueur. Wrap in heavy-duty foil or plastic storage bag. Store in cool dry place or refrigerate. Age fruitcake for at least one week before serving.

SERVES 8

This spectacular tart with a tangy cranberry and marmalade filling is ideal to serve with a steaming cup of fresh-brewed coffee or espresso. Don't let the length of this recipe deter you — it's surprisingly easy to make.

TIP

The baked tart can be wrapped in foil and frozen for one month.

Cranberry-Orange Cookie Tart

Preheat oven to 350°F (180°C)
10-inch (25 cm) tart pan with removable bottom, greased

FILLING

2 cups	fresh or frozen cranberries	500 mL
2/3 cup	granulated sugar	150 mL
1/2 cup	orange juice	125 mL
1/2 cup	orange marmalade or raspberry jam	125 mL

PASTRY

2 cups	all-purpose flour	500 mL
1/2 cup	granulated sugar	125 mL
1/4 tsp	salt	1 mL
2/3 cup	cold butter, cubed	150 mL
1	egg	1
1 tsp	vanilla	5 mL
1	egg yolk	1
	Confectioner's (icing) sugar (optional)	

1. Filling: In a medium saucepan, combine cranberries, sugar and orange juice. Bring to a boil; reduce heat and cook, stirring often, for 6 minutes or until thick and jam-like. Stir in marmalade. Remove from heat; let cool.
2. Pastry: In a large bowl, combine flour, sugar and salt. With a pastry blender or two knives, cut in butter until mixture resembles fine crumbs. In a small bowl, beat egg with vanilla; stir into dry ingredients. Gather dough into a ball and on lightly floured board, knead three to four times until smooth. Shape dough into two discs, one slightly larger than the other. Wrap each in plastic wrap; refrigerate for 1 hour.

3. On a lightly floured surface, roll the larger dough portion into a 12-inch (30 cm) circle. Fit dough into tart pan. Trim edges of pastry, leaving a ½-inch (1 cm) overhang. Fold the overhang into the pan and press into pastry to reinforce the sides of the tart. Prick dough in several places with a fork.
4. Spoon cranberry-jam mixture into tart shell. Roll out remaining dough on lightly floured surface into a 10-inch (25 cm) circle. Cut into twelve ¾-inch (2 cm) strips. Using a long spatula to lift them, arrange six strips of dough, spaced about ½-inch (1 cm) apart, over jam filling. Arrange remaining strips at right angles to first strips to create a diamond shaped-pattern. Trim edges; press pastry strips against sides of tart to seal. In a small bowl, beat egg yolk with 1 tsp (5 mL) water; brush over pastry strips and edges.
5. Bake for 40 to 45 minutes or until golden. Let cool on rack for 15 minutes. Remove pan rim; let cool completely. Just before serving, sift with confectioner's sugar, if desired.

SERVES 8

Intimidated by baking a pie? Don't be. This one is a breeze to bake. The filling just takes just a matter of minutes to assemble. It goes a long way to satisfy any sweet craving.

VARIATION

Chocolate Pecan Pie

Line pie plate with pastry; freeze 15 minutes or until firm. Microwave ½ cup (125 mL) semi-sweet chocolate chips at Medium for 2 minutes or until melted. Stir until smooth; let cool slightly. Spread pastry bottom with melted chocolate; refrigerate until set. Pour in pecan filling.

Pecan Pie

Preheat oven to 375°F (190°C)
9-inch (23 cm) pie plate, lightly greased

	Pastry for single crust 9-inch (23 cm) pie crust (see recipe, page 351)	
2	eggs	2
¾ cup	packed brown sugar	175 mL
¾ cup	golden corn syrup	175 mL
2 tbsp	butter, melted	25 mL
1 tsp	vanilla	5 mL
1¼ cups	whole pecans	300 mL

1. On a lightly flavored surface, roll pastry out to a 12-inch (30 cm) round. Fit into lightly buttered 9-inch (23 cm) pie plate or fluted tart pan with removable bottom. Trim dough leaving a ¾-inch (2 cm) border. Fold under rim of dough and flute pastry edge. Refrigerate.
2. In a bowl, beat eggs. Stir in brown sugar, corn syrup, melted butter and vanilla until smooth.
3. Coarsely chop 1 cup (250 mL) pecans (chop nuts into three pieces each). Stir into filling.
4. Pour into prepared crust; sprinkle top with remaining ¼ cup (50 mL) whole pecans. Bake in preheated oven for 35 to 40 minutes or until filling is set around edges but is slightly moist in the center. Cool pie completely on wire rack. Serve at room temperature.

SERVES 8

Living in Niagara in the heart of peach country, I can't wait for the first baskets of rosy-blushed peaches to appear at neighboring roadside stands in late July to make my all-time favorite pie.

Ginger Peach Pie

Preheat oven to 425°F (220°C)
9-inch (23 cm) pie plate, lightly greased

	Pastry for double-crust 9-inch (23 cm) pie (see recipe, page 171)	
6 cups	sliced, peeled peaches (about 8)	1.5 L
1 ½ tsp	grated lemon zest	7 mL
2 tbsp	fresh lemon juice	25 mL
¾ cup	packed brown sugar	175 mL
¼ cup	cornstarch	50 mL
¼ cup	finely chopped candied ginger (optional)	50 mL

1. On a lightly floured surface, roll out half of the pastry into a 12-inch (30 cm) round. Roll pastry loosely around rolling pin; unroll into pie plate and trim edges.

2. In a large bowl, toss peaches with lemon zest and juice; stir in brown sugar, cornstarch and candied ginger, if using. Spoon into prepared pie shell.

3. Roll out remaining pastry and fit over filling. Trim leaving a ½-inch (1 cm) overhang. Tuck top edge of pastry under bottom edge. Press edges together with a fork or flute edges with fingers to seal. Cut steam vent in center and make small slashes using a knife.

4. Bake in preheated oven for 15 minutes; reduce temperature to 375°F (190°C). Bake for 35 to 40 minutes or until pastry is golden and filling is bubbly. Place on rack to cool. Serve warm with ice cream, if desired.

SERVES 8

Tart, sweet and lemony — who can resist indulging in a slice of this tempting pie?

TIP

Make sure to seal edges of crust with meringue to prevent the meringue from shrinking when baked.

VARIATION

Sky High Lemon Meringue Pie

For a very high meringue, use 5 egg whites and increase sugar to ⅔ cup (150 mL).

Lemon Meringue Pie

Preheat oven to 425°F (220°C)
9-inch (23 cm) pie plate, lightly greased

	Pastry for single crust 9-inch (23 cm) pie (see recipe, page 351)	
FILLING		
1 cup	granulated sugar	250 mL
¼ cup	cornstarch	50 mL
Pinch	salt	Pinch
4	egg yolks	4
½ cup	fresh lemon juice	125 mL
2 tbsp	butter, cut into pieces	25 mL
1 tbsp	finely grated lemon zest	15 mL
MERINGUE		
4	egg whites	4
¼ tsp	cream of tartar	1 mL
½ cup	granulated sugar	125 mL

1. On a lightly floured surface, roll out pastry into a 12-inch (30 cm) round. Roll pastry loosely around rolling pin; unroll into pie plate. Trim edge leaving a ½-inch (1 cm) overhang; turn pastry edge under and flute edge. Prick with a fork and line with a sheet of parchment paper or foil; fill with dried beans or pie weights.
2. Bake in preheated oven for 10 minutes or until edges are set. Remove pie weights and bake for 5 to 6 minutes more or until pastry is light golden. Place on rack to cool.
3. Filling: In a medium saucepan, combine sugar, cornstarch and salt; whisk in 1½ cups (375 mL) cold water until smooth. Add egg yolks and lemon juice. Cook over medium heat, whisking constantly, until mixture comes to a boil. Boil, stirring constantly, for 1 minute; remove from heat. Whisk in butter and lemon zest until butter is completely melted. Let mixture cool for 10 minutes; pour into pie shell. Let cool completely until filling is set, about 2 to 3 hours.

4. Meringue: In a large bowl, using an electric mixer, beat egg whites and cream of tartar until soft peaks form. Gradually add sugar, a spoonful at a time, until stiff glossy peaks form. Spread over lemon filling, making sure to seal edges of the crust. Make decorative swirls with the back of a spoon.
5. Bake in preheated 350°F (180°C) oven for 10 to 12 minutes or until light golden. Place on rack to cool; refrigerate. To serve, cut with sharp knife dipped in hot water.

SERVES 8

This classic pie is the highlight of Thanksgiving dinner for my two children, Pat and Nicole, when they come home from university. The whipped cream topping is a must to complete the holiday indulgence!

Pumpkin Pie

Preheat oven to 425°F (220°C)
9-inch (23 cm) pie plate, lightly greased

	Pastry for single crust 9-inch (23 cm) pie (see recipe, page 351)	
2	eggs	2
1 cup	packed brown sugar	250 mL
2 cups	pumpkin purée (not pie filling)	500 mL
1 cup	half-and-half (10%) cream	250 mL
1 1/2 tsp	ground cinnamon	7 mL
1/2 tsp	ground allspice	2 mL
1/2 tsp	freshly grated nutmeg	2 mL
1/4 tsp	ground cloves	1 mL
1/4 tsp	salt	1 mL

1. On a lightly floured surface, roll out pastry into a 12-inch (30 cm) round. Roll pastry loosely around rolling pin; unroll into pie plate. Trim edge leaving a 1/2-inch (1 cm) overhang; turn pastry edge under and flute edge. Refrigerate until ready to fill.
2. In a bowl, beat eggs with brown sugar. Stir in pumpkin purée, cream, cinnamon, allspice, nutmeg, cloves and salt until spices are well combined.
3. Pour filling into pie shell; bake in oven for 15 minutes, then reduce temperature to 350°F (180°C). Bake for 35 to 40 minutes more, until tip of knife inserted in center comes out clean. Place on rack to cool; refrigerate.

SERVES 6 TO 8

Intimidated by the thought of making two-crust pies? Try this simple free-form pie — it only needs a single pie crust and looks like it came from a pastry shop.

TIP

Store-bought pastry for a single crust pie can be used instead of the suggested homemade pastry.

Farmhouse Apple Pie

Preheat oven to 375°F (190°C)
Large baking sheet, lightly greased

PASTRY

1¼ cups	all-purpose flour	300 mL
1 tbsp	granulated sugar	15 mL
Pinch	salt	Pinch
½ cup	butter, cut into pieces	125 mL
2 tbsp	cold water (approx.)	25 mL

FILLING

4	apples, such as Golden Delicious, Spy or Granny Smith, peeled, cored and sliced	4
⅓ cup	granulated sugar	75 mL
¼ cup	finely chopped pecans	50 mL
½ tsp	ground cinnamon	2 mL

1. Pastry: In a bowl combine flour, sugar and generous pinch of salt. Cut in butter with a pastry blender or two knives to make coarse crumbs. Sprinkle with enough water to hold dough together; gather into a ball. Flatten to a 5-inch (12 cm) circle; wrap in plastic wrap and refrigerate for 30 minutes.
2. On a lightly floured surface, roll pastry to a 13-inch (32 cm) round; transfer to large baking sheet. Using a sharp knife, trim pastry edge to form an even circle.
3. Filling: Starting 2 inches (5 cm) from edge, overlap apple slices in a circle; arrange another overlapping circle of apples in center. In a bowl, combine sugar, pecans and cinnamon; sprinkle over apples. Fold pastry rim over apples to form a 2-inch (5 cm) edge.
4. Bake for 35 to 40 minutes or until pastry is golden and apples are tender. Place on rack; let cool. With a spatula, carefully slide pie onto serving platter.

SERVES 8

When you arrive home with your bounty of rosy apples in the fall, whip up this family treat. You won't regret it. A thick slice of warm-from-the-oven pie topped with a scoop of vanilla ice cream is pure comfort food no one can resist.

VARIATION

Apple Walnut Crisp

Omit pastry shell. Arrange apple filling in 9-inch (2.5 L) round or square baking dish. Prepare crumble topping. Toss with ½ cup (125 mL) chopped walnuts or pecans. Sprinkle evenly over fruit. Bake in preheated 375°F (190°C) oven for 35 to 40 minutes or until apples are tender and topping is golden.

Cinnamon Apple Crumble Pie

Preheat oven to 425°F (220°C)

	Pastry for single crust 9- or 10-inch (23 or 25 cm) pie shell (see recipe right)	

FILLING

8 cups	sliced and peeled tart apples, such as Macintosh	2 L
½ cup	granulated sugar	125 mL
2 tbsp	all-purpose flour	25 mL
1½ tsp	ground cinnamon	7 mL
¼ tsp	freshly grated nutmeg	1 mL

CRUMBLE TOPPING

¾ cup	old-fashioned rolled oats	175 mL
½ cup	all-purpose flour	125 mL
⅔ cup	packed brown sugar	150 mL
½ cup	cold butter, cut into pieces	125 mL

1. On a lightly floured surface, roll out pastry to a 12-inch (30 cm) round. Fit into a lightly greased deep 9-inch (23 cm) pie plate; trim pastry leaving ½-inch (1 cm) border. Fold under rim of dough and decoratively flute the edges. Refrigerate.
2. Filling: In a large bowl, toss apples with sugar, flour, cinnamon and nutmeg. Spoon into prepared pie shell, packing lightly.
3. Crumble Topping: In a bowl, combine rolled oats, flour and brown sugar; cut in butter using a pastry blender or fork until mixture resembles coarse crumbs. Sprinkle over apples, packing lightly.
4. Bake in lower third of preheated oven for 15 minutes; reduce temperature to 350°F (180°C) and bake for 40 to 45 minutes more or until apples are tender.
5. Place on rack to cool. Serve warm or at room temperature with ice cream, if desired.

TIP
Traditional pie pastry is made with shortening, but I prefer to make mine using butter and shortening. The reason? Not only does the buttery taste come through, but butter produces a golden crust. Another plus: the pastry is easy to handle and roll.

Single Crust Pie Pastry

1/4 cup	cold butter	50 mL
1/4 cup	shortening	50 mL
1 1/4 cups	all-purpose flour	300 mL
1/4 tsp	salt	1 mL
2 tbsp	ice water (approx.)	25 mL

1. Place butter and shortening in a bowl; freeze for 20 minutes or until firm. Cut into bits.
2. In a food processor, combine flour, salt, butter and shortening. Process to make fine crumbs. Transfer to a bowl; stir in water and gather dough into a ball. (Add just enough water to hold dough together.) Alternative method: Place flour and salt in bowl. Using a pastry blender, cut in butter and shortening; no need to put in freezer to make fine crumbs. Stir in water and toss; gather dough into a ball.
3. With floured hands, flatten dough into a 5-inch (13 cm) round. Wrap in plastic wrap; refrigerate for 1 hour.

SERVES 6 TO 8

Saucy fruit topped with a light cake batter makes one of the most soothing desserts ever created. This version hails from Quebec, where sweet and snappy Macintosh apples are paired with amber maple syrup.

TIP

Once opened, make sure to store maple syrup in the refrigerator. It also can be frozen.

Warm Maple Apple Pudding

Preheat oven to 350°F (180°C)
8-inch (2 L) square baking dish, greased

4 cups	peeled and sliced Macintosh apples	1 L
2/3 cup	maple syrup	150 mL
1/3 cup	raisins	75 mL
1 cup	all-purpose flour	250 mL
1/4 cup	granulated sugar	50 mL
1 1/2 tsp	baking powder	7 mL
1/2 tsp	baking soda	2 mL
1/4 tsp	salt	1 mL
1/4 cup	butter, cut into pieces	50 mL
1	egg	1
1/2 cup	buttermilk	125 mL
1 tsp	vanilla	5 mL

1. In a saucepan, bring apples and maple syrup to a boil; simmer 3 minutes or until softened. Add raisins. Pour into prepared baking dish.
2. In a bowl, combine flour, sugar, baking powder, baking soda and salt. Cut in butter using pastry blender or two knives to make fine crumbs. In a bowl, beat egg, buttermilk, and vanilla. Pour over flour mixture; stir just until combined.
3. Drop by large spoonfuls onto warm apple slices. Bake in preheated oven for 30 minutes or until top is golden and cake tester inserted in center comes out clean. Serve warm with ice cream, if desired.

Bread Pudding with Caramelized Pears (page 356) ➢

SERVE 6

What could be more quintessentially comfort food that homespun baked apples? Here they take on an entertaining flair with a splash of rum. Terrific served warm.

TIP

If baking apples ahead, reheat in the microwave at Medium-High for 4 to 5 minutes or until warm.

VARIATION

Instead of rum, replace with additional water and 1 tsp (5 mL) vanilla.

Baked Apples with Buttered Rum Sauce

Preheat oven to 350°F (180°C)
Shallow baking dish just large enough to hold apples

6	medium apples, such as Spartan or Cortland	6
1/2	lemon	1/2
1/3 cup	chopped pecans	75 mL
1/3 cup	sultana raisins	75 mL
2 tbsp	butter, cut into pieces	25 mL
3/4 cup	packed brown sugar	175 mL
1/4 tsp	freshly grated nutmeg	1 mL
1/4 cup	dark rum or brandy	50 mL

1. Core apples; peel skins starting at top leaving 1-inch (2.5 cm) band at bottom. Rub apples with lemon half to prevent browning. Arrange in baking dish.
2. In a bowl, combine pecans and raisins; stuff into apple cavities and top with butter.
3. In a small saucepan, combine brown sugar, 1/3 cup (75 mL) water and nutmeg; place over medium heat and bring to a boil, stirring, until sugar is dissolved. Stir in rum. Pour over apples. Bake in oven, basting occasionally with sauce, for 45 to 50 minutes or until apples are just tender when pierced with a knife.
4. Place in individual serving dishes and drizzle with sauce. Serve warm.

< Lemon Fool with Fresh Berries (page 361)

SERVES 8

I look forward to indulging in this old-fashioned dessert when local berries and rhubarb are in season. But it's also good in winter, when I turn to my freezer for my stash of summer fruits. Serve the cobbler warm and top with good-quality vanilla ice cream.

TIPS

If using frozen fruit, there's no need to defrost before using.

If you prefer to bake the cobbler earlier in the day, reheat in 350°F (180°C) oven for about 15 minutes.

VARIATION

Blueberry-Peach Cobbler

Use 2 cups (500 mL) fresh or frozen blueberries and 4 cups (1 L) sliced peaches. Reduce sugar to 2/3 cup (150 mL).

Strawberry-Rhubarb Cobbler

Preheat oven to 400°F (200°C)
9-inch (2.5 L) round or square baking dish

4 cups	chopped fresh rhubarb	1 L
2 cups	sliced strawberries	500 mL
3/4 cup	granulated sugar	175 mL
2 tbsp	cornstarch	25 mL
1 tsp	grated orange zest	5 mL

BISCUIT TOPPING

1 cup	all-purpose flour	250 mL
1/4 cup	granulated sugar	50 mL
1 1/2 tsp	baking powder	7 mL
1/4 tsp	salt	1 mL
1/4 cup	cold butter, cut into pieces	50 mL
1/2 cup	milk	125 mL
1 tsp	vanilla	5 mL
	Additional granulated sugar	

1. Place rhubarb and strawberries in baking dish. In a small bowl, combine sugar, cornstarch and orange zest; sprinkle over fruit and gently toss.
2. Bake in preheated oven for 20 to 25 minutes (increase to 30 minutes if using frozen fruit) until hot and bubbles appear around edges.
3. Biscuit Topping: In a bowl, combine flour, sugar, baking powder and salt. Cut in butter using a pastry blender or fork to make coarse crumbs. In a glass measure, combine milk and vanilla; stir into dry ingredients to make a soft sticky dough.
4. Using a large spoon, drop eight separate spoonfuls of dough onto hot fruit; sprinkle with 2 tsp (10 mL) sugar.
5. Bake in preheated oven for 25 to 30 minutes or until top is golden and fruit is bubbly.

SERVES 6

When you pair fresh ripe peaches with a crumbly nut topping, it's a juicy sweet treat. Served warm with ice cream, it's the ultimate comfort-food dessert.

TIP

Fresh peaches work best, but in a pinch you can substitute 1 can (28 oz/796 mL) peaches, drained and sliced. Omit the cornstarch.

Irresistible Peach Almond Crumble

Preheat oven to 375°F (190°C)
8-inch (2 L) baking dish, greased

FRUIT		
4 cups	peeled and sliced peaches or nectarines	1 L
2 tsp	cornstarch	10 mL
1/3 cup	peach or apricot preserves	75 mL
TOPPING		
1/2 cup	old-fashioned rolled oats	125 mL
1/2 cup	all-purpose flour	125 mL
1/3 cup	packed brown sugar	75 mL
1/3 cup	sliced blanched almonds	75 mL
1/4 tsp	ground ginger	1 mL
1/3 cup	butter, melted	75 mL

1. Fruit: In a bowl toss peaches with cornstarch; stir in preserves. Spread in baking dish.
2. Topping: In a bowl, combine rolled oats, flour, brown sugar, almonds and ginger. Drizzle with butter; stir to make coarse crumbs. Sprinkle over fruit.
3. Bake in preheated oven for 30 to 35 minutes or until topping is golden and filling is bubbly. Serve warm or at room temperature with ice cream, if desired.

SERVES 6 TO 8

In the old days, bread puddings were an economy dish, simply made with stale bread and custard. But there's nothing humble about this recipe. The golden pear topping flecked with raisins transforms it into a special dessert fit for company.

TIPS

Use homogenized milk to give this pudding an extra creamy texture.

Can't figure out the volume of a baking dish? Look for the measurements on the bottom of dish or measure by pouring in enough water to fill completely.

Bread Pudding with Caramelized Pears

Preheat oven to 350°F (180°C)
8-cup (2 L) baking dish, greased
Shallow roasting pan

6	slices egg (challah) bread or white sandwich bread	6
2 tbsp	butter, softened	25 mL
4	eggs	4
1/3 cup	granulated sugar	75 mL
2 tsp	vanilla	10 mL
2 cups	hot milk	500 mL

PEAR TOPPING

1/3 cup	granulated sugar	75 mL
4	pears, such as Bartlett, peeled, cored and sliced	4
1/2 tsp	freshly grated nutmeg	2 mL
1/3 cup	raisins	75 mL
1/4 cup	sliced blanched almonds	50 mL

1. Trim crusts from bread; butter one side of each bread slice. Cut into four triangles each; layer in prepared baking dish, overlapping the triangles.
2. In a large bowl, whisk together eggs, sugar and vanilla. Whisk in hot milk in a stream, stirring constantly. Pour over bread.
3. Pear Topping: In a large nonstick skillet over medium heat, cook sugar and 2 tbsp (25 mL) water, stirring occasionally, until mixture turns a deep caramel color. Immediately add pears and nutmeg (be careful of spatters). Cook, stirring often, for 5 minutes or until pears are tender and sauce is smooth. Stir in raisins; spoon evenly over bread slices. Sprinkle almonds over top.
4. Place baking dish in larger shallow roasting pan; add enough boiling water to come halfway up sides of dish. Bake in preheated oven for 40 to 45 minutes or until custard is set in center. Remove from water bath; place on rack to cool. Serve either warm or at room temperature.

SERVES 6

There is no more sinful and satisfying combination than rich dark chocolate and whipped cream. Serve small portions of this silky classic. It's rich. And wonderful.

TIPS

Mousse can be made up to three days ahead. It also can be frozen; let defrost in the refrigerator for several hours or overnight.

Bittersweet (not to be confused with unsweetened bitter chocolate) refers to dark European chocolate. It's recommended in this recipe for its superior flavor and can be found in supermarkets and fine bakeries. If unavailable, semi-sweet baking chocolate can be substituted.

Ultimate Chocolate Mousse

2	eggs	2
1/2 cup	milk	125 mL
1/3 cup	granulated sugar	75 mL
6 oz	bittersweet or semi-sweet chocolate, finely chopped (6 squares)	175 g
1 tsp	vanilla	5 mL
1 1/2 cups	whipping (35%) cream	375 mL
2 oz	bittersweet or semi-sweet chocolate at room temperature (2 squares)	60 g

1. In a metal bowl, whisk together eggs, milk and sugar until smooth. Place over a saucepan of simmering water; cook, whisking constantly, for 4 minutes or until foamy and hot to the touch. Remove bowl from heat; whisk in chopped chocolate until melted. Stir in vanilla.
2. Refrigerate for about 15 minutes, whisking every 5 minutes, until mixture cools and is slightly thickened. (Do not chill chocolate until completely set.)
3. In another bowl, using an electric mixer, beat cream until stiff peaks form. Whisk one-third of the whipped cream into the chocolate mixture to lighten it; gently fold in remaining whipped cream until well combined.
4. Spoon mousse into six stemmed wine glasses or serving dishes. Cover with plastic wrap and refrigerate 4 hours or overnight.
5. With a vegetable peeler, shave curls of chocolate onto a sheet of waxed paper; garnish mousse with chocolate curls just before serving.

SERVES 4

Why rely on expensive store-bought puddings, when you can make nourishing homemade ones that take little time to make on the stovetop or in the microwave? Milk puddings are also a great way to boost calcium.

TIPS

Whole milk gives a creamier consistency than lower-fat 1% or skim milk in this easy-to-make dessert.

If cooking pudding in the microwave, be sure to use a large bowl to prevent boil-overs.

VARIATION

Butterscotch Pudding

Cook pudding as directed. Substitute ½ cup (125 mL) butterscotch chips for the chocolate chips; reduce sugar to ¼ cup (50 mL).

Kids' Favorite Chocolate Pudding

⅓ cup	granulated sugar	75 mL
¼ cup	cornstarch	50 mL
2¼ cups	milk	550 mL
⅓ cup	semi-sweet chocolate chips	75 mL
1 tsp	vanilla	5 mL

1. In a medium saucepan, whisk together sugar and cornstarch; add milk, whisking until smooth. Place over medium heat; cook, stirring, for 5 minutes or until mixture comes to a full boil; cook for 15 seconds.
2. Remove from heat. Stir in chocolate chips and vanilla; blend until smooth. Pour pudding into individual serving dishes. Let cool slightly; cover surface with plastic wrap to prevent skins from forming on surface. Refrigerate.

Microwave Method

1. In an 8-cup (2 L) glass bowl or casserole dish, whisk together sugar and cornstarch; add milk, whisking until smooth. Microwave at High for 3 minutes. Whisk well; microwave at High for 3 to 4 minutes more, whisking every minute, until pudding comes to a full boil and thickens. Stir in chocolate chips and vanilla.

SERVES 6

When it comes to comfort food, I put rice pudding at the top of my list. It's creamy, it's luscious and oh-so-satisfying.

TIPS

If short-grain rice is unavailable, use long-grain rice (not converted) instead. Long-grain rice is not as starchy, so reduce the amount of milk to 4 cups (1 L) in total. Combine long-grain rice with 3½ cups (875 mL) of the milk and continue with recipe as directed.

Be careful of spillovers: add a walnut-size piece of butter to rice mixture to reduce milk from foaming.

Instead of using vanilla for flavoring, add a 3-inch (8 cm) strip of lemon peel to the milk-rice mixture when cooking. Remove before serving.

Creamy Rice Pudding

½ cup	short-grain rice, such as Arborio	125 mL
5 cups	homogenized milk	1.25 L
⅓ cup	granulated sugar	75 mL
½ tsp	salt	2 mL
1	egg yolk	1
¼ cup	sultana raisins	50 mL
1 tsp	vanilla	5 mL
	Ground cinnamon (optional)	

1. In a large saucepan, combine rice, 4½ cups (1.125 L) milk, sugar and salt. Bring to a boil; reduce heat to medium-low and simmer, partially covered, stirring occasionally, for about 45 to 50 minutes until rice is tender and mixture has thickened.
2. Beat together remaining ½ cup (125 mL) milk and egg yolk; stir into rice mixture, stirring, for 1 minute or until creamy. Remove from heat. Stir in raisins and vanilla.
3. Serve either warm or at room temperature. (Pudding thickens slightly as it cools.) Sprinkle with cinnamon, if desired.

SERVES 6

This self-saucing French custard was the rage in the 70s. Now that French cuisine is back in vogue, so too is this appealing dessert that is surprisingly easy to make and serve.

TIP

Can be made up to two days ahead of serving.

Crème Caramel

Preheat oven to 325°F (160°C)
6 individual ramekins or 6-oz (175 mL) custard cups
13-by 9-inch (3.5 L) baking pan

CARAMEL		
½ cup	granulated sugar	125 mL
¼ cup	water	50 mL
CUSTARD		
2	eggs	2
2	egg yolks	2
½ cup	granulated sugar	125 mL
1 tsp	vanilla	5 mL
2 cups	homogenized milk	500 mL
½ cup	whipping (35%) cream	125 mL

1. Caramel: In a heavy-bottomed medium saucepan, combine sugar and water. Place over medium heat until sugar melts; increase heat to medium-high and cook until sugar mixture boils (do not stir). When syrup has turned a rich caramel color, remove from heat; pour into ramekins. Quickly rotate dish to spread caramel evenly over bottom.
2. Custard: In a bowl, whisk together eggs, egg yolks, sugar and vanilla. In another saucepan, heat milk and cream over medium heat until almost boiling. Pour hot milk mixture in a thin stream into egg mixture, whisking constantly. Strain through a sieve into prepared ramekins.
3. Arrange in baking pan; carefully pour in boiling water to come 1 inch (2.5 cm) up sides of dish. Place pan in oven; bake for 25 minutes or until tester inserted in center comes out clean. Let cool to room temperature; refrigerate. To serve, run a knife around edges to loosen custard. Invert onto serving plate.

SERVES 6

Here's an updated version of the traditional "fool" — an old-fashioned dessert with fruit or berries folded into whipped cream or custard. This dessert is ideal for entertaining since it can be assembled earlier in the day.

TIP

Instead of individual serving dishes, layer berries and lemon fool in a 6-cup (1.5 L) deep glass serving bowl.

Lemon Fool with Fresh Berries

2 tbsp	cornstarch	25 mL
2/3 cup	granulated sugar	150 mL
1 tbsp	grated lemon zest	15 mL
1/3 cup	fresh lemon juice	75 mL
2	egg yolks	2
1 cup	whipping (35%) cream	250 mL
3 cups	fresh berries, such as sliced strawberries, raspberries or blueberries	750 mL
	Additional berries, mint sprigs and grated lemon zest	

1. In a small saucepan, combine cornstarch with 1/2 cup (125 mL) cold water; whisk until smooth. Add sugar, lemon zest, juice and egg yolks; cook over medium heat, whisking constantly, until mixture comes to a full boil; cook for 15 seconds. Remove from heat; pour into a large bowl. Let cool slightly. Cover surface with plastic wrap; refrigerate for 2 hours or until chilled. (Recipe can be prepared to this point up to a day ahead.)
2. In a bowl, using an electric mixer, whip cream until stiff peaks form. Whisk lemon mixture until smooth. Whisk in one-quarter of the whipped cream; fold in remaining whipped cream.
3. Arrange half the berries in six parfait or large wine glasses. Top with half the lemon fool; layer with remaining berries and lemon fool. (Recipe can be prepared to this point and refrigerated for up to 4 hours.) To serve, garnish with whole berries, mint sprigs and grated lemon zest.

SERVES 12

Worth every calorie! That's what everyone says who has sampled this luxurious variation of the Italian classic. Never since the heyday of cheesecake have we been so smitten.

Lemon Tiramisu

13- by 9-inch (3 L) shallow baking dish

SYRUP

¾ cup	water	175 mL
¼ cup	granulated sugar	50 mL
⅓ cup	frozen lemonade concentrate, undiluted	75 mL

FILLING

¾ cup	granulated sugar	175 mL
1 tbsp	cornstarch	15 mL
1 tbsp	grated lemon zest	15 mL
½ cup	fresh lemon juice	125 mL
2	egg yolks	2
2 cups	mascarpone cheese	500 mL
1 cup	whipping (35%) cream	250 mL
1½	packages (each 7 oz/200 g) dry ladyfingers	1½
4 oz	bittersweet or semi-sweet chocolate, grated (4 squares)	125 g
2 cups	strawberries, halved	500 mL
	Mint sprigs	

1. Syrup: In a saucepan, combine water and sugar; bring to a boil over high heat; let boil for 1 minute. Remove from heat; stir in lemonade concentrate. Let cool.
2. Filling: In a saucepan, stir together ½ cup (125 mL) sugar and cornstarch. Whisk in lemon zest, juice and egg yolks. Cook, stirring constantly, over medium heat until thickened, about 5 minutes. Do not boil. Remove from heat; pour in bowl and cover surface with plastic wrap to prevent skin from forming. Refrigerate until lukewarm, about 25 minutes.
3. In a large bowl, beat mascarpone with remaining ¼ cup (50 mL) sugar; beat in lemon curd until combined.

TIP
This dessert can be made up to two days ahead. Just add the final strawberry and chocolate garnish an hour or two before serving.

4. In another bowl, beat whipping cream with electric mixer, until stiff peaks form. Using a spatula, fold whipped cream into mascarpone mixture just until no white streaks remain.
5. Using half the ladyfingers, quickly dip each in lemon syrup, then line bottom of baking dish. Spread with half the lemon cheese filling. Repeat with remaining ladyfingers and filling to form second layer. Cover with plastic wrap and refrigerate at least 4 hours or up to two days.
6. Just before serving, sprinkle with grated chocolate; garnish with strawberry halves and sprigs of fresh mint.

SERVES 10 TO 12

A fresh twist on classic trifle, this sensational recipe stars seasonal fruits drizzled with a special orange custard cream. Traditional jam also gets replaced by tart-sweet raspberry sauce. I can count on this surprisingly light dessert to fit in well at a summer barbecue or a winter holiday meal.

TIPS

Try any combination of fruits — raspberries, blueberries, sliced strawberries, halved green and red grapes, peeled kiwi slices, orange sections, apple, pear and pineapple pieces, cut into ½- to ¾-inch (1 to 2 cm) cubes.

Toss fruits that discolor in 1 tbsp (15 mL) lemon juice; drain before using.

For a decorative top, spoon 2 tbsp (25 mL) of the raspberry sauce into a small plastic sandwich bag. Press mixture into one corner of the bag. Poke a small hole in tip of bag using a skewer and pipe mixture in a thin stream over top in a zigzag or lattice pattern.

To toast almonds: Place on baking sheet in 350°F (180°C) oven for 7 to 9 minutes or until lightly toasted.

Fresh Fruit Trifle

½ cup	granulated sugar	125 mL
1 tbsp	cornstarch	15 mL
½ cup	orange juice	125 mL
2	egg yolks	2
4 oz	cream cheese, cubed and softened	125 g
2 tsp	grated orange zest	10 mL
¼ cup	orange-flavored liqueur or orange juice	50 mL
1 cup	whipping (35%) cream	250 mL
1	frozen pound cake (10 oz/298 g), cut into ¾-inch (2 cm) cubes	1
	Raspberry Sauce (see recipe right)	
6 cups	prepared fresh fruits	1.5 L
3 tbsp	toasted sliced almonds	45 mL
	Fresh or frozen raspberries	
	Mint sprigs	

1. In a small saucepan, whisk together sugar, cornstarch and orange juice until smooth; beat in egg yolks. Cook over medium heat, whisking constantly, for 3 minutes until mixture comes to a full boil and thickens. Remove from heat. Beat in cream cheese, orange zest and orange-flavored liqueur until smooth.
2. Transfer custard to a bowl and cool. (Can be made one day ahead, covered and refrigerated.) In a bowl, using an electric mixer, whip cream until stiff peaks form. Fold into orange custard just before using.
3. Arrange half the cake cubes in bottom of a 10-cup (2.5 L) trifle or straight-sided glass serving bowl. Drizzle with half the raspberry sauce. Add half the fruit pressing an occasional piece of fruit flat against sides of the bowl. Spoon half the orange custard cream over fruit.

4. Layer with remaining cake cubes, patting down lightly. Spoon remaining raspberry sauce over and top with fruit mixture. Spread with rest of orange custard cream.

5. Cover and chill for at least 4 hours or up to one day ahead. Just before serving, sprinkle with toasted almonds and garnish with raspberries and mint.

Raspberry Sauce

1	package (10 oz/300 g) frozen unsweetened raspberries, defrosted	1
¼ cup	granulated sugar	50 mL
1½ tsp	cornstarch	7 mL
2 tsp	fresh lemon juice	10 mL

1. Place raspberries in a fine sieve set over a bowl. Using a rubber spatula, press berries to extract juice and remove seeds. There should be 1 cup (250 mL).

2. Place in a saucepan; stir in sugar and cornstarch until smooth. Bring to a boil over medium heat, stirring constantly, until thickened. Remove from heat. Let cool; add lemon juice. Cover and refrigerate. The sauce can be made up to two days ahead.

SERVES 12 TO 16

This fabulous crowd-pleasing dessert can be made ahead and tucked away in the freezer to serve at a moment's notice.

Frozen Skor Bar Mousse

Preheat oven to 275°F (140°C)
2 cookie sheets, lined with parchment paper
13-by 9-inch (3 L) baking dish

MERINGUE		
3/4 cup	confectioner's (icing) sugar	175 mL
1/4 cup	cocoa powder	50 mL
4	egg whites, at room temperature	4
1/4 tsp	cream of tartar	1 mL
3/4 cup	superfine sugar	175 mL
MOUSSE		
1 1/2 cups	milk	375 mL
4	egg yolks	4
1/3 cup	granulated sugar	75 mL
5 oz	bittersweet or semisweet chocolate, chopped (5 squares)	150 g
1/3 cup	coffee liqueur or strong coffee	75 mL
2 cups	whipping (35%) cream	500 mL
6	Skor candy bars (each 1 1/4 oz/39 g), finely chopped	6
1 tbsp	cocoa powder	15 mL

1. Meringue: Trace two 12-by 8-inch (30 cm by 20 cm) rectangles on parchment paper; turn paper over and place on cookie sheets.
2. In a bowl, sift confectioner's sugar with cocoa powder. In a large bowl, using an electric mixer, beat egg whites with cream of tartar until soft peaks form. Beat in sugar, a spoonful at a time, until stiff glossy peaks form. Using a rubber spatula, fold in cocoa mixture in two additions.
3. Spoon meringue onto parchment rectangles evenly to edges. Bake in oven for 1 1/2 hours or until crisp and dry, rotate cookie sheets halfway through to bake evenly. Place on rack; let cool. Peel off paper. (Meringues can be wrapped in foil and stored in cool dry place for up to three days.)

TIP
Mousse can be made ahead and frozen for up to two weeks.

4. Mousse: In a heatproof bowl, whisk together milk, eggs yolks and sugar. Place over saucepan of simmering water; cook, whisking often, for 8 minutes, or until thick enough to coat a spoon. Remove from heat. Add chocolate and stir until melted; stir in coffee liqueur. Let cool to room temperature. Cover and refrigerate, stirring occasionally, for 4 hours or until thickened.
5. In a bowl, whip cream; stir one-third into chocolate mixture. Fold in remaining whipped cream. Set aside 1⁄3 cup (75 mL) chopped Skor bars; fold in remaining candy into chocolate mixture.
6. Place one meringue in baking dish, trimming to fit, if necessary. Spread with half the mousse. Top with remaining meringue; spread with remaining mousse. Sprinkle with reserved candy. Wrap in heavy-duty foil. Freeze for 8 hours. Sift cocoa powder over top. Transfer to refrigerator for 30 minutes before cutting into squares.

SERVES 12

No cooking is involved in this sensational dessert! It's only a matter of assembling layers of pound cake, luscious strawberries, creamy mascarpone and dark chocolate. Sinful — and oh so simple.

TIP

Instead of the mascarpone cheese, you can use 1 package (8 oz/250 g) light cream cheese.

Strawberry Mascarpone Trifle with Chocolate

1 cup	mascarpone cheese	250 mL
2/3 cup	granulated sugar	150 mL
2 tbsp	orange juice	25 mL
1 tbsp	grated orange zest	15 mL
1 1/2 cups	whipping (35%) cream	375 mL
5 cups	fresh strawberries	1.25 L
1/3 cup	orange-flavored liqueur or orange juice	75 mL
1	frozen pound cake (10 oz/298 g)	1
4 oz	bittersweet or semi-sweet chocolate, grated (4 squares)	125 g
	Mint sprigs	

1. In a bowl, beat mascarpone cheese with sugar, orange juice and zest until creamy. In another bowl, using an electric mixer, beat cream until stiff peaks form; fold into mascarpone mixture until smooth.

2. Set aside 1 cup (250 mL) small whole strawberries. Slice remaining berries and place in a bowl; stir in orange-flavored liqueur.

3. Cut cake into 1- by 1/2-inch (2.5 by 1 cm) pieces. Arrange half the cake cubes in bottom of an 8-cup (2 L) glass serving bowl. Top with half the sliced strawberries, including some juice. Spread with half the mascarpone mixture; sprinkle with half the grated chocolate. Repeat layers with remaining ingredients.

4. Cover and refrigerate at least 4 hours and up to 12 hours before serving. Garnish with reserved whole strawberries and mint sprigs.

SERVES 10

Surprisingly easy to prepare, this impressive frozen dessert is sublime when fresh berries are in season.

TIP

Instead of orange-flavored liqueur substitute the same quantity of undiluted frozen orange juice concentrate.

Strawberry Ice Cream Cake

9-by 5-inch (2 L) loaf pan, lined with plastic wrap with ends hanging generously over sides of pan

1	frozen pound cake (10 oz/298 g)	1
6 cups	fresh strawberries, hulled	1.5 L
6 tbsp	orange-flavored liqueur	75 mL
4 tbsp	fresh lime juice	50 mL
1⁄3 cup	granulated sugar	75 mL
4 cups	strawberry ice cream, softened slightly	1 L
	Whipped cream (optional)	

1. Slightly defrost pound cake. Trim dark crusts from top and sides of cake; cut into 24 slices, each 1⁄4-inch (0.5 cm) thick.
2. Quarter and slice 2 cups (500 mL) berries. Place in bowl with 3 tbsp (45 mL) orange-flavored liqueur and 2 tbsp (25 mL) lime juice. Set aside.
3. In a food processor, purée remaining berries, orange-flavored liqueur, lime juice and sugar; pour into a bowl.
4. Spread scant 1⁄4 cup (50 mL) strawberry purée in pan. Layer with 8 slices of cake, arranging them lengthwise with slightly overlapping edges. Spread cake with scant 1⁄4 cup (50 mL) strawberry purée, then top with 2 cups (500 mL) ice cream and another scant 1⁄4 cup (50 mL) strawberry puree.
5. Repeat layers of cake, strawberry purée, ice cream and strawberry purée. Arrange remaining cake slices on top and spread with 1⁄4 cup (50 mL) strawberry purée. Fold plastic wrap over top, pressing gently down on cake. Freeze for 8 hours.
6. Stir reserved purée into sliced strawberry mixture. Cover and refrigerate.
7. To serve, place cake in refrigerator for 30 minutes to soften slightly. Lift out of pan and remove plastic wrap. Cut into slices and arrange on serving plates. Top with a generous spoonful of strawberry mixture and a dollop of whipped cream, if desired.

SERVES 8 TO 10

This delectable ice cream cake is a simple assembly of store-bought ice cream layered with tart lemon curd and raspberries.

Lemon Raspberry Ice Cream Torte

9-inch (2.5 L) springform pan

1 1/4 cups	chocolate baking crumbs	300 mL
3 tbsp	butter, melted	45 mL
3/4 cup	store-bought lemon curd (not spread)	175 mL
2 tsp	fresh lemon juice	10 mL
1 1/2 cups	fresh raspberries	375 mL
6 cups	vanilla ice cream, softened slightly	1.5 L

1. In a bowl, combine chocolate crumbs and butter. Press into bottom of pan. Freeze for 15 minutes or until firm.
2. In a bowl, whisk lemon curd with lemon juice. Spread 2 cups (500 mL) ice cream in pan. Spread with half of the lemon curd mixture leaving 1-inch (2.5 cm) border around edge. Freeze for 1 hour or until firm. Spread with 2 cups (500 mL) ice cream.
3. Meanwhile, in a food processor, purée 3/4 cup (175 mL) raspberries; spread over ice cream leaving 1-inch (2.5 cm) border around edge. Freeze for 1 hour or until firm.
4. Spread with remaining ice cream and top with remaining lemon curd. Lightly press remaining whole raspberries into lemon curd. Wrap well and freeze overnight or up to two weeks ahead.
5. To serve, place in refrigerator for 20 minutes to soften slightly. Remove sides of pan, place on serving plate and cut into wedges.

SERVES 6

Here's a kid-friendly treat that is as much fun for them to make as it is to eat.

TIPS

Chocolate sauce thickens slightly if made in advance; microwave briefly on defrost until warmed slightly and easy to spread.

If Skor bits are not available, use 2 chopped Skor bars (each 1 oz/39 g) instead.

Crunchy Ice Cream Sandwiches with Chocolate Sauce

8-inch (2 L) square baking pan, lined with plastic wrap with ends hanging generously over sides of pan

1 cup	finely chopped crunchy granola bars	250 mL
1/2 cup	finely chopped pecans	125 mL
1/2 cup	Skor bits	125 mL
4 cups	mocha almond fudge or butterscotch ripple ice cream, softened slightly	1 L

CHOCOLATE SAUCE

3/4 cup	whipping (35%) cream	175 mL
1/2 cup	semi-sweet chocolate chips	125 mL
1/2 tsp	vanilla	2 mL
	Strawberries or raspberries	

1. In a bowl, combine granola bar crumbs, pecans and Skor bits. Sprinkle half of the crumb mixture into prepared pan; spread with ice cream. Sprinkle remaining crumbs over top; using back of a spoon, pat gently. Cover with foil and freeze for 8 hours or until firm.
2. Chocolate sauce: In a saucepan, heat whipping cream over medium heat until piping hot; remove from heat. Whisk in chocolate chips until melted and smooth; stir in vanilla. Let cool slightly; transfer to a covered container and refrigerate.
3. To serve, lift dessert out of pan and cut into six pieces. Spread chocolate sauce on serving plates and top with ice cream sandwiches. Garnish with berries.

MAKES 1½ CUPS (375 ML)

I like to have this versatile, easy-to-make sauce in the fridge for impromptu desserts. It's great poured over ice cream; it's even better when you add sliced bananas or strawberries and a dollop of whipped cream. To create a scrumptious brownie sundae, place a large brownie on a dessert plate, top with a scoop of ice cream and pour sauce over.

TIP

Keep the sauce in a covered container in the fridge for up to one month. The sauce thickens when refrigerated, so let it come to room temperature before using; it will then pour easily.

Amazing Marshmallow Fudge Sauce

1 cup	canned evaporated milk	250 mL
¾ cup	semi-sweet chocolate chips	175 mL
1 cup	miniature marshmallows	250 mL
1 tsp	vanilla	5 mL

1. Pour evaporated milk in a large glass bowl or casserole dish; microwave at High for 2 to 2½ minutes or until almost boiling. Add chocolate chips; let stand for 2 minutes to melt. Stir well. Add marshmallows; microwave at Medium for 1½ to 2 minutes or until marshmallows are melted. Add vanilla; stir until smooth. Let cool to room temperature before using. Sauce thickens as it cools.

MAKES 1¼ CUPS (300 ML)

Here's another great sauce for pouring over ice cream. You can also drizzle it over cake, apple pie or fresh fruit.

TIP

Let sauce come to room temperature before using. Sauce can be stored in a covered container in fridge for up to one month.

Quick Butterscotch Sauce

¾ cup	packed brown sugar	175 mL
¾ cup	whipping (35%) cream	175 mL
¼ cup	golden corn syrup	50 mL
½ tsp	vanilla	2 mL

1. In a large glass bowl or casserole dish, combine brown sugar, cream and corn syrup. Microwave at High, stirring twice, for 5 to 6 minutes. Add vanilla; let cool to room temperature. Sauce thickens as it cools.

National Library of Canada Cataloguing in Publication

Burkhard, Johanna
300 best comfort food recipes / by Johanna Burkhard.

Includes index.
ISBN 0-7788-0059-8

1. Cookery.
I. Title. II. Title: Three hundred best comfort food recipes.

TX714.B876 2002 641.5 C2002-901843-9

Index